THE TEXAS CIVIL RIGHTS PROJECT

THE TEXAS CIVIL RIGHTS PROJECT

How We Built a Social Justice Movement

JIM HARRINGTON

University of Texas Press Austin

Printed in the United States of America
First edition, 2025

♾ The paper used in this book meets the minimum requirements of ANSI/NISO Z39.48-1992 (R1997) (Permanence of Paper).

Library of Congress Cataloging-in-Publication Data

Names: Harrington, James C., 1946– author.
Title: The Texas Civil Rights Project : how we built a social justice movement / Jim Harrington.
Description: First edition. | Austin : University of Texas Press, 2025. | Includes bibliographical references and index.
Identifiers: LCCN 2025001828 (print) | LCCN 2025001829 (ebook)
ISBN 978-1-4773-3234-4 (hardcover)
ISBN 978-1-4773-3235-1 (pdf)
ISBN 978-1-4773-3236-8 (epub)
Subjects: LCSH: Harrington, James C., 1946– | Civil rights lawyers—Texas—Biography. | Texas Civil Rights Project. | Civil rights—Texas—History. | Civil rights movements—Texas—History. | Human rights—Texas—History. | Legal assistance to the poor—Texas—History. | Community organization—Texas—History.
Classification: LCC KF373.H373 A3 2025 (print) | LCC KF373.H373 (ebook) | DDC 340.092 [B]--dc23/eng/20250407
LC record available at https://lccn.loc.gov/2025001828
LC ebook record available at https://lccn.loc.gov/2025001829

doi:10.7560/332344

The University of Texas Press gratefully acknowledges the Jess and Betty Jo Hay Endowment for its support of this publication.

CONTENTS

FOREWORD

In Texas, the name Jim Harrington is synonymous with justice. Justice for immigrants, justice for those who are differently abled, justice for all who are entitled to vote, justice for those who encounter the police, justice for those imprisoned, justice for farmworkers, justice for, well, all. Period.

The Texas Civil Rights Project (TCRP), a Texas institution, is also synonymous with the name Jim Harrington. In this book, Jim's recollections of the TCRP's founding, he recounts its humble beginnings, major successes, and everything in between.

This is as much a piece of legal scholarship as it is a memoir. It's as much a series of case studies of legal victories as it is a how-to manual on civil rights litigation in Texas. It is academic, poignant, funny, and full of important lessons in the pursuit of justice for everyone possible. One might say it's a primer for those interested in civil and human rights and blending legal support activism and community activism to further those rights.

In addition to being the founder of the TCRP, Jim Harrington would wear many hats: lawyer, community organizer, husband, dad, grandad, friend, vegetarian chef, priest, and all-around good troublemaker. I was a young legal aid lawyer in Austin when Jim left the Texas Civil Liberties Union and opened the iconic Texas Civil Rights Project under the aegis of the Oficina Legal del Pueblo Unido, Inc. (Law Office of the People United). I have a vivid memory of Jim, his former wife, Rebecca, and their three children marching through the streets of Austin with César Chávez and Dolores Huerta. I remember being proud that so many citizens participated in a rally to promote and celebrate the human rights of all people. Jim helped lead that march, and I was so proud to know him and witness his leadership in action.

Later I became a judge, and our professional paths crossed when Jim appeared in my court as a litigator. While we often agree on political matters, we did not always agree on established legal and procedural matters in the courtroom. That means I sometimes ruled in his favor, sometimes against him. Needless to say, we both thought we were right, but we held each other in such high regard that we could disagree agreeably.

Years later we attended the same church. We each came to our faith community from very different faith traditions, and yet we found ourselves, and many others, in solidarity of faith and service to others. We noticed that many other lawyers and legal professionals also gravitated to communities of faith in service to those in need. Of course, ever the overachiever, Jim became an Episcopal priest while I simply sat in the pews to listen and learn—as I still do.

Jim and I have also traveled together. We traveled to Türkiye on an interfaith journey designed to compare and contrast Islamic and Christian traditions. We were meant to learn and to teach. Again, overachiever Jim wrote a couple books about the experiences. I continued (and continue) to study, listen, and learn; Jim has much to teach in those books and certainly in this masterful work, his latest contribution to so many who may or may not be aware of his value to us all. Traveling fed Jim's interest in history, culture, and international law, and his trips informed his civil rights and human rights initiatives. Similarly, the work of the TCRP was informed by and built upon the civil rights and human rights work of many champions of those movements long before the organization's inception. This book chronicles that work and provides a compelling history of civil rights work in Texas that spans five decades.

Jim and I became lawyers to be in service to others. We always wanted to be the voice of the voiceless, a megaphone for those whose voices have been reduced to whispers or outright silenced. While we used our professional time, talent, and treasure in different ways, we both stayed on the path toward a more perfect justice system. We envision a justice system that serves all—rich and poor, educated and uneducated, documented and undocumented—regardless of background or circumstance, regardless of innate characteristics over which no human being has control. Yes: a justice system for all, no exceptions.

While the focus of much of the work of the TCRP was on individual cases and clients, a large part of the practice sought to bring about systemic change. The TCRP's impact litigation led to significant changes across many institutions. I watched in awe as the TCRP sued the Supreme Court of Texas, an institution steeped in tradition. The lawsuit challenged the court to use its administrative power to ensure access to justice for all in our state. That bold move led to the creation of the Texas Access to Justice Commission, its mission to "improve the quality of justice in civil matters for low-income Texans by developing initiatives that increase access and reduce barriers to the judicial system."

Like the justice system we strive for, this book is for everyone. For students of the law, legal enthusiasts, community organizers, those looking for a lesson in professionalism, readers who love a good yarn as well as a little political intrigue. Jim recounts the highs and lows of his own and the TCRP's fights for justice, the struggle to keep the doors of a small but mighty civil rights law firm open, the stories of the men and women they fought for. And he does not leave out the stories of the men and women who fought alongside him in the battle for justice.

LORA J. LIVINGSTON
Retired Judge, 261st Civil District Court of Texas

Judge Livingston graduated from the UCLA School of Law and served as a Reginald Heber Smith Community Lawyer Fellow at the Legal Aid Society of Central Texas before entering private practice. She subsequently served as an associate judge for the Travis County district courts and was elected to the 261st District Court in 1998, becoming the first African American woman to serve as a Travis County district judge. She retired in 2022 and continues to be a vigorous legal services advocate, nationally and in Texas, for poor and low-income people.

THE TEXAS CIVIL RIGHTS PROJECT

INTRODUCTION

PAST AS PROLOGUE

Justice on the Horizon?

> It means a great deal to those who are oppressed to know that they are not alone. Never let anyone tell you that what you are doing is insignificant.
>
> DESMOND TUTU

Some people along the way have called me a "badass." I never aspired to be a badass and usually don't think of myself as one. For me, my career was all about being a zealous advocate for people who are poor, disenfranchised, and oppressed. What matters is their lives, their stories, their histories, their hope, and walking alongside them on the journey toward justice.

Being part of any movement for justice, I admit, is pretty badass. That is certainly true of the Texas Civil Rights Project and the people with whom we collaborated. One colleague, herself a fervent activist, made her own assessment by gifting me with a pair of bright-red professional boxing gloves, which I hung from the bookcase behind my desk.

This is not a pure memoir in a literary sense, since I have endeavored to make this more about those with whom I labored in the vineyard, striving boldly for human rights and dignity, than about me. While I may be the writer of these pages, authorship belongs as much to those whose lives intersected with mine. As the Irish say, a fortunate wind blew us together.

Friends and family coaxed me gently into this writing project after years of my own resistance. Perhaps they had heard the same war stories and proffered rocking-chair analyses enough to want me away from the patio and dinner table and in front of the computer, out of harm's way as it were.

I demurred because an account such as this seemed daunting and time-consuming (and it was). Moreover, my well-refined Irish guilt prompted me to seriously question whether my time would be better spent on another undertaking directly enriching others' lives.

They prevailed, convincing me that an account of the Texas Civil Rights Project and what I call its "step-predecessor," the South Texas Project (STP), had merit as one of the many facets of the civil rights struggle in Texas. More important for me, this was a way of paying respectful tribute to the people at the grassroots, *la gente*, who fought the good fight and committed themselves to the struggle, quite often at personal cost.

Friends cautioned me to frame this undertaking more in thematic perspectives than in chronological order and, above all, to avoid making it a dull read about legal cases, however significant they might be. They suggested that my reflections and understanding of the times might be of value to others. I trust this wasn't disguised flattery. Maybe a reader or two might find a few kernels of worthy social analysis and helpful suggestions for years yet to come. Perhaps this will light the flame in a fellow traveler to make "good trouble, necessary trouble," as the late John Lewis famously said.

I have attempted to be faithful to their advice and have woven together ruminations on nearly a half-century of work with the Texas Civil Rights Project and the projects before its creation. Some anecdotes relay humorous events. Some reflections are poignant, and some experiences are deeply moving.

This history chronicles victories and losses (some quite painful), happy moments and sad times, joy and sorrow. It relates accounts of courageous people who stepped forward to better their lives and those of others, living, passed on, and yet unborn, and took on powerful adversaries. I have tried to open the door into the world of those we served, to feel the pain, anguish, dignity, and pride of success they brought to us.

I frankly admit that I do not recollect all the memorable events over the last half-century or completely recall them correctly. The *bola de años* has taken care of that, but I have done my best to accurately recall and knit it all together. English has no good, nuanced translation for *bola de años*. It means the years have rolled on and taken their toll.

Many winters have passed, as Northern Plains Native Americans would put it. That I was coming up on my seventieth winter counseled the decision to retire from TCRP and turn my eyes toward other labors of a different kind and scale.

My intent is to recount trying to do civil rights work rooted in the community and people's aspirations in Texas, a state often inimical to human rights. Our task was to offer supportive legal assistance to change society. Over the years, it is fair to say, TCRP became grounded as an institutional bulwark for the community that other social and political institutions had to take into account, if not pay heed. That was how the media perceived us as well, which strengthened our clout.

I decided early on to be a badass. I didn't define myself that way but as intending to fight as fiercely as possible for what was right. The people I worked with had suffered enough at the hands of Anglo lawyers, and my name was not going to be found on that list.

Nor would there be any backslapping or posttrial happy hour to work out a compromise deal with opposing counsel whose aim wasn't to help fix a bad situation. That was not an absolute rule, but it was an operative principle. Judges were not exempt, either.

The people I represented would call the shots, not me. An example was a session with a San Antonio judge in a disability rights case against the Bill Miller Bar-B-Q chain, which we had sued because of a slew of inaccessibility issues. He tried to get me to compromise and select just some access issues that were important and let the others slide, kind of like halving the baby. That discussion was short-lived, and the chain became fully accessible.

My dad's example probably accounted for some of my stubborn bent, although he's no longer around to defend himself. Ted Kennedy's eulogy for his brother in 1968 mentioned Bobby's perpetual sense of outrage at injustice. I recognized that in myself and realized it had to be channeled into justice work.

My part in TCRP is not small, but my aim is to focus the lens on what the community and TCRP did together for greater equity. TCRP always strove to focus on those for whom we advocated. Our goal was to be part of the valiant team, not its captain, making justice. Everyone helped carry the ball. I was lucky to be a player.

TCRP took guidance from individuals and grassroots organizations trying to better the lives of those around them. We did our best to be their protector, advocate, and servant leader, to take direction from them and not the other way around.

Law is a tool, not an end in itself. Justice is the goal of all human rights undertakings—everything in "right relationship," as the philosophers and

Scriptures put it. Right relationship is not status quo and does not appear on the scene without arduous struggle and fundamental social readjustment. Right relationship means the people have power, all the people.

Two memories about keeping law in perspective always stayed on my mind as an attorney. One is a meeting between the labor leader César Chávez and a dozen prospective volunteer lawyers on a chilly Saturday morning in a small vacant rural house in the Rio Grande Valley in December 1976. The local United Farm Workers (UFW) branch was beginning to reorganize.

There were the customary polite handshakes and warm greetings. We all were in awe of César, of course. He was our hero. After the pleasantries, we finally sat down on old folding chairs in a circle filling out the small, empty living room of the unheated house.

César started the meeting with generous thanks and then before long made a seemingly impolitic comment, which only he could get away with, that he did not like working with most lawyers. They spent too much time telling him how various laws impeded the UFW from doing something. He wanted lawyers who would figure out how to do something when the law was an obstacle and assist the movement when the law needed bending. That memory stuck and represented for me the UFW mantra: *¡Sí, se puede!* "Yes, it can be done!"

That became the TCRP mantra, too. We turned it into a verb to better convey its message: how to creatively use the law, how to think outside the box, so that the law could help, not hinder, those we served. How to sí-se-puede.

From then until his death eighteen years later, it was my privilege to represent César and the UFW in Texas and learn from him. He was a brilliant strategist at using litigation hand-in-glove with organizing. He could be charming in person with audiences but also fierce in summoning people to action. He was like a grandfather with our young kids at breakfast when he stayed overnight. He would sit at the end of the table while they were eating their cereal before leaving for the school bus and chat them up about school, what they liked, favorite class—the regular questions. He was always smiling and laughing with them.

The second memory is a pithy summary of César's point: a wizened migrant farm laborer and dogged UFW organizer, Baltazar "Don Balta" Saldaña, expressing gleefully a few times that "we have a lawyer on our side." He knew from experience how essential that was for any gritty organizing and hard-fought social action to join forces with a legal team.

Don Balta, as we respectfully called him, had lost his right hand in a farm accident but could still outwork any two other people. His sons and daughters, then young adults, had the same labor ethic and dedication to the movement. They migrated from McAllen to California's fields, a broiling 1,800-mile desert drive, every year for much of their lives and were proud *huelguistas* (UFW strikers), whenever César needed them.

One cannot get a hawk's-eye view of TCRP without seeing how it was rooted originally and firmly in the South Texas Project, which I've characterized as our step-predecessor. STP's philosophy and grassroots model held firm for nearly five decades. That continuity was our heart and soul.

TCRP's legal docket coursed with issues of poverty, class, race, disability, equality, sex, ethnicity, privacy, due process, police, discriminatory structures and systemic practices, voting, and criminal procedure. They often intersected and were always intertwined.

TCRP was unique in being the only community-based civil rights organization of its kind in Texas, perhaps the country. We lived under a hybrid model, blending statewide or national impact litigation with on-the-ground community legal assistance. Our emphasis was on developing and protecting human rights in Texas. Our assistance came without cost to those who needed it. Our only regret was that we had the capacity to help only about five percent of those who sought us out, such was the need.

As I cautioned earlier, this memoir has a thematic approach to better center the issues in which we concentrated our efforts. The lawsuits and organizing ventures recounted in these pages often happened at the same time. Nothing was short-term. It went on for years. Unlike criminal trials that are focused on a particular incident and happened relatively quickly, civil trials, which were our hallmark, are protracted (probably a year or two from the time the case is filed until it concludes).

Stacking different events on top of each other as they took place chronologically would invite insufferable confusion and require something like a scorecard. The reader can imagine what life and work were like with the activities happening parallel to other events and often interacting, one with another.

This book is a tribute to all those with whom I had the privilege to labor—brave clients, stalwart staff, devoted grassroots activists, pro bono attorneys, and family—without whom nothing told in these pages could have happened.

I must also recognize and credit my former wife, Rebecca Flores, who became an indefatigable UFW organizer and leader (and a terrific mother to our three children). In many ways, she is the Texas brand of the UFW cofounder Dolores Huerta: steadfast, always present, never mincing words.

We labored closely together for years to interlock organizing and legal backup. She could fill a memoir herself about her work. Indeed, a documentary (*Under the South Texas Sun*) is underway about her life. As a tribute to the farmworkers' deep respect and love for her, the city of Elsa dedicated a street to her, deservedly so.

As time barreled on, I saw more clearly that people's struggles today lived in the struggles of those who went before. Today's struggles, like theirs, help bend the long arc of the moral universe a bit more toward justice, as Martin Luther King Jr. envisioned. The arc doesn't bend itself. Progress is slow, excruciatingly slow, and requires robust hope to hold greed, corruption, and power in check and help bring about their great reversal.

For me, our responsibility is not just to our community and grandkids, who follow us into a life we try to make better for them. We have a weighty duty to continue the arc-bending of the many who preceded us and who lived with the hope that we would carry forward their struggle against oppression, resisting the vortex of evil. This is how we keep faith with our inheritance from them.

Many sacrificed to get us where we are today. Many were killed, lynched (some in obscene spectacle fashion), burned, mutilated, lost jobs, and endured much, trusting that we would take the torch from them, run a marathon or two with it, and then pass the torch to the next group of runners. And no time to do a pit stop for handwringing.

The marathoners' stories in this book show dignity amid the struggle in which they were caught up. They claimed their self-worth and helped others do the same against degrading individual and institutional treatment. The undertow of justice carried us all along in its uncertain current.

I tried to work and live closely with the people I served. Bryan Stevenson of the Equal Justice Initiative calls this "getting proximate" on issues of race and injustice. Being proximate is as much a learning encounter as a sharing experience. In so many ways, they propelled my growth as a person and taught me much about human rights as a way of life and not just a cause.

Getting proximate, I believed, included being content with a lower salary than one might expect even for a nonprofit group. It was a good reminder of the financial stress most people face daily, which often alters the direction of their lives. If someone's car broke down, they didn't have AAA to call. We depended on friends and neighbors to help fix the vehicle. Getting proximate also meant not expecting a standard forty-hour workweek.

Few were the days I did not wake up in the morning, grateful and honored to be at the people's side. And when the work was harder than usual and the brick wall almost impenetrable, I took inspiration from them.

For those with and for whom I worked, with humility and gratitude, I offer this recollection of an era that destiny let me share with them. And that's pretty badass.

1

THE EARLY YEARS

From Michigan's Strawberry Fields to South Texas

My early years in Lansing, Michigan, were normal and uneventful. Nothing presaged Texas. Our family was tight-knit and supportive, an important value for my dad, whose own father had died young, when my dad was only three years old. My mom and dad urged us ahead in sports (I was a lousy leftie at softball), church activities (altar boy), work (peddling newspapers at 6 a.m., even in freezing cold and blizzards), and scouting (Eagle Scout here). The family income was lower middle-class, so our vacations were mostly camping along Lake Michigan's beaches and in the Upper Peninsula, which we loved.

The normalcy ended in 1960 when, after eight years of primary at Resurrection School, I decided to study to be a Catholic priest, beginning as a high-school freshman at the Pontifical College Josephinum, a seminary in Columbus, Ohio, which the bishop chose for me. I was there eight years, for high school and college.

Our required daily college garb was a black topcoat-style cassock that buttoned across the chest, with red piping, red buttons, cuffed sleeves with buttons, and a long red sash. For our heads, it was a three-wing black biretta with a black silk pom-pom. But the snazzy attire didn't fit where many of our hearts were. We were moving away from that clerical era into contemporary society, often to the authorities' consternation.

My classmates were an eclectic gathering of ninety-two students from around the country, mostly chosen on academic potential. They were smart, funny, and made for good friends. Everyone brought different talents, and we bonded well together, sometimes mischievously.

It's hard to pinpoint why I did what I did. The regular amenities of high school life were not particularly inviting to me personally. Doing something larger to help people appealed more. The civil rights movement was picking up steam, and social justice attracted me. For some reason, I developed an interest in politics around fifth grade. Given the world around me at the time, the church, which was part of our family life, seemed like the best option; its recruitment program in those days began with ninth grade.

Until then, the major formative life figures for me were my folks and my grandmother on my mom's side, who lived three blocks away. The path to her house was well-traveled. My grandmother profoundly inspired me, more than I have words for. Her compassion and spirituality ran deep. She was religious but not pietistic or judgmental. She was a wonderful, generous woman who cared about, and attended to, the community about her. She was a lousy cook, but her heart made up for that deficit a hundred times over. She shared her sparse retirement with family and poor people.

It was a pleasure getting my grandmother out on a farmworkers boycott line at age eighty, carrying the red-and-white UFW flag with the black Aztec eagle. Her frame was slight, wrapped in a light-blue cloth coat on that chilly autumn afternoon in front of a Lansing grocery store, but her resolution was as solid as her grip on the flagstick. She helped mold me, more than she ever knew.

My mother taught me how to organize. My father showed me how to be steadfast and a bit stubborn in doing what's right and not waste any time at it. I'm told Molly Ivins once called me "crusty" in one of her audiobooks. My dad would have liked that. Those skills and values played out in spades in my later life, and I have always been grateful.

Our parents impressed on us that, while others had more than us, we had more than others and that we should share and give back, even if all we had was our time. They gave a good deal of their time in different volunteer projects. Scouting was one, which was something they could wrap us in as kids. My dad, a handyman by avocation, would answer anyone's call for help, especially fixing electrical wiring or light carpentry work in friends' or neighbors' houses. Their giving back to the community carried on with all us six kids as we grew older.

THE HUNTER PARK INCIDENT

An early life event drew together the influences of my parents and grandmother and portended the future. At age fifteen, after my freshman seminary year, I was at Hunter Park one warm summer evening near my home, hitting golf balls, when another kid my age came by and joined me. He was Cuban, I learned.

A police officer showed up after a while and asked where we lived. After finding out my friend was Cuban, the officer told him he had to leave. We were the only two people in the fourteen-acre park. The cop let me stay. Outraged, I went to the next city council meeting and complained about the cop's discriminatory treatment of my new pal.

The following day, the local *Lansing State Journal* daily newspaper printed a news item about my council visit, identifying me as a seminarian. Within twenty-four hours, the local parish priest stopped by the house to tell my parents and me that the bishop disapproved of my actions, that aspiring clerics should not make waves.

This astounded me. One would have thought a religious leader would encourage speaking out against racism. Regardless, I paid no heed to the good bishop; nor did I become more circumspect about my actions. These two brushes with authority orientated me toward later life in ways neither the police nor bishop anticipated—or might have desired.

THE KICK-START: TEXAS MIGRANTS IN MICHIGAN

My eventual journey to Texas, unknowable at the time, began on a lark in 1961, when I was a Josephinum high-school freshman. The seminary curriculum required us to begin a five-year language track as sophomores and continue on into our college years. Our only options were German or Spanish.

A group of us rebellious upstarts (a politer term than "smartasses") hatched an ill-fated plan that, if we petitioned for French, the authorities would respect our request and initiate a French program. It was naïve thinking for the conservative Josephinum, directly under Vatican control, where I spent eight years.

The authorities, who prided themselves on discipline, reacted predictably (in hindsight) and arbitrarily assigned either German or Spanish to us mutinous French-seekers as they saw fit and to teach us a lesson. I drew Spanish, and it redirected my entire life.

Our professor, Father Paul "Pablo" Sicilia, a young priest from Pennsylvania, cajoled us for five years to learn the language and immersed us in

Spanish-speaking cultures. He was particularly fond of Mexico, where he studied and worked summers in Indigenous mountain communities. His dedication was inspiring and carried me along in his direction more than he realized.

So in college, when a summer job opened up with the Catholic Diocese of Lansing working among migrant workers in southwestern Michigan, I jumped at it, although I knew absolutely nothing about migrants. I was soon to learn. I could both do ministry and use my Spanish. I began working with migrant folks in that area for seven summers, wearing two different hats.

At the time, about 80,000 farmworker families, including 20,000 children, migrated to Michigan farmlands during the summer, mostly from the Rio Grande Valley in Texas, to harvest strawberries, blueberries, raspberries, peaches, and other carefully handpicked crops. From there, they went north to reap tree fruit, typically cherries. Somewhere between 25,000 and 35,000 migrants worked in Michigan's southwestern tri-county corner where I was during those summers.

Their 1,500-mile drive north from South Texas took twenty-fours at best, usually closer to thirty. Their old cars—packed full to the brim with kids, food, and the family's clothes—traveled long ways through inhospitable territory (they knew never to stop in New Braunfels, for example). A breakdown on the road was a feared and not uncommon event, with severe financial consequences and lost time they could ill afford. Kids often missed the last week or two of school and the first week or two because of harvest schedules, something their parents regretted, but they had no choice.

The migrant housing the families resided in was appalling and shameful. "The camps," as everyone called them, were dirty (muddy when it rained), degrading, cramped, and bedeviled by vermin. Families lived in converted barns and ramshackle single-room cabins, sometimes as many as twenty shacks on a farm. Many times, families didn't know each other and were thrown together randomly by the grower. No indoor toilets, just stinking outhouses. Electricity by extension cord. Cooking on small propane tabletop stoves. Lousy refrigeration for provisions. Outdoor water hoses for bathing and for washing cookware and dishes.

The camps could have been transported from an impoverished region of the world, and no one would have known the difference. They were a stunning contrast to the growers' well-appointed homes nearby. Wealth and abject poverty were close neighbors, plantation capitalism in our face, to use a phrase of Reverend James Lawson, a civil rights movement spiritual guide. Workers had no choice but to tolerate it because of their own poverty and economic necessity.

Wages from stooping over all day in the fields were barely life-sustaining. Young children picked crops, too, for the family's sustenance and earned even less. The grueling harvests began in the chilly predawn dew and continued long into the hot, sunbaked afternoons. People had to pick crops on Saturdays as well.

Activists, do-gooders, church volunteers, and sympathetic government officials showed up, intent on improving the families' miserable living and labor conditions and offering a modicum of dignity. Everyone did their best to bring at least some justice to the fields. This was all so heartrending to us. We had nothing but respect and profound compassion for people having to live and labor under such unremitting conditions, working hard so their kids would have a different life when they grew up. The experience moved me profoundly, deepened my compassion, and angered me for the injustice of it all.

President John F. Kennedy's clarion call in his winterly outdoor inaugural address on January 20, 1961, resonated deeply for many of us high school and college-age idealistic folks: "Ask not what your country can do for you—ask what you can do for your country." It was a challenge to take up, and many of us did. His timing was perfect. The civil rights movement was taking hold. A new era was birthing, and we could do our part. Kennedy was youthful, dynamic, humorous, and eloquent. He reached into my soul and pulled the best out of it in terms of serving others, especially those living in poverty and on the margins. Kennedy lit a fire in us. His assassination broke my heart.

Between 1966 and 1972, I worked with the Catholic Diocese of Lansing for five years and then two years with United Migrants for Opportunity, Inc. (UMOI), a Great Society poverty program that rankled local political and business leaders for meddling in their communities' unjust way of life. I eventually became director of the church program and built it up to twenty-four staff members. These summers were radicalizing for me and instructive on how the gloves of power wrapped themselves tightly around our necks.

We do-gooders joined together to fashion summer programs for young migrant children, provide Saturday evening dances for teens, arrange college scholarships for young adults (one eventually became general counsel for the United Auto Workers), enforce minimum wage laws, set up health clinics, help distribute food commodities and vouchers, visit migrant camps in the evenings with appropriate information, conduct adult education, and attend to people's religious needs. We did our jobs with vigor, out of compassion for the workers and their families. The growers sneered at us as outside agitators, as indeed we were and proud of it. The organizing skills learned from those summers served me well for the future.

Young UMOI lawyers took on wage issues, which abounded, and freedom of access to the camps, from which the growers were increasingly barring us troublemakers. They wanted no one talking with the workers about anything.

Inevitably, thanks to UMOI, a federal lawsuit came about over the camp-access issue. A young nun in our church program, Sister Betty LaBudie, became a star witness against Joe Hassle, one of the area's more notorious growers, who physically barred her from distributing migrant health clinic leaflets in his camps. He had four camps, as I recall, all in varying degrees of deterioration. We thought his last name was appropriate to his persona.

Sister Betty was attractive, kind, and charming. She was a member of the Sisters of St. Joseph in nearby Kalamazoo. She had a smile and a pair

MIGRANT HEALTH REDUX

Ironically, while I was writing this memoir, the Midwest Stream Forum for Agricultural Worker Health 2023 invited me to keynote their Austin conference. It was a great honor and a full-circle thing, speaking to health care workers from Michigan, where my feet got wet a half-century earlier, helping migrants.

More impressive and personally moving was that over half of them or their parents had come out of the migrant stream. Our desire and aspiration fifty years earlier had come true. It was striking and sad how bad the conditions continued to be after all the years, but inspiring how our successors doggedly continued the struggle. They were carrying forward the torch with aplomb, hope, and joy.

of twinkling eyes that could beguile even a sinner. Judge Noel Fox listened intently while she recounted her attempts to visit migrants and how Hassle rudely and unceremoniously expelled her from a camp. She could not have been a better witness.

Sister Betty set the stage for the noon break, which was when Hassle and his attorneys found out through the bailiff that the judge attended Mass every day during lunch hour. Bowing to the suddenly inevitable, they quickly settled midtrial, granting us access, and we went back to visiting the camps in the evenings. Court precedent was now on our side. That put an end to the growers trying to block visitors to their abysmal, blighted camps.

I left the seminary in 1968 after college and began graduate studies in philosophy, first at the University of Texas in Austin and then the University of Detroit. Church structures were not conducive to the kind of social justice life toward which I was being drawn. The hierarchy kept tight reins over how clergy could get involved in social justice work, if at all. Organizing was not on the table. It always intrigued me how the desire to help people in a way consistent with my religious principles drew me into the seminary and then ultimately drew me away from the seminary.

Of the ninety-two of us who entered the seminary in 1960 as high school freshmen, only eight remained by the end of college in 1968. And all of us left the Josephinum after graduation. Only one of our group went on to be ordained elsewhere. The seminary experience was bizarre in some respects and good in others. Some left scarred. For others, like me, it was a mixed bag. I have always been grateful for the excellent education and intellectual challenge of my classmates. And while the disciplinary regimen was excessive and sometimes absurd, like something out of a Dickens novel, I did need the discipline.

Leaving the seminary put me at risk of military conscription for a war that I and many others believed was immoral. A malfunctioning kidney kept me from having to face being a conscientious objector to the Vietnam War, much to my father's relief as well. One evening he told me, his firstborn, that I would have to move out of the house because I would not take up arms, a decision that pained him since we got along well. But he was a man of principle.

He was a World War II vet, having served in the Seventh United States Army. He was at the liberation of the Werl prisoner and labor camp but would never speak about what he saw (other than to say it was "horrible"). His twin brother, a United States Marine, was permanently disabled in the Pacific, having lost part of his skull on the left side of his head, which paralyzed that side of his body.

The morning after my dad issued my marching orders, I was in the emergency room with an acute kidney infection. The medical situation disqualified me from the draft and gave my dad, and me, a pass. I eventually lost the left kidney to a Texas surgeon's knife in 1976.

Interestingly, my dad changed his view of the war and, two years later, wrote a letter supporting my brother-in-law's application for conscientious objection. I didn't learn of this until I was wrapping up this memoir and was quite surprised. I regret I never had a chance to talk with him about his change of heart.

I wrapped up a master's degree in Spanish Existentialism at the University of Detroit in 1970 and enlisted in the University of New Mexico's PhD program in the same academic direction. By then I had already made up my mind to go work in the Valley with farm laborers there. I felt drawn to the burgeoning United Farm Workers movement. All the activists were heading to join the UFW in California, where the union was based. I chose otherwise, moving instead to South Texas, where I knew many of the workers and the need there was just as great as in California.

My summers with migrants in Michigan galvanized my desire to move to the Valley, where the UFW also had a presence. My intent was to be a philosophy professor there (an ultimately naïve idea) and join the movement. While I was in grad school, though, my plans took a sudden lightning bolt on a Saturday morning. The memory is still vivid. I used to get up early on Saturdays to watch an episode of *Underdog* (the original vintage).

That wintery January morning, right before the show, I suddenly sat upright in bed and heard myself saying, "You have to go to law school." It was quite an experience, and nothing like it has happened before or since. Perhaps by then my subconscious had put two and two together that being a lawyer made more sense than pursuing philosophy in terms of my goal: helping farmworkers. Besides, the sole philosophy professorship in the Valley already had an occupant.

Only in writing this memoir have I realized the cartoon irony—that I would spend my life toiling in underdog situations.

After the "Underdog Saturday" revelation, I switched over to studying law at the University of Detroit. I stayed in Motown another three years, where I met Rebecca Flores and we married. Appropriately enough for two student activists, we ran into each other at the Detroit UFW's grape boycott office.

Hailing from San Antonio, Rebecca was doing graduate social work in community organizing at the University of Michigan after the Black Action Movement had shut down U-M until it opened up more minority undergraduate and graduate scholarships. It was a fortuitous escape from the secretarial track to which San Antonio schools pushed *mexicanas* at the time. She became a steadfast UFW organizer and leader. Having picked cotton with her family as a young migrant girl, her heart was deep in the movement.

Before her family of eight moved to San Antonio, Rebecca spent eight years as a little girl, starting at age five, working in the fields near her farm home near Poteet and migrating to different states during the summer. She was fond of pointing out later as an organizer that nobody could challenge her credentials as not knowing what she was talking about. And nobody ever did.

My philosophy master's degree did come in handy, though. I taught an evening business ethics course in UD's business school, which helped pay my law-school tuition. It was an atypical course, I am sure. Two of my texts, for example, were Herbert Marcuse's *One-Dimensional Man* and Eldridge Cleaver's *Soul on Ice* (with appropriate omissions).

During the two summers before moving to Texas, while in law school, I joined UMOI because a new bishop fired me from my church position. He did not approve of the activist direction in which I was moving the migrant program. Amazingly, he said passing out health clinic information was too political. The growers had complained to him. Sister Betty's day in court probably sealed the deal. Bishops tend to frown on church activists—and activist nuns particularly.

Little did the good bishop know that distributing health information was but the proverbial iceberg tip. With other groups, we had helped organize a noon protest rally at the Capitol Building in Lansing on a summer weekday in 1970. About four hundred farmworkers and advocates took over the Rotunda, raucously chanting demands for higher wages and stricter enforcement of field and labor camp health regulations.

A few protesters caught Governor William Milliken trying to sneak out of the building through a side stairwell. He had no choice then but to address the assembled demonstrators and promise reform, which was weak and almost imperceptible in coming.

I visited the labor camps as a UMOI paralegal, no longer wearing the church hat, although the prior church association conveniently overlapped in the workers' minds, which was helpful for credibility purposes. Many of the tasks were the same: passing out health clinic information, talking about issues that affected them, and eating with the families in the camps after their workdays ended.

People offered us food, usually tacos of homemade flour tortillas and beans. Families were so generous with their food even though it was a drain on their meager incomes. We tried to take something to share with them. It was an important lesson for me in cultural hospitality.

Michigan allowed third-year law students to acquire a student bar card, which permitted us to handle civil lawsuits and criminal misdemeanors under an attorney's supervision. It's like the driver's training permit that allows teens to drive with a licensed adult in the car.

The only civil case I tried with that permit, with a local legal aid lawyer serving as second chair, was for a family of five who traveled to Michigan after a grower, with whom they had worked three prior summers, had promised them employment again.

When they arrived 1,500 miles and three days later, they found out he had hired someone else without having the decency to inform them beforehand. The local judge poured us out, siding with the grower, one of the county's biggest, and denied any damages to the family for having detrimentally relied on the grower's promise. Of course, the national origin demarcations were as one might expect. How could we lose, given the facts; but we did.

I mention this case because it was not an unusual happenstance for migrant families. It was distressingly typical both in occurrence and in the disrespect with which growers treated the workers: as commodities, not as persons with families. Immoral in my book.

A LAW-SCHOOL CLASS: COPS ON THE WITNESS STAND

Later in my career, when suing police became a focus of our litigation, we could not automatically assume that police would always tell the truth, to different degrees and for varied reasons, under oath at trial.

I learned this as a student intern in the University of Detroit Law School criminal defense clinic. UD's law school pioneered in hands-on legal clinics, which are now common at law schools. The clinic program attracted me to the school, along with being able to use my philosophy degree to teach an evening ethics course at the university's business school to pay the bills.

I was shocked when my first experience with police testifying under oath happened and am now shocked by my naiveté then. That experience was a growth tutorial. Fortunately, it happened before I headed to Texas.

Nowadays smartphones catch the police being less than honest or fence them into a place where they cannot dissemble. Smartphone technology was not as available during most of my tenure suing cops as it is today. If you lived in the white community, you believed that police were mostly honest. If you lived in a minority community, you discovered reality early on.

My rite of passage happened in a double trial I was handling with my student bar card. The trial involved Detroit's notorious police STRESS tactical unit (an acronym for "Stop the Robberies, Enjoy Safe Streets"), which the mayor eventually had to disband because of the cops' brutality and the number of innocent people they killed. The clinic assigned me two cases, defending two young African American men. Two white STRESS cops had stopped them on the freeway, beat them up on the side of the road, and then charged them with assaulting officers.

A jury heard both cases together and acquitted one of the men and hung on the second man's verdict. At the retrial of the hung case, the same two officers testified again but with completely different stories. Was the second round of testimony fabricated to get a conviction? Or was the first? Maybe both? Their lies were not small and were, potentially, egregious enough to send two innocent men to jail.

This stunned me, and I did my best to impeach the officers with my recollection of their prior testimony. Impeaching them was difficult without an official transcript of the first trial. It never crossed my mind that I would need to impeach the police so drastically. The jury quickly acquitted the second man and handed me a solid experience lesson.

Given what we know now about police dissembling or outright lying under oath and DNA exonerations in recent years, I often wonder how many innocent people are in prison today, and have been unfairly incarcerated over years past, because police testified against them without candor and truthfulness. How many lives have police ruined because of their lack of integrity? There are plenty of honest cops who are truthful, but there are enough who aren't that we can't be sure; in preparing for a trial, we have to assume the worst.

There is one more story about the Detroit police I need to share: being placed under surveillance by its Red Squad (known for questionable and at times illegal tactics to gather intelligence against activist citizens). While in law school I did volunteer work in the Hispanic community and joined in activist actions like picketing for UFW at stores during the grape boycott and anti–Vietnam War marches. Shortly after moving to South Texas, because of a class action lawsuit by the National Lawyers Guild, I received notice that the Detroit Police Department had maintained a Red Squad "subversive" file on me.

The surveillance had to do with my living near a Black Action Movement auto-plant organizer and parking my car in front of his house. Absurd, but not surprising. The Red Squad was disbanded in 1974 after thirty years of unconstitutional activity. I always assumed throughout my career that the potential of secret government surveillance was present, but it never changed how I did anything.

SOUTHBOUND: 1,700 MILES IN THE REARVIEW MIRROR

Law school was over in May 1973, and I wore a UFW "Boycott Grapes" button on the front of my graduation cap at commencement. It went well with the elegant purple stole, though my fashion choice was not exactly pleasing to others or my parents. Now it was off to Texas to take the attorney bar examination. Rebecca, who had wrapped up her master's in social work a year earlier from the University of Michigan, and I did the long, hot-summer drive, carrying all our worldly possessions in a vintage white Ford Mustang and a canary-yellow Datsun pickup.

I was lucky to find a job with the South Texas Project ahead of time after one of its two lawyers left. He had just resigned when my letter to the local UFW arrived, asking if the union had any job openings. The union did not but gave my inquiry to STP, which shared space in the UFW building and had the newly vacated position available. Another serendipitous quirk of fate.

In those days, the local judges of your Texas county of residence had to approve attorney candidates before they could take the bar. I had set up residence in Hidalgo County at the beginning of law school. When it came time to apply for the bar, I had to fly to the Valley to meet in person with the judges, four at that time.

One judge, Magus Smith, voted against me when he learned my worksite would be at the UFW center. *¡Ya Mero!*, the union newspaper, had published a piece characterizing him as a bigot. The article featured a photograph of one of those racist Black jockey statues in front of his house. He was the only naysayer, but he illustrated the purpose of the procedure, since abandoned, of "character screening" future lawyers. One more vote and my life might have been quite different.

With some serious anxiety, I turned down a Reginald Heber Smith Fellowship, sponsored by the federal Office of Economic Opportunity, to work at a local South Texas legal aid office. Even though the "Reggie" was better financially, assured stability, and offered a job with Valley poor people, it was the more activist STP tugging at me that won out. Blind trust in what was yet to come carried me along. Rebecca secured a moderately paying health-related job for a year, which helped enormously as our first of three children, a son, came along in mid-1974.

ARRIVING TO WORK RIGHT BEFORE *LA CANÍCULA* ROLLED IN

After cranking through the Texas bar exam in Austin six days earlier, I showed up on July 16, 1973, at the South Texas Project in the newly built UFW center on the northwest corner of Business U.S. 83's intersection with Morningside Road (since renamed for César Chávez) between San Juan and Alamo. It was a sweltering, humid Monday morning. I was nervous, of course, and had no idea what I was getting into as I pulled open the solid, black front door. But I was ready to file class action lawsuits and save the world (naiveté and more than a bit of hubris on my part).

Farmworkers and volunteers built the center in 1972, complete with offices and union hall, on the corner of a ten-acre plot donated by the Catholic Diocese of Brownsville. They named the center "El Cuhamil," a Náhuatl word referring to an Indigenous family's small garden patch by their home. The Mexican muralist Artemio Guerra graced two walls of the large hall with vivid canvas murals in Diego Rivera's social realism style, depicting the agricultural labor struggle.

People constructed a huge, colorful UFW eagle insignia close to the street intersection, which the land abutted. At night, some unfriendly individuals decorated the cinder-block edifice with the pockmarks of bullets.

The white, square, cement-block union building had no air conditioning. That was tough enough, but *la Canícula* (aka the dog days of summer) was about to hit, when even the Valley's sizzling summer currents paused for a month. Without air conditioning in the building, the legal papers always had a mildly damp quality about them.

Nearby growers sometimes sprayed residue pesticides in generous amounts over the union building. Their crop dusters flew past at low level, letting the building's ceiling fans suck in the eye-stinging, stinking chemicals along with the sultry air through the open windows. The pesticide dousing didn't stop until the law changed to require identification numbers on the undersides of the planes' wings.

TAKEAWAYS

When I stepped across the front threshold on July 16, I was joining a ten-year rebellion against oppressive Anglo rule. I did not realize that at the time. Nor did I appreciate how much the movement would become part of me and vice versa.

MEETING FIFTY YEARS LATER

This memoir was in its final stages when I was walking in an elementary school hall with a PTA leader, planning a legal clinic for immigrant parents, as a teacher who was leading her young students approached. She suddenly called out my name. She remembered me from when she was a young migrant in Berrien County, Michigan, and I would visit her camp and talk with her parents. The best part of this serendipitous experience was that she had gone from being a migrant worker to teaching kids the same age she was when we first met fifty years before.

2

SOUTH TEXAS IN THE 1960S AND 1970S

Upheaval, Resistance, and the Origin of the South Texas Project

Before coming to the Rio Grande Valley in 1973 I had attended college and then law school, watching from afar as the winds of civil rights activism blowing across the nation in the late 1960s swept into South Texas and stirred up a rebellion against oppressive Anglo-controlled political and economic power structures. My summers with farm laborers drove my interest and drew me to the Valley.

"Anglo" in this context refers to the white, non–Hispanic/Latino community. It has common usage in South Texas, along the Mexican border, and in related literature.

The high-profile organizing of César Chávez and Dolores Huerta, founders of the United Farm Workers, and their fellow travelers captured the nation's imagination, infused the civil rights movement with momentum, and sent a tidal wave of hope across Texas and into the Rio Grande Valley.

Three major "movement events" helped remake the political landscape of the Valley by the time I arrived in 1973, fresh from law school, and adjusted the compass for my work.

THE MARCH TO AUSTIN

Early in my tenure, a 490-mile march to Austin became an early show of strength for agricultural workers. The United Farm Workers movement, operating then as the UFW Organizing Committee, burst onto the South

Texas scene in 1966–1967 with a series of labor strikes and harvest stoppages by seven hundred farm laborers against corporate melon-growers in Starr County.

La Casita Farms, the largest of the three major agricultural businesses in Starr County and a subsidiary of Hardin Farms in California, was the major focus. Melons are the biggest crop in Starr County, and La Casita produced a quarter of the county's harvest. In 1967, La Casita brought in $5 million for its melons.

The melon pickers demanded living wages. They were averaging $0.40–$0.60/hour amid inhumane labor conditions. These were seasonal workers who had to patch together a crop-based livelihood, often migrating across different areas of the country to sustain their families. The federal minimum wage had not applied to them since its inception in 1938, an unpardonable sin of Congress.

In 1966 Congress upped the federal minimum beginning in 1967, to $1.40/hour for the general workforce. For the first time, agricultural laborers came under federal law, but at a miserly $1/hour.

Melon harvesting occurred in May and June, after the scorching daytime sun had set in. The days were grueling. Melons are heavy to gather and pack, especially for hours on end. Young kids would join their parents in the fields as soon as school ended for the summer break. Families needed to scrape every little bit of income they could.

Starr County was one of the poorest areas of the Rio Grande Valley, which itself was deeply depressed economically. The Valley's fertile soil was lucrative for the growers, but its residents and workers had an awful-hard time of it. The ranchers, growers, and bankers held them in a stranglehold. Raw exploitation.

The *mexicanos* (as the community often called itself) lived in abject poverty and labeled the Rio Grande Valley "El Valle de Lágrimas" (The Valley of Tears). *El Valle* stretched a hundred miles along the Rio Grande, from Brownsville to Roma and a bit beyond.

When agribusinesses stood behind their wall of intransigence and rejected the very idea of raising wages, the melon harvesters' strike activity coalesced into a 490-mile march to Austin, kicked off by 120 strikers and supporters on July 4, 1966. They intended to meet with Governor John Connally on Labor Day and demand that he convene a special session of the legislature to create a $1.25/hour statewide minimum wage for all Texas workers.

BACK IN AUSTIN FIFTY YEARS LATER . . .

On September 11, 2016, Rio Grande Valley farmworkers and hundreds of backers took part in a commemorative march from St. Edward's to the Capitol. Five of the original La Casita *huelguistas* (strikers) were able to attend and proudly bear witness. Guadalupe Guzmán, at seventy-eight years old the most senior of the five, brought her son, who started picking melons at age ten.

More and more people joined the two-month march in the oppressive July and August heat as it curved over to Corpus Christi and then San Antonio. Others lined the route, cheering as marchers passed by under the summer sun (or pouring rain). Supporters and churches along the way offered food, drink, music, overnight lodging, and their backing. It was an astonishing event, unmatched by any Texas protest before. It lit a prairie fire of activism.

Connally fled Austin "to go hunting." He did deign to stop his limousine in New Braunfels and tell the marchers that he would not oblige their request and they should return home.

The people rebuffed Connally and marched on. After arriving in Austin the afternoon before Labor Day, they gathered at St. Edward's University and bunked there for the night. The next morning, they began the march up Congress Avenue to the Capitol with music, flags, and colorful protest signs. César Chávez joined them, along with other civil rights, labor, and political leaders. By the time *La Marcha*'s rally was underway at the Capitol, ten thousand allies had gathered in solidarity.

. . . AND IN THE VALLEY

Fifty-four years after the march to Austin, farmworkers (including original melon strikers) took part in the unveiling of an official Texas historical marker in Starr County commemorating the march. Librado de la Cruz, arrested seven times during the strike, attended in a wheelchair. Similar historical markers are now erected along the march route in Hidalgo and Willacy Counties. Much of all this is due to Rebecca Flores's organizing talent.

ENTER STAGE RIGHT: TEXAS RANGERS

After the march to Austin, union organizing and strikes continued into the 1967 melon season. In brazen cahoots with Texas Rangers, the growers brutally crushed the strikes.

Texas Rangers were a fierce group, originally established as a quasi police force to enforce law and order on the early frontier. Despite their pop culture glorification in films, TV shows, and books, the Rangers have a deeply racist and cruel history that admits of no whitewashing.

The *mexicano* community widely feared and reviled the Rangers, who lynched and shot Mexicans and Mexican Americans at will and with impunity on both sides of the border. Residents in Mexico called them *los diablos tejanos* (the Texas devils). Texas *mexicanos* derided them as *los rinches* (a pejorative Spanish coinage for "rangers"). So many were the innocent victims of Rangers between 1910 and 1920 that the era became known as *la hora de sangre* (the hour of blood). Derogatory Spanish-language ballads were sung along the border about the Rangers, the most famous being "El Corrido de Gregorio Cortez" in 1905 that gave rise to the *corrido* genre of music.

Rangers in South Texas openly colluded with local growers to keep their farm labor employees oppressed. It was Rangers who crushed the 1936 spontaneous strike of 1,200 onion harvesters in Webb County for higher wages led by La Asociación de Jornaleros, an independent union of Mexican American workers from different occupations.

The Rangers' last gasp at infamy was breaking the Starr County strikes, even to the point of drawing rebuke from the United States Supreme Court in 1974 in a lawsuit that made a slow trek up there from Starr County. The court's written decision, delivered the year after my arrival in the Valley, outlined the Rangers' treachery and malicious deeds against workers and organizers.

Captain A. Y. Allee, the first-named defendant in the Supreme Court case, oversaw the Rangers' malevolent antiunion activities. Allee himself led the "violent and brutal" arrests of two union organizers, which Justice William Douglas detailed in the court's ruling. One man was hospitalized with a brain concussion. X-rays showed the Rangers struck him so hard on the back that his spine was curved out of shape. The other organizer suffered multiple abrasions. Rangers broke one of his fingers and tore off the nail. It makes one cringe to imagine the excruciating pain this out-of-control force so wantonly inflicted.

The Supreme Court opinion recounted other Ranger-instigated incidents to break the strikes. In one, UFW pickets, to protest transporting produce from the Valley on the Missouri Pacific Railroad, had gathered at the train tracks that ran through Mission, Texas. The Rangers arrested Reverend Ed Krueger and Magdaleno Dimas, a lead UFW organizer, and held their bodies so close to the passing train that their faces were only inches from the railcars speeding past.

No one had ever beaten *los rinches* in court before, nor so dramatically. Because of the excoriating court decision, Texas legislators, led by their Mexican American colleagues and the progressive bloc at the time, finally reined in the Rangers and put them under the thumb of the Texas Department of Public Safety, the state police. The Rangers organization had to take on the trappings of professionalism and jettison its tough "one riot, one Ranger" motif, which Rangers had cynically cultivated over the

CAPTAIN ALLEE THREATENS TO SUE

In 1972, the Valley's UFW newspaper, *¡Ya Mero!* (*Now Is the Time!*), ran a front-page photo of Allee, arms crossed, smilingly chomping on a cheap, stubby cigar, as was his wont, and looking rather paunchy in his Ranger outfit. Across the middle of the photo was the slogan *¡Abajo los Rinches!* (Down with the Rangers!) in red letters resembling dripping blood.

Allee took umbrage at the photo and accompanying article and threatened a lawsuit for slander. *¡Ya Mero!* was up to the challenge, published his cease-and-desist letter, and dared him to sue. His bullying days were coming to an end. Truth, after all, is an absolute defense against a slander charge. It would not have been pretty for Allee to argue his case to Hidalgo County jurors, some of whose families would have had an unfortunate family history with the Rangers.

Rubbing it in, *¡Ya Mero!* printed large posters of the front page as a fundraiser. One hung on my wall until damaged by an office fire in 2013. I had subscribed to *¡Ya Mero!* long before arriving in the Valley.

years by terrorizing the *mexicano* community at whim. Captain Allee had to retire in ignominy.

After retiring, Allee pistol-whipped a young Hispanic clerk in a Carrizo Springs store for accidentally ringing up the wrong charge for a five-gallon jug of water ($1.75 instead of $1.35). That was a pattern in his career, including pistol-whipping a highway patrol officer who had ticketed his wife.

Allee diligently earned his reputation as an unrepentant racist. He was a representative symbol of the Rangers' aggression, but not an exclusive one. Others also filled those boots.

Although the 1966 march and melon strikes didn't yield immediate success (the legislature passed the minimum wage in 1969), they ignited a brushfire across the state. Together, they were a catalyst for the Chicano human rights movement in Texas. It was the movement's Rosa Parks moment.

A seed of justice was growing now in fertile soil, fertilized by the high court's stunningly sharp censure that brought a semblance of justice served to the brutish Rangers.

Volunteers who had been involved in aiding the Starr County strikes moved on to other local organizing actions. They plugged in to programs initiated by President Lyndon Johnson's War on Poverty. They formed La Raza Unida, a separate political party, to move away from the local Democratic Party's *patrón* structures that controlled Valley politics.

EDCOUCH-ELSA STUDENT WALKOUT

On and off high school and university campuses throughout Texas, youth, mostly Mexican Americans, began to organize, inspired by the farmworkers' courage. They called themselves "Chicanos," originally an Anglo classist and racist slur toward low-income Mexicans that activists reclaimed as their own. As Valley UFW members pressed harder for their rights, these young folks looked for ways to drive the movement forward.

Edcouch-Elsa High School students, virtually all of them Mexican American, were getting itchy and pushing back against the school district's in-your-face racism. They organized together in 1968 and demanded an end to being punished for speaking Spanish on campus and being discouraged from pursuing college ambitions. When the Anglo-controlled school board summarily spurned their demands without even a gesture of dialogue, two hundred students walked out of school.

The Edcouch-Elsa students took a cue from Kingsville Gillett Junior High School students who had walked out for similar reasons eight days earlier on April 14. As that group marched toward another junior high, Kingsville police arrested every student and broke their efforts. Walkouts had begun a year earlier in seven East Los Angeles schools (15,000 students).

The Edcouch-Elsa protest grabbed the national spotlight. The students were articulate in the media: Why, after all, should administrators jeopardize the students' education and their futures simply because they spoke their family language with friends at school? And why did the school channel them into trades and steer them away from college? Does any reason but bigotry explain this?

The Anglo power structure held tight. School officials retaliated with expulsions and suspensions. They had some students arrested and jailed. The students' classmates responded by serenading them in evening vigils outside Hidalgo County's old, dilapidated jail, singing "De Colores," which had become a movement anthem.

The La Joya Independent School District, forty miles away, was the only district that would accept the expelled students. The owner of the Tienda Amarilla grocery in Elsa covered the cost of busing the students daily there and back so they could continue their educations. Had it not been for him, those kids would have had to repeat the school year and wait to graduate—not that school administrators cared one bit. It was a dark commentary on the Valley's establishment, how it could take away, apportion, and deny education to the *mexicano* community at will.

The Edcouch-Elsa walkout was a hinge moment in Rio Grande Valley history and for the broader Chicano civil rights movement. Walkouts spread to Uvalde and Crystal City in the fall, foretelling the epicenter of the new La Raza Unida political party. The resistance leapfrogged across Texas and the country to as many as a hundred schools.

THE PHARR RIOT

In February 1971, the so-called Pharr Riot rocked South Texas like an earthquake. It began at City Hall in the small town of Pharr, which borders McAllen on the east, as a peaceful protest by the Mexican American community against overarching local police brutality and Anglo oppression. A coalition of local groups and individuals organizing as Unión y Fuerza (Union and Strength) spearheaded the resistance.

The City Hall protest began with a small group. As the day wore on, the protest expanded exponentially. The local constabulary, panicked by the enormity of the gathering crowd, unleashed powerful fire department water hoses at the demonstrators and shot tear gas at them. They were following the playbook of the police in the South against African American protesters.

Order broke down, and the police fatally shot an innocent bystander, Alfonso "Pancho" Flores, in front of Estanislado Ramos's small barbershop six blocks away. Reportedly, a nearby officer was aiming at Ramos through the window of his barbershop. He missed. His bullet ricocheted off the rain gutter and hit Flores in the head. Ramos was likely targeted for being an activist. He had one of the few *mexicano* businesses in the rigidly segregated town, and the local Raza Unida party held meetings there.

Pancho Flores's slaying ignited an intense political campaign that deposed the Anglo-controlled government and elected a Mexican American mayor for the first time. César Chávez attended Flores's memorial, which helped rev up political organizing. Pharr's new council revamped the city's police regime.

Fifty years to the date, Pharr officials unveiled a Texas Historical Commission marker in front of the former Ramos barbershop, commemorating the "Pharr Riot" and the political organizing in its aftermath as "important events in Texas' Chicano Movement [that] advanced civil rights and political participation."

The marker's words are an understatement. "Another catalyst" in the movement would be more historically accurate. Nor should this memorial placate us into thinking anything other than it being a single signpost among many on the long road to justice. No backsliding, move forward.

SOUTH TEXAS WATER RIGHTS PROJECT

In 1972, the national ACLU decided to lend help to the cause by creating a water rights project in the Valley and housing it at the UFW offices in south McAllen, where the union had set up shop after the Starr County uprising.

David Fishlow, a volunteer with the Texas UFW and editor of its *¡Ya Mero!* newspaper, guided this arrangement with the ACLU. David Hall, already on the scene as a forceful movement lawyer, became director of the new South Texas Water Rights Project. Its dual design was to fight the discriminatory exclusion of Valley *colonias* from local water districts and to assist UFW organizing.

Colonias are wretchedly poor, rural Hispanic communities. At the time, they were unregulated subdivisions located outside municipal boundaries; housing was less expensive there. Most *colonias* lacked infrastructure such as paved roads, street lighting, sewer systems, trash pickup, postal service, and so on. Nor was there police protection. Residents had to rely on the county sheriff, who was without resources to adequately patrol the *colonias*.

About 1,200 *colonias* with varying numbers of residences are dispersed throughout the Valley, mostly families of farm laborers and other low-income occupants. The *colonias* are places of punishing poverty and prone to flooding.

Like other Southwestern states, Texas has state-created water districts, twenty-five altogether. They are municipalities with elected governance. In 1972, a district's function was to manage flooding and to allocate potable water within its geographic boundaries for human consumption and agricultural irrigation.

Water district boards had the power to include or exclude residential communities within the district. If a district excluded a residential area, it no longer had to provide drinking water. The Anglo growers and ranchers governed the districts through trickery and connivance, such as burying English-only election advisories and meeting notices on the courthouse bulletin board and holding meetings during the workday.

The growers and ranchers could, and did, jeopardize people's lives and health at pleasure.

They excluded *colonias* with abandon so they could reserve the water for their crops and cattle, depriving *mexicano* rural communities of drinkable water. It was a raw exercise of power and greed without moral boundaries. Curtailing a natural resource on which poor people depended for livelihood was shameless oppression.

There are also *colonias* without potable water that were never part of a water district or municipality. Alex Moreno, one of the UFW organizers assaulted during the La Casita strike and mentioned by name in the *Allee v. Medrano* Supreme Court case (the litigation against the Ranger captain, discussed above), became executive director of the nonprofit Colonias de Valle, Inc., which aided in bringing water to *colonias* through private and government funding sources.

He helped engineer a very unfavorable *U.S. News & World Report* 1976 Bicentennial article with photographs about Colonia Balboa adjacent to south McAllen. That prompted the city finally to incorporate the *colonia* and extend municipal services. Bad publicity does not attract tourists and "snowbird" dollars to the "Magic Valley," as a common sales pitch puts it.

Being denied clean water meant that misery and disease abounded. In excluded areas, people would have to truck in water in fifty-five–gallon barrels that might have once contained harmful chemicals or lead. The barrels sat outside small *colonia* homes in the Texas sun. Overall, health data for the Valley is more wretched than for other regions of the country. As a parent, I shudder at the very thought of having to raise kids without clean water for drinking and washing. Unimaginable.

The *colonia* reality was only one marker of the oppression that the Anglo power centers visited upon the Mexican American community. Every facet of life danced to the racism and class structures at play. Sometimes it was a tale of two cities in one.

The east–west railroad line across the Valley ran through a long string of border towns, with Anglos residing on one side of the track, *mexicanos* on the other. The differences were stark and shameful: two separate communities united by geography but forcibly divided by heritage, a tool to perpetuate class divisions.

Wealth and power gathered on one side of the railroad line, poverty and oppression on the opposite. It was as night is to day, as they say, except that the phrase does not capture the suffering visited upon poorer people. A few *mexicanos* made it across the tracks, including those who would protect the system and offer their services as border watchdogs, attuned to Anglo interests.

The historical record and narratives of the Valley fill far too many volumes of rampant injustice and heavy-handed repression.

EARLY LITIGATION AT THE SOUTH TEXAS PROJECT

Under David Hall's adroit leadership, the South Texas Project helped shepherd three major federal lawsuits. Two, cocounseled by the Mexican American Legal Defense and Education Fund (a nonprofit civil rights advocacy group of Texas origin formed in 1968), challenged the *colonias*' exclusion from water districts.

Eventually, the water district litigation was lost due to an intervening US Supreme Court decision authored by then-Justice William Rehnquist in a similar California water district case. The high court ruled that denying drinking water to Mexican American *colonias* did not violate the equal protection guarantees of the Fourteenth Amendment to the United States Constitution. The Court had decided it was okay to take away from people a common, necessary natural resource that they once possessed!

The water district lawsuits were not a total defeat. What is the classic adage? Losing the battle but winning the war. This is so because in 1975 the legendary Congresswoman Barbara Jordan of Houston helped bring Texas under the jurisdiction of the Voting Rights Act of 1965, which among other things banned municipalities from excluding geographic areas from their jurisdictions if doing so would diminish minority representation. The law was retroactive. The law also required bilingual access, such as ballots and election notices in Spanish. Being covered by the Voting Rights Act meant that many *colonias* stayed within the water districts.

The third case attacked the gross underrepresentation of Hispanics on Hidalgo County grand juries, which had a heavily Anglo tilt in a county that was 80–85 percent Mexican American. The grand jury case succeeded in the Supreme Court, an enormous victory for justice in South Texas. I detail the saga of grand jury reform in Texas in chapter 4.

MY FIRST ASSIGNMENTS AT THE SOUTH TEXAS PROJECT

The South Texas Project had four people on staff: two lawyers, a legal assistant, and a paralegal. David handled the systemic change lawsuits. Yours truly attended to the individual legal needs of UFW members. The handful of lawsuits described below, handed to me minutes after I walked through the front door, reflected common issues impacting South Texas justice.

Minimum Wage: A Regular Valley Problem

My very first lawsuit in 1973 was on behalf of Fidel Desiga, who had a minimum wage claim that he was not receiving time-and-a-half pay for overtime hours, as required by law. He was one of the lucky farmworkers who drove a tractor and thus came under the regular federal minimum wage law, which was a munificent $1.60/hour. The law entitled him to time-and-a-half overtime pay for working more than forty hours per week. The minimum wage for regular farm laborers at the time was $1.30/hour, with no overtime pay.

Fidel's lawsuit settled quickly, as he had kept meticulous documentation of his hours. The settlement was substantial because the underpayment had occurred for months despite entreaties to his boss. Suing was risky because his employer might have replaced him on the spot, not an uncommon fate for Valley workers asserting their rights. He was a pleasant man, and softspoken, but single-minded that his family needed what he should have received for his labor.

Sadly, a couple years later, the tractor Fidel was driving overturned and crushed him to death. He was in his mid- to late thirties and left behind a young family. This was before federal law required rollover bars on farm

BETWEEN THE EYES

Sometimes a person learns humility in the most unexpected ways. Not too long after my start in the Valley, a farmworker and his teenage daughter came in to discuss a case. They sat together, barely fitting between the wall and the desk in my hot, cramped office.

I held forth for a half-hour in Spanish about his case, boasting to myself in my mind that I had Spanish nailed down. They politely listened. When I finished, he quietly turned to his daughter and asked, "¿Qué dijo?" (What did he say?). "¿Qué dijo?" will come up again later in this memoir.

equipment like tractors. Fidel was a victim of tardily enacted federal regulations for agriculture. Still today, agricultural labor in Texas is one of the state's most dangerous occupations, trading first place with construction depending on the season of the year.

Another minimum wage issue was whether the Valley piece rate reflected the federal minimum hourly requirement. Farmworkers harvest crops by buckets, sacks, pounds, and the like. Theoretically, payment for what they harvest by the piece must average out to the federal hourly minimum.

The Texas Department of Agriculture would publish a piece-rate schedule that growers relied on to ensure they were complying with federal law (e.g., $.35/bag of onions). The department, which agricultural employers controlled politically, set the rate low to maximize growers' profits. This meant that field laborers rarely received the federal minimum, coming in under the mark.

I held my first-ever press conference in August 1973 at the UFW center. Without air-conditioning in the building, the heat was sweltering, ratcheted up a few more degrees with the TV stations' floodlights. With a great deal of fanfare we laid out large, hand-drawn graphs demonstrating how farmworkers would need to approximate superhuman strength and capabilities to achieve the federal hourly wage at the official Texas piece rate. The charts did the trick. The media loved them. The state's agriculture commissioner, in the face of the adverse publicity, agreed to reevaluate the piece rate, but nothing ultimately came of it of course.

By sheer happenstance, while writing this book, I met a former agriculture department employee directly involved in the piece-rate issue at the time. She confirmed that the message had come down from on high to slow the reassessment process such that it would be forgotten. No raising the piece rate. The typical Texas government two-step.

A Cattle-Dipping Vat in Your Backyard

Simultaneously with Fidel Desiga's suit, I took up a lawsuit for the people of Santa Maria, a small town of four hundred souls. There was a private cattle-dipping vat smack in the middle of the town. A dipping vat is a huge bathing pool of chemicals that ranchers run cattle through and immerse them in to kill ticks that cause cattle fever. Dipping is a legal requirement before transporting them north to slaughter. A tick eradication quarantine boundary arches around South Texas.

A vat operation is incredibly filthy, stinking, and odious. Just imagine the manure left behind. Unloading and reloading cattle in the middle of the small town was dirty, noisy, and noxious, even worse when they herded cattle into town on hoof instead of cattle trailers, although that was quite bad enough.

The Anglo owner was about to build a new, even larger dipping vat to replace the old one. The citizens were very upset. An expanded vat would only increase the stinking odors that wafted across the little *mexicano* town, not to mention all the residual manure. We filed a suit on behalf of the residents to block the new vat.

Texas law considers a cattle-dipping vat to be a per se nuisance. That means its location must be far enough away not to adversely affect neighbors or even the larger community. Otherwise, the law presumes it a nuisance in and of itself ("per se" means "on its face"), and so the owner must remove it or not build one in the first place.

Our chances seemed slim because the private owner was a politically powerful county commissioner. However, good winds were behind us. The judge accepted our per se nuisance argument and ordered the commissioner to find a new vat location elsewhere. It was my first time getting a court-ordered injunction from a judge. It was an exhilarating feeling for me and a joyful day for Santa Maria.

That somebody would build a dipping vat in the middle of a poor residential area reflected the Valley's unabashed power structure. The Anglo growers and ranchers wielded power and cared not one whit how they adversely and arbitrarily affected those without power—the *mexicano* communities.

Blowing Smoke and Sugarcane

Another memorable case that came my way in mid-1974 involved Rio Grande Valley Sugar Growers, Inc. The agribusiness was seeking a permit from the Texas Air Control Board to burn 30,000 acres of sugarcane (200–300 acres/day) before machine-harvesting it. The operation produced 1.5 million tons of sugarcane each year.

Burning a cane field is a way of removing the "trash," the leaves and tops of the sugarcane plant, so only the sugar-bearing stalks remain. Machines then move through the field, harvesting the cane. Burning in the Valley, whether sugarcane or something else, can result in stark, in-your-face environmental racism.

Burning sugarcane pollutes nearby waterways with acid rain, increases greenhouse gas emissions, and depletes soil nutrients and microbial life. It can harm wildlife caught in the flames, which shoot high into the air above the fields.

Burning is an extraordinarily filthy process. Clouds of oily ash drift near and far with the wind. The sticky ashes dirty people's laundry, yards, and housing, especially of those living in the *colonias* near the flaming acreage. The ash drift is unhealthy to breathe, especially for older people and individuals with respiratory ailments, who already have limited medical care access because of their poverty.

Machines can harvest the cane without burning it. The alternate process is slower and more cumbersome, but it is doable. Burning is unnecessary. Yet landowners preferred it because it is efficient and increases profits. Other places in the world that once customarily torched cane were scaling back burning, except in Texas, where it continued to expand.

Various Valley community groups opposed burning cane for a variety of reasons apart from the environmental. Burning reduces the number of harvesters needed. The farmworkers union looked at the effort to block cane-burning as a way of employing 500–1,000 more field laborers, who would clean the trash with machetes before machines moved in. This would economically benefit the Valley at large.

We partnered with a small legal project, American Friends Service Committee in San Benito, to sue the Air Control Board and prevent it from issuing the permit. Because it was a state agency, we had to file the case in Austin. Nutritional Enrichment, Inc., a local community-based, health-related foundation, was the lead plaintiff.

It did not take long for us two Valley attorneys—both very new to the profession with law school barely in hindsight—to run into a buzzsaw of money and high-powered attorneys, as well as an elected judge far from the Valley who, like all Texas judges, depended on campaign contributions. We were not sitting on a balanced seesaw. We lost.

What set us back more than anything was being late to the game. The growers' cooperative had already built their sugar refining mill for $28 million and were gearing up to begin burning in December 1973.

Whether we could have prevailed if a solid organizing effort to stop the burning had begun a few years earlier before the mill was built is an open question, probably answered negatively, given the economic forces at play. But it would have been well worth the fight.

The mill shut down in 2024 due to a lack of enough water to run the operation, the result of a treaty dispute with Mexico over allotment of irrigation water from the Rio Grande, the border river separating the United States and Mexico.

Another Early Lawsuit: Discrimination

Another early case was an employment discrimination claim for Juanita Cantú, who was seeking a routine promotion with her US Customs job at the Hidalgo Port of Entry on the border, but some Anglo good old boys blocked her advancement. They misjudged her resolve to assert herself into their hitherto closed group. Her lawsuit unblocked the logjam.

We also later oversaw two successful pattern-and-practice discrimination lawsuits for Mexican Americans at the Weslaco hospital and for women and Mexican Americans at KGBT in Harlingen, the Valley's TV and radio dynamo broadcasting in English and Spanish. We partnered with community groups to petition the Federal Communications Commission to revoke KGBT's broadcast license, which was up for renewal,

MOTHERS CARRYING KIDS THROUGH FLOODWATERS

Developers built *colonias* on floodplains existing among the flood-control levees that weave throughout the Valley because it was cheaper to do so. As a result, torrential or prolonged rains would inundate the *colonias*. Few roads were paved. Most streets became mud.

One memory has a permanent place in my mind. I was driving south of Pharr early one school day. Las Milpas, a large *colonia* close to town, was under water after a few days of heavy rain. The yellow school bus could not drive into the *colonia* to pick up the kids because of the flooding. The bus had stopped on the raised highway that ran alongside the colonia.

Mothers were walking through the muddy, shin-deep water, carrying their kids to the bus. Such was the moms' dedication that their kids get an education and advance beyond the life of abject poverty in which the family lived. Witnessing this profoundly moved me.

and settled when KGBT bowed and substantially improved its employment practices.

The Anglo vanguard needed some help moving out of the way—and we obliged them.

TRANSITIONING FROM A SPECIAL PROJECT INTO A COMMUNITY CIVIL RIGHTS WORK

David Hall did a very worthy job, shepherding the South Texas Project into the Valley's struggle for justice. Less than two years after my arrival in El Valle de Lágrimas, David went off to become executive director of the newly created, federally funded Texas Rural Legal Aid (now known as Texas RioGrande Legal Aid, with the same "TRLA" acronym).

That left me, still a legal neophyte, in charge. This came with some hefty responsibilities and an undreamed-of opportunity to forge a new direction for STP, to anchor it in the community, an approach I carried forward to the Texas Civil Rights Project.

The ACLU funded STP at $20,000/year, which we divided among four staff at $5,000/year as salaries. The national Methodist Church covered our health expenses. The median national personal income was $12,050 at that time. Nor did we have funds for litigation. To say we were a shoestring operation is close to an overstatement.

We were desperate for more funding. That pressed me to organize Oficina Legal del Pueblo Unido, Inc. (Law Office of the People United), a tax-exempt nonprofit grassroots foundation, and set about raising direly needed money.

Oficina Legal became the vehicle to receive four years of funding from the Catholic Campaign for Human Development, which was underwriting community organizing projects at the time. That group wanted to support us but could not send money through the ACLU because of the abortion issue.

Bishop John Fitzpatrick of Brownsville, a solid ally, had our back on this and other matters. We secured the funding. In time, we raised our salaries with an overall budget of about $90,000. The UFW center, which housed STP, continued to furnish office space and cover utilities.

Little did I imagine that Oficina Legal would later provide a launching pad for the new Texas Civil Rights Project. So much of what I learned—

and had to learn—early on was important to later forming and guiding TCRP.

What moved us quickly into becoming a community civil rights organization was a series of lawsuits against the McAllen police. This expanded our focus beyond farm labor issues and grand jury reform into other human rights issues facing the people. The people began to see us—and we began to see ourselves—as opening a new civil rights path in South Texas. That path became wider as time went on.

TAKEAWAYS: MY FIRST TWO YEARS AT THE SOUTH TEXAS PROJECT

Showing up is important. I spent a few hot Saturday mornings husking maize that grew on eight acres of the union's property. I was surprised by people's reaction when the lawyer would join them. That created confidence on all levels. I learned the lesson and practiced it for five decades: show up and be part of whatever the community is doing.

Word spreads. As with other minority groups, the Mexican American community rapidly spreads the word (*chisme*) among itself. The scuttlebutt on the street might not always be 100 percent accurate, but it was usually accurate enough to work with. A corollary of this is that farmworkers "know things," much more so than the majority culture credits them. How much innate wisdom and practical talent abounded was a real eye-opener for me. Given my background and training, this was a lesson in humility; and I was grateful for it.

People appreciate what you do. Grapefruit, oranges, lettuce, or vegetables from whatever harvest was underway would show up at the office. Or maybe some bean tacos with homemade tortillas. One day, a large wooden sculpture of the UFW's Aztec eagle logo against the red-and-white background showed up. An inmate from the Valley had made it at the prison workshop and had someone deliver it. I never learned his name, unfortunately—only that it was for the "union attorney." It was in my office since that day and now takes place of pride on a wall in my home.

It was a great privilege to arrive in the Valley at that period and do my best to help further the justice work begun by others. I met many of these stalwart individuals and collaborated with some of them, ordinary people doing extraordinary things.

3

POLICE BRUTALITY, ACT I

McAllen's C-Shift Animals

I learned early on that, as a civil rights lawyer, you move ahead not knowing what's coming next or even the scale of what's about to happen. This was true for a sequence of cases at the South Texas Project against the McAllen Police Department that unfolded one after another and eventually garnered national and international opprobrium.

The McAllen lawsuits had their beginning in a single, vicious police beating and escalated because of a happenstance discussion with two brothers before filing their lawsuit. Theirs was the third to go to trial in this sequence.

Some background: the first lawsuit (these were all civil actions filed in federal court by private citizens for violations of their civil rights under federal statute) was in 1976 on behalf of Guadalupe "Lupe" Cano, a clean-cut eighteen-year-old high-school student. An officer arrested Lupe for public intoxication at a nightclub one evening in November 1975. Lupe became physically ill in the back of the squad car, and the police hosed him down outside the station when they arrived and then pummeled him into unconsciousness inside, cutting his face and badly bruising him.

We won a favorable jury verdict, which drew considerable media publicity, much to our happy surprise. Police lawsuits are tough to win, which makes any victory sweeter. More McAllen victims at the hands of cops began showing up at the front door. As we won more lawsuits, the line grew longer.

The second jury trial involved two other young high-school students, Mike Robles and his older cousin Lisandro Espinoza. Lisandro went into a nightclub one evening to take a quick peek for a friend. Mike, a minor, remained in the car.

Mike was of slight stature for his fifteen years. He had some developmental disabilities and difficulty speaking and hearing. He was sitting in the passenger seat of the car—counting his pennies, as he testified—when the police showed up. After some hasty questioning, the cops arrested Mike for suspected auto theft. They took him away without checking his claim that he was waiting on his cousin in his cousin's car. The police were hard-pressed at trial to explain why they thought Mike was heisting an auto.

Lisandro came out of the club and found that Mike was gone. When he heard that the police had been in the parking lot, he went to the police station to check whether Mike was there and, if so, to bring him home.

Mike was still in the booking area when Lisandro arrived, upset at what had happened. He let the officers know. The police didn't cotton to Lisandro's attitude and beat both him and Mike, slamming Lisandro against a wall. Margie Robles, Mike's mother and Lisandro's aunt, became irate at what had happened and pressed forward with litigation. We prevailed in that jury trial, too. Another happy outcome.

But what was different about this case compared to the other police brutality lawsuits against McAllen was that Margie came from a more middle-class setting than the other kids the police beat. It soon became clear that, unlike people from a lower economic bracket, middle-class folks will give deference to the police; but if they betray that deference, then it goes downhill hard and fast for the police.

The third lawsuit, the one with the farthest-reaching consequences, involved Celso and José Guerrero—two brothers, early twenties, of small stature—whom the police had arrested and severely beaten at the police station. Their case broke open a logjam.

Celso and José came by the office after work the evening before I was to file their case. During our conversation and almost as an afterthought, Celso shared a bombshell: "Don't forget to get the videotape." The brothers reported that, while the police were assaulting them, one of them shouted to someone to turn off the video camera so it would not record the beating.

It seemed beyond the pale that cops would be so foolish to videotape themselves whipping up on people in the booking area. This was decades before the ubiquitous, painful, and sometimes horrifying recordings of police brutality that today circulate on the internet.

Nevertheless, to be prudent, I drafted a perfunctory order to preserve all existing tapes and took it with me when I went to file the case in Brownsville. The United States District Court judge, Reynaldo Garza, signed my draft order without any questions, to preserve all videos.

On the way back to the office, I looped over to the McAllen Police Department and dropped off the order for the police chief, still not totally believing there would be videotapes of the officers' brutality. As fate would have it, the chief routinely handed off the order to Captain James Borman. That was the game-changer.

After the jury returned its verdict in favor of the Guerrero brothers, we decided to rachet up our police litigation and moved forward with a class action suit against the city. Besides seeking damages for victims, the idea was to pursue a court order requiring systemic change in the department. Such an order would protect people from the kind of ongoing brutality playing out in our lawsuits. It would also determine if the city owed damages to the plaintiffs in addition to what they won against individual culprit officers.

Before the class action could commence against McAllen itself, US District Judge James DeAnda, who was newly appointed and presiding over the police litigation, ruled that we would have to complete the trials on each individual's legal claims. This turned out to be a fortuitous decision, although none of us had a clue at the time. As it happened, DeAnda's decision added pressure on us to win the individual trials to proceed against the city in the class action.

Joe Richard Flores, a newly licensed attorney, joined the South Texas Project in September 1980 during the police trials and showed his skill at sizing up juries and their take on witnesses' credibility. Together we successfully litigated eight separate jury trials over a five-year period on behalf of ten victims, losing only one case. We added eight more people to the class action with the court's approval. Altogether there were seventeen plaintiffs bringing claims against twenty-six officers. Other potential plaintiffs decided against suing the police for various reasons, including fear of retaliation.

The victims were young men, typically arrested for alcohol-related offenses, whom the police then thrashed at the station. The beatings happened at night at the hands of the department's late-night shift, designated as the "C-Shift."

Judge DeAnda, whose son was a Houston police officer, did not take kindly to our lawsuits and was often harsh with respect to his rulings. One trial, for example, involved the parents of young Eddie Longoria, who unfortunately had died in a traffic accident a year before his brutality case

BANISHING A BIASED NEWSPAPER REPORTER

One fun part of the McAllen police trials, admittedly with a smack of retribution, was sidelining the *McAllen Monitor*'s reporter assigned to cover the cases, Virginia Armstrong. She was a good friend of Mayor Othal Brand.

During city council meetings, Armstrong chain-smoked small, slim cigars at the press table, above which hung a black-and-red "No Smoking" sign. She enjoyed impunity. No one dared upset her. She had a poison pen and free rein at the *Monitor*. She was so pro–City Hall that locals labeled her reportage "Brand-speak."

Armstrong was against our cases and wrote disparaging comments about the trials. Her narrative was so off-base that an observer would not believe that she had really been present. Her articles would refer to me as a "civil rights" lawyer. Yes, "civil rights" in quotes. That was her way of commenting negatively on civil rights generally, and on our clients, in her backhanded style.

As the trials went on, it became clearer that the class action would implicate the mayor. Because she and Brand customarily breakfasted together at a local omelet restaurant, I decided to subpoena her as a potential witness. That would block her from attending any of the individual trials and reporting back to Brand. It would also dead-end her lousy, biased reporting on our cases, both the individual cases and the class action to come.

Under standard court procedure, a subpoenaed witness cannot be inside the courtroom to watch when not testifying unless the attorneys agree to allow it. It was a fun conversation in the courthouse hallway when Armstrong found out she was under subpoena and thus according to the rules she could not attend hearings and any of the related trials. She begged me to let her off the hook. I just smiled and pulled the fishing line a little tighter. This turned out to be a good move because the *Monitor* assigned a different reporter, Gail Sammons, whose coverage was more objective and fair-minded.

came to trial. Eddie was a short young man with a beguiling smile and curly black hair. He was his parents' only child, and they doted on him.

McAllen officer B. T. Wilson had beaten Eddie, only fifteen years old. Wilson, who was six inches taller and sixty pounds heavier, slugged the young teen with such force that he knocked him into a brick wall, breaking a tooth and lacerating the inside of his cheek.

The trial pressed down hard on his parents, who had to relive their son's brutalization by Wilson while still grieving his death. It saddened them, but they wanted to move forward out of a desire to exact justice upon Wilson for what the officer had done to their son. We wanted to do our best for them and for their deceased child.

For reasons related to arcane rules of evidence, we had a tough time getting the parents' testimony in front of the jury regarding Eddie's medical and emotional problems following the beating. DeAnda kept saying that applicable rules precluded the parents' testimony because Eddie was deceased and that they couldn't testify about his verbal communications with them unless there was other evidence supporting those statements. We had plenty of evidence, and we would have had more had we known of the police videos at the time.

I pushed back, which angered the judge. That I would not back down stoked his ire even more. He began berating me in front of the jury, one time almost shouting that he was going to hold me in contempt and declare a mistrial. It was excruciatingly embarrassing to stand in front of the jury and the Longoria family while he excoriated me. I'm sure my face was as red as my tie, and I hoped they didn't think I was as bad a lawyer as the judge was implying. I remember my body temperature jumping a few notches. It was the roughest trial of my life—but we prevailed. The jury awarded actual and punitive damages to Eddie's parents.

After concluding deliberations the jurors sent out a note that they had reached a verdict but could not elect a presiding juror to deliver the verdict because they were all afraid that the judge would rebuke and scold the foreperson. To his credit, Judge DeAnda found this amusing and sent a "not to worry" note back to the jury. He was gracious and even a bit apologetic in the end.

Somewhere along the line, as the trials played out, the lawyers met in the judge's chambers for a pretrial matter. He tilted slightly back in his chair behind his desk as we stood around (one never sat down in a judge's office unless invited). He took off his glasses, rubbed the bridge of his nose, and joked with a certain amount of truth that he had done his best to help the city but that we were still running the table.

BEATING THE CRIMINAL CHARGES BROUGHT AGAINST MY CLIENTS

I also had to handle any criminal trials resulting from charges police filed against the young men, which were usually public intoxication, resisting arrest, assault, or something similar.

Avoiding any convictions from the confrontation with the cops is crucial to civil rights trials. A conviction goes a long way toward resolving disputed facts in favor of the police and in fact precludes a civil lawsuit against them.

One criminal case involved officer B. T. Wilson, also the defendant in Eddie Longoria's civil case. In 1979, he assaulted and arrested Pedro Dennett and Juan Martínez at a nightclub because they were flirting with a woman who, unknown to them, turned out to be Wilson's girlfriend. Wilson, even though off-duty at the time and having tipped a few at the club, arrested both men for public intoxication. At the police station, he assaulted them outside the booking area in the carport entranceway. A video captured the beating.

Both Dennett and Martinez were military police on leave to visit their families. Their criminal trial had an amusing moment. Wilson testified about the standard characteristics that police memorize to prove somebody is intoxicated (slurred speech, unsteady on their feet, alcohol on their breath, bloodshot eyes, that kind of stuff).

When it was the defendants' turn to testify, I asked Dennett and Martinez about their duties as MPs and whether they had arrested people for public intoxication on the base. Of course, they said, a good number. I went through all the same intoxication characteristics with each of them about Wilson, as he had done regarding them. And then I asked if Wilson appeared to be intoxicated. They both answered affirmatively. The jurors enjoyed the irony and smiled a bit.

After listening to me almost parade around the courtroom, righteously declaiming American justice and praising the MPs for their service (it was the afternoon before Thanksgiving, after all), the six jurors adjourned to deliberate. They did not even sit down in the jury room. They did a

UNDULY INFLUENCING THE JURY?

One jury-related event is worth mentioning. After a successful trial on a consumer case for TCRP's community architect friend, long after moving to Austin, the losing party, outraged at an adverse jury verdict, filed a complaint against me with the State Bar for "unduly influencing the jury." That seemed humorous (if not bizarre), since that's pretty close to exactly the job of a lawyer. The State Bar of course ignored the complaint, but I would bet they also chuckled a bit at this farce.

quick survey on their feet, chose the presiding juror, turned around, and returned the verdict: "Not guilty." To say they took a whole minute would be a stretch.

I loved handling trials and arguing appeals. Being on your toes (and often on your feet) gets the adrenalin flowing. Jury trials are especially fascinating, with more than a bit of theater. Jurors love to watch a certain amount of posturing and playacting by the attorneys moving around the courtroom and even getting close to the jury box. It's often helpful to the case.

Trial judges are cutting down on the drama, however. Nowadays, they often require would-be thespian attorneys to stand behind a podium and prevent them from moving around the courtroom. That has made trials less interesting and less gripping and usually causes a juror or two to take in a quick snooze.

BRUTAL POLICE VIDEOS SUDDENLY APPEAR

It took four years to find out that police videos indeed existed. It occurred almost haphazardly as three McAllen officers were testifying on our behalf at a pretrial hearing before the class action was to get underway. This trio came forward and offered to testify for the plaintiffs against the C-Shift officers who did the beatings; they were disgusted by their colleagues' brutal conduct.

In preparing each case for trial, out of due diligence, we repeatedly asked the city attorney assigned to the lawsuit if there were videos of the beatings and always received a negative response.

The city attorneys would reply that indeed a camera was affixed to the wall in the booking area. The camera was there, they affirmed, only so the front desk officer could monitor the booking room in case something suddenly came up to which other police needed to respond, but no recordings.

The city's responses did not seem unreasonable, and there did not appear to be any reason to doubt them. Lawyers are supposed to trust their colleagues. In retrospect, the question is whether this was deliberate dissembling on their part or were knowingly relaying someone else's lie.

Adding to my current skepticism is that, along the line, we learned that Mayor Brand and the police chief at the time had ordered the videos' destruction. Did their attorneys know this? Fortunately, Captain Borman didn't play games and resolutely abided by the federal judge's order.

Borman was one of the three officers who came forward to testify for us. As it turned out, he changed the course of the litigation. During the pretrial hearing, answering a throwaway question, when lawyers might stretch for a Perry Mason moment, I asked him about the tapes, as if they existed (though I still doubted they did). I don't know why I tossed out the question spontaneously.

Then came the bombshell. Borman testified that yes, indeed, there were videos—six years' worth, in fact. He himself kept them shelved and cataloged after the former chief had given him the court order to preserve evidence. It turned out that he had saved seventy-two tapes of police brutality at the station. He had routinely erased another seventy or so before receiving the court's order.

Even more astonishing was Captain Borman's testimony that the police would check out videos of the beatings from his office and watch them for entertainment at parties. It is hard to find an adjective for this; maybe "sadistic" would fit.

McAllen faced a day of reckoning in 1980 when Judge DeAnda ordered the graphic videos released to the public. They showed police taunting, slapping, kicking, punching, and hurling arrestees to the ground. The victims were Mexican American boys or young men. The police who wreaked the brutality were mostly Anglo, but some were Mexican American themselves.

Most of the videotaped McAllen police beatings occurred during the late-night shift, the "C-Shift," whose officers took perverse pride in their

LEGITIMACY, THANKS TO PHIL DONAHUE

The McAllen litigation and videos drew the attention of *The Phil Donahue Show*. They invited four of us as guests on the show: plaintiffs Margie Robles and Guadalupe Cano, the professor and sociologist Delores Reed-Sanders, and yours truly.

When we arrived in Chicago late on Mother's Day (the show was Monday), a blizzard and a limousine from the show awaited us. It was the first limo ride with a chauffeur for all of us. The temperature was eighty degrees when we left the Valley and had dressed accordingly. We were rather chilled.

Since the show was in Chicago, I asked for tickets for my mother in Lansing, not that far away. My mom, an avid Phil Donahue fan, was ecstatic to meet (and swoon over) him in person. Donahue legitimized my work in my parents' eyes. They always had questions about my life's trajectory, that I was off somewhere in La Mancha with Don Quixote. Allaying their misgivings was never on my agenda. It was clear from the beginning that they would always have questions about what I was doing—and in Texas of all places. I had to follow my heart.

The *Donahue* show went well. Our appearance was a celebratory hit with the Valley media. Lupe Cano did well, telling his story. Donahue was sympathetic and showed some rough video clips. The McAllen police switchboard lit up with complaints.

brutality. In one video an officer shouts: "You ever been snakebit? Well, now you've been C-Shift bit!"

The C-Shift cops formed a comradery and bragged about their brutality. Their slogan: "Kick ass; ask questions later." They created black t-shirts emblazoned in gold with their self-styled "C-Shift Animals."

There were also unexplained gaps in some videos, raising the presumption that the police tampered with them at the time of a beating. How much other graphic brutality might have been recorded but erased despite Judge Garza's earlier order to the contrary?

The videos were so bad that they became a national and international sensation on TV news networks. One McAllenite reported viewing them while in Paris. Television and radio stations in Reynosa, Mexico, on the border warned people to think twice about shopping in McAllen, which had grocery stores catering to Mexico residents.

Police sources reported that, whenever the videos played somewhere, the department switchboard would light up with callers complaining about the brutality. It was intriguing that people from around the state and country would get on the phone and call to register their denunciations.

The videos would air again in political ads during the fierce 1981 mayoral election between incumbent Othal Brand and challenger Dr. Ramiro Casso, a race that itself attracted national publicity. The police switchboard would get overactive again. One wonders how many brutal incidents escaped recording because the police turned off the camera.

The ultimate irony was that the McAllen Police Department installed the cameras with federal funding promised by Richard Nixon during his law-and-order campaign for president. Something designed to protect the police from unfounded accusations came back to haunt them or, as the C-Shift Animals might say, "It snakebit 'em."

THE CLASS ACTION HEADS TO TRIAL

Trial day finally arrived on March 16, 1981, as to whether the city of McAllen itself was responsible to the seventeen named plaintiffs and the class for tolerating a "pattern and practice" of police brutality in the legal vernacular. The class included anyone who would have an encounter with the McAllen police in the future, which could be a very large group.

We had seventy-two arrows in our quiver in the videos plus the three officers testifying for us against twenty-six policemen. McAllen hired Carol Vance, a renowned, if not infamous, former Harris County district attorney, to assist the city attorney.

After we concluded the plaintiffs' opening statement to the jury, detailing the evidence of all the perverse incidents over the years of which we knew, Judge DeAnda called a recess and summoned all us lawyers to his chambers. He sat down, as we stood around in a semicircle. He took off his glasses, squinted a bit, and said to the city's lawyers: "You know, if only half of what Harrington says is true, you are in big trouble with this jury. Have you looked at the jurors? They are not on your side. Have you thought about settling the case?"

They had not, but they certainly did at that point. After a long day of intense negotiations, the city agreed to pay $500,000 to the plaintiffs in addition to the financial awards already won from juries in their individual lawsuits. The settlement funds were apportioned to the seventeen plaintiffs, according to the severity of the police misconduct they had endured, as measured by the jury verdicts.

The city accepted a court order to implement a special training program for officers on how to deescalate situations and how to manage arrests and booking events appropriately. A criminal justice expert from Sam Houston State University would oversee the training.

The city also agreed to create the Police Human Rights Commission to monitor the police. The panel of five would include four members drawn from different geographical and demographic areas of the city to ensure representation of Mexican Americans and McAllen's poorer areas.

When the smoke finally cleared after five years, the city was on its third police chief, the earlier two being casualties of the scandal. The third was soon to follow. McAllen had suffered a deep, self-inflicted public relations gash and paid out nearly $750,000, a respectable sum for 1981 (about two and a half million bucks today).

Quite unbelievably, right in the middle of the McAllen police chaos in 1981, then-Governor Bill Clements nominated Othal Brand to serve on the Texas prison system board. You cannot make this stuff up.

It created a political uproar. Newspapers across the state published adverse editorials and lampooning cartoons. Brand publicly threatened to sue them. At the state senate's confirmation hearing, videos of police beatings during Brand's mayoral tenure were shown. Much of the state media was in attendance, which gave even more currency to the videos.

State Senator Hector Uribe of Brownsville blocked the nomination. There was no handwringing when the governor bowed to inevitability and withdrew Brand's name from consideration.

Brand duly put off senators of both parties by his propensity to sue people who criticized him. True to form, Brand filed a $2.5 million slander lawsuit against the *Brownsville Herald* afterward, claiming that the newspaper's reporting on the McAllen police lawsuits had caused Uribe to scuttle Brand's nomination. A consummately asinine lawsuit.

Brand's bullying style presaged our modern politics.

THE AFTERMATH: BREACH, SHENANIGANS, AND NEW LEADERSHIP

Right out of the gate, McAllen broke compliance with the settlement agreement by not properly constituting the Police Human Rights Commission. Mayor Brand had engineered the appointment of individuals who did not represent the diversity and demographics of McAllen.

McAllen conducted its own burial. One gravedigger was a mayor who tied himself up in a lie about ordering the destruction of the videos. Another was a city commissioner who, while speaking to a group of police wives, offered a bottle of champagne to anyone who would burn the tapes (jokingly, he later said). That ignited Judge DeAnda's ire: "McAllen has been castigated all over the country. This is not a matter to joke about. I am tired of this Mickey-Mousing around. I am not going to put up with it anymore."

Then the city's insurance company, which agreed to pay half of the class action settlement (the city paid the other half), tried to argue that the plaintiffs from the seven individual jury trials should not receive any money from the settlement against the city because they had already received money awards.

The insurance company's bad faith and chicanery were astonishing. We rebuffed its effort to reduce the settlement payments. The company took it up on appeal. The appellate court sent it back for resolution.

We then had a jury trial about the intent of the settlement, and we prevailed once more. Because I had to be a witness in the trial about what we negotiated, George Powell of Texas Rural Legal Aid ably represented the plaintiffs, just as he had in the earlier phases of the marathon police litigation. It was a good partnership.

One of the three officers who came forth to testify for us against the C-Shift Animals, Captain Alex Longoria, became McAllen police chief in 1985, the first Hispanic in the position, and reformed the department. He was a genial fellow, well-liked, a ten-year veteran, and respected across the board. He testified about officers being trained to "get even" and that only the "toughest" cops were picked for the C-Shift. He also discussed the internal peer pressure that kept officers from reporting miscreant colleagues.

C-SHIFT ANIMALS FACE FEDERAL CRIMINAL CHARGES

The local United States Attorney could not ignore the public uproar and the violent videos and filed three indictments—criminal charges—in January 1982 against five former McAllen officers, all of whom had resigned after juries found them liable for damages in our lawsuits. There probably would have been more indictments if the federal government had not delayed so long and had shown more initiative.

The officers in two indictments pleaded guilty. One, Robert Ramos, who was head of the department's internal affairs division, which speaks volumes, had ordered subordinate officers to beat a young man in a field after a chase because "I have too many lawsuits pending." He had three civil rights cases at the time. He settled two, and the jury ruled against him in the third, a lawsuit we had brought. Ramos was also one of the three or four officers responsible for creating the C-Shift Animal subculture. Ramos was in command of the graveyard shift for a while and transferred out any officers he deemed not aggressive enough.

The third indictment involved the worst beating video, that of Pedro Dennett, the same individual mentioned above with a successful verdict against officer B. T. Wilson in a second encounter with the police. The video showed the three officers repeatedly punching him and smashing his head against the booking counter while twisting his arms behind him. Dennett's agonizing screams could be heard over the thudding sound of the cops' punches. It was hard to watch and not recoil.

And yet a trial jury acquitted the former officers. The acquittal was utterly dumbfounding in light of the video and provoked community outrage. Their defense was an omen of what was to come in later criminal trials of police: the videos do not show everything that happened to justify the use of force. It was clearly at odds with what the video showed, but apparently it gave the jurors enough on which to hang their hats.

The jury verdict precluded Dennett from filing a civil rights lawsuit over this incident because it resolved the facts in favor of the police. We could not allow this stark miscarriage of justice to go unanswered. We organized a massive Sunday afternoon "March of Solidarity" against injustice and police brutality. We began with a demonstration in Archer Park, McAllen's central plaza, with speeches, music, and prayers. When I spoke from the park's central bandstand, the anger and passion manifested by the crowd struck me—seething discontent against the police. I was grateful and even proud to have played a role in curtailing such rampant police abuse against the Hispanic community.

From Archer Park we marched, four hundred and fifty people in all, five blocks to the federal building and continued the protest there. The demonstration lasted two hours. We had our own C-Shift t-shirts, yellow with black lettering (reversing their colors): "I survived McAllen PD," sticking it back in the face of the police. LULAC—the powerful League of United Latin American Citizens—joined the protest; and Dr. Hector García, the hallowed founder of the GI Forum, who was quite elderly, sent a personal representative.

But calm was not to settle over McAllen.

B. T. Wilson, sued twice as a McAllen officer and an infamous C-Shift Animal, went on to become a Hidalgo County sheriff's deputy and, sure enough, landed in federal court again, losing a case in which he grotesquely sexually harassed a woman. That he found employment as a deputy with two civil rights adjudications against him and his graphic violence on videotapes should have raised more than an eyebrow. Quite a pathetic commentary on how easy it was to be a bad cop.

TRYING TO SELL THE CITY HOSPITAL: OTHAL BRAND REBUFFED BY THE VOTERS

While the McAllen police cases were ramping up toward the coming class action trial, Brand proved himself a nemesis in another matter. In 1980, he tried to ram through a sale of the city hospital to the Hospital Corporation of America so that it would be out of McAllen's control. The hospital had long provided health care for indigent people, but HCA would have no such responsibility. It had a less-than-admirable entrepreneurial reputation.

Farmworkers in McAllen's Colonia Balboa and neighboring communities would be the most negatively affected. McAllen General was one of two regional hospitals at the time. The other was in Harlingen. Health care for poor people had already long passed the crisis marker. The sale would have nearly gutted what was left.

Along with attorney George Powell of Texas Rural Legal Aid, we filed a lawsuit and blocked the mayor's gambit, convincing the judge that the city charter prohibited such a sale. Brand then engineered a referendum in 1981, attempting to amend the charter.

Dr. Ramiro Casso, a well-respected community physician and longtime Valley figure, along with other doctors, headed the opposition, which included the UFW as a major team member and Rebecca Flores as the organizer. The farmworkers did "human billboarding," a union tactic of lining people along intersections with campaign signs, this time waving "Vote no" signs.

The community came together solidly against the proposed hospital sale, and the charter amendment gave up the ghost in the Saturday referendum. "Buried in the dust" would be more descriptive of the election result.

Eventually Brand stepped back, and the city brought everyone to the table and negotiated an arrangement with Methodist Hospitals to take over management of the city facility and continue providing indigent health care. It was a good arrangement.

BRAND RUNS FOR REELECTION, AND THE *C-SHIFT ANIMALS* VIDEOTAPE SERIES REAPPEARS

As the McAllen police litigation began winding down and the hospital referendum flopped, Brand announced for reelection that same year. Dr. Casso decided to throw his hat into the ring.

Casso, fifty-eight at the time, was a longtime, deeply committed, soft-spoken civil rights activist. If he ever called you and turned on his gentle, charming voice, you knew he would end up kindly cajoling you into doing something for the movement. The *mexicano* community loved him. He was known and respected for providing medical care at a discount and sometimes at no charge. It was said he delivered half the babies in McAllen, which likely was close to the truth. No one doubted it.

The campaign was bitter and heated, and 6,500 new voters signed up. Casso's fierceness on the campaign trail was surprising. He pulled not a punch. The race drew national attention because of the McAllen police mess on Brand's watch. The brutal videos appeared on people's television screens in campaign ads, and the police switchboard lit up again.

Brand sent his McAllen employees to fields as far away as possible—as was customary for Valley growers—so they would not have time to return, clean up, and vote in the city before 7 p.m. He also intimidated voters by personally videotaping them at polling places.

Rebecca helped organize the Casso campaign and did an amazing job, but Brand managed to get reelected by fewer than nine hundred votes. He poured a barrel of money into his campaign and painted Casso as a radical who would upend the status quo. Brand did not leave much subtext to the racist fears he was stoking with the city's heavily Anglo population. Nor did Casso waste any words in powerfully calling him out for it on election night.

Brand, as was his wont whenever he sought revenge, sued Casso afterward. During the campaign Casso had accused Brand of having presided over the C-Shift police brutality and ruling McAllen with an iron fist like an "ayatollah," a reference to Iran's autocratic governance.

David Casso, who had interned with TCRP as a law clerk, represented his father all the way to the Supreme Court of Texas and won a precedent-setting victory. David's case changed the burden of proof in libel lawsuits to make it easier for a defendant like his father to have groundless

VIRGINIA ARMSTRONG REDUX: CAUGHT MAKING FAKE NEWS

The McAllen mayoral race was tight between Casso and Brand. The *Monitor* reporter Virginia Armstrong, Brand's pal, was on hand at City Hall to watch the tallies come in.

The next morning, a Sunday, the *Monitor* prominently reported that four people (who, although unnamed, were clearly Rebecca, two others, and me) had rampaged through City Hall, overturning desks and wreaking havoc. It was a dumbfounding fabrication, even for Virginia. I know, because I was there. It was her way of discrediting the movement against Brand.

We wasted no time. First thing Monday morning we filed a slander suit against her and the *Monitor*. To its credit, the *Monitor* reported the suit and quickly settled, paying modest damages. We wanted to make our point that Virginia Armstrong, no matter how hard she tried, and the *Monitor* were not going to remake reality or pull things back to where they had been.

slander suits dismissed and more difficult for plaintiffs like Brand to pursue them.

Brand also sued *The Nation* magazine over an unflattering article about him and the election, mentioning *patrón* politics and using Casso's "ayatollah" quote. I represented *The Nation* and had the case summarily dismissed by the trial judge on free press grounds. Brand did not appeal.

Brand knew that none of his slander cases would ever get past the First Amendment firewall. Nor would he risk a jury trial that he would lose ignominiously. However, filing a suit meant his opponent had to hire legal counsel and go through legal machinations to successfully dismiss Brand's suit, all at great financial cost.

Brand was one of the early aficionados of this kind of SLAPP suit (Strategic Lawsuit Against Public Participation) until the legislature shut them down with the Texas Citizens Participation Act. SLAPP suits were baseless, harassing lawsuits by individuals with money to scare their critics away from relaying negative publicity about them. Brand was a master practitioner.

TAKEAWAYS: CREDIBILITY CAN MAKE ALL THE DIFFERENCE

Reflecting back fifty years later on the McAllen police cases, I think they gave the South Texas Project great credibility in that we were willing to take on an abusive arm of the Anglo power structure and do so publicly. And win. It was a community win, which brought together different parts of local society. Our credibility quotient drew other cases to us. People who were itching to change the status quo invited us to their organizing meetings to see what kind of litigation options were available. I became part of the community effort, more than just a lawyer.

This was critical in other work underway at the South Texas Project during this period. Police abuse was not the only serious flaw in South Texas's criminal justice system. Discriminatory grand juries was another, and it became a priority item on our agenda. In the next chapter I describe how we strove with community leaders to reform this unjust aspect of the criminal justice system in Texas.

4

TEXAS GRAND JURY REFORM

Sidelining the Good Old Boys

While the various McAllen police lawsuits were unfolding and farmworkers were stepping up their organizing efforts (described in chapter 5), we were engaged in yet another stream of litigation: grand jury reform.

Moving political power away from a fiercely entrenched South Texas Anglo structure was slow and had to struggle forward on multiple fronts. The push for grand jury reform began in 1972, the year before I arrived, and eventually became a major litigation focus.

The granite cornerstone of the establishment edifice was control over the criminal justice system, especially county grand juries, which decide who should be indicted, that is, whom to formally accuse of a felony crime and send to trial.

Although only a few flesh-and-blood stories show up in this chapter, the successes and benefits described here affected all Texans then, as they do today and will into coming years, protecting an unknown number of people from wrongful criminal prosecution. Such injustices disoriented and distorted defendants' lives and those of their families.

WHY TAKE ON GRAND JURIES IN TEXAS?

Texas is one among about half the states in the nation that require grand juries to issue indictments or formal charges for felonies. Prosecutors cannot bring these major crimes (as compared to lesser misdemeanors) on their own. Grand juries were originally designed in part as a democratic check on abusive government power, as a bulwark protection from any government unleashing its authority against a person for corrupt reasons.

Fair grand juries are critical to sustaining an evenhanded criminal justice system. They do not always function that way. The most problematic junctures of the criminal justice system, whether by design or practice, are places where officials can exercise discretion in the wrong direction. Therein seeps the decay of bias, both overt and latent. Grand juries are one of those discretion junctures.

A common thread weaving through US Supreme Court cases over the years is limiting official discretion when it has become a pathway for discrimination or denied due process to disfavored or unfavored individuals or groups.

Over time, prosecutors and judges devised ways to mold the grand jury system into their image and likeness. Grand juries became tools to map the establishment's criminal justice priorities according to economic and social class and race. Their preferred way was to handpick grand jurors, who meet in secret. The result was a system that did their bidding, not check their actions. Texas grand juries followed this rubber-stamp game plan.

To curb prosecutors' manipulation of grand juries, a national movement began galvanizing in the 1940s toward making juries more representative of the community. It picked up steam. The Supreme Court got on board in 1975 and declared the "fair cross-section" requirement to be the law of the land: a jury pool had to be a microcosm of the population. This applied to grand juries that indict people and to trial juries that sit in judgment of criminal cases after indictment.

The pronouncement was welcome but not always followed closely, partly because the justices failed to hand down helpful guidelines, as is often the case with breakthrough rulings. In essence the Court is saying, "This is wrong. Figure out how to do it the right way." The South Texas Project would help counties do it the right way.

Whether we're speaking of a grand jury or a trial jury, the idea is to lay a case before a quintessentially democratic body for a decision. A cross-sectional jury has jurors with diverse perspectives, experiences, and interests, seen through the prism of their individual belief, structure, race, gender, ethnic background, and social and economic status.

A jury is fair and impartial when it fairly represents group differences and hashes them out rather than eliminating them. Evaluating police conduct, for example, is an area of jury deliberation that needs perspectives from minority and poor communities, since their interactions with police often are at variance with the majority community's experiences. Men also tend to view physical violence against women differently than do women, some would say more unsympathetically or even callously.

Having set such a goal, how do we achieve it? The easiest and fairest way is by lot, randomly drawing from a properly constituted jury wheel that represents the community. The legal phrase "jury wheel" was originally a random-selection mechanism, like those used for raffles: a round wire cage that someone cranked before drawing jurors' names. Jury selection is now random by computer, but the old phrase remains in use.

As it skillfully has done in myriad other areas, Texas found a way to circumvent the goal of truly community-based grand juries by using the so-called key-man system throughout the twentieth century for selecting "intelligent" grand jurors, as the statute put it. "Intelligent" is a classic code word, of course. Discrimination ran rampant.

The Supreme Court's 1975 decision had no impact on Texas grand jury selection. The judge picked three to five commissioners (the key men). They in turn selected fifteen to twenty potential grand jurors, among whom the judge selected the final twelve as the grand jury.

The result was neither unexpected nor shocking. Grand juries typically looked like an assorted group of the judge's friends, associates, political cronies, and social class. Since the establishment suppressed minority voting, the judges, who were elected, came out of the power structure, duly anointed to do its bidding. The key-man system was derisively referred to as "pick-a-pal."

Grand jurors received a small honorarium and a few other perks from the judge, who assured them that the district attorney, also selected by the powers that be, would soften their burden of deliberation by preparing and presenting the cases to them for felony charges. Without articulating it, the system was expecting them to quickly add their imprimatur to the prosecutor's recommendations as to whom to prosecute and for what crime.

Nor did prosecutors and judges clarify to grand juries their independent subpoena and investigatory powers. Too much knowledge might lead to a jury having its own mind. It was a clever, insidious manipulation of a centuries-old procedure designed to limit state power, not be its choirboy.

Texas grand juries, true to form, functioned as good-old-boy networks, not as instruments of justice. Consistently underrepresented or wholly absent were women and minority, poor, and young individuals. In the Rio Grande Valley, as in other areas of Texas, Anglos with economic and political dominance adeptly manipulated this system. Indictments tended toward business and property crimes and away from personal violence cases, and of course none were brought for police violence, brutality, and killings. Scholars refer to this as a "gateway control" function.

One can wonder how many people were wrongly convicted because of a skewed justice system set in motion against them. Studies show that, regardless of actual guilt or innocence, once a person is brought into the criminal justice system the odds of leaving it with a conviction are about 72 percent for a host of reasons unrelated to actual guilt or innocence.

Poverty is a major reason. Poor people are more likely to plead guilty to get out of jail and back to work. Court-appointed attorneys (constitutionally required public defenders) offer a lesser caliber of representation compared to expensive criminal defense lawyers and are more likely to guide clients toward entering a plea bargain. Even though there is a legal presumption of innocence, the operative presumption is guilt in the eyes of the judge, jury, prosecutor, and court-appointed counsel. Where there's smoke, there's fire. Other factors come into play as well, but these are the most salient.

Being among the 28 percent that escapes conviction frequently depends on one's economic resources. Simply being indicted and charged with a crime, whether guilty or innocent, creates an enormous risk of jail time, financial penalties, and adverse employment consequences. The odds are worse if the person cannot afford bond and remains locked up until trial months later, unable to work. The pressure on them to plead guilty and avoid trial is heavy despite the draconian consequences.

As is often the case with Texas institutions, the logic of justice does not always carry the day. What helps move along the Lone Star horse and buggy is a sharp snap of the whip: litigation. The South Texas Project saddled up.

RODRIGO PARTIDA'S SUPREME COURT VICTORY REVERBERATES AND SHAKES UP THE STATUS QUO

David Hall, my illustrious and intrepid predecessor, took up an initiative to reform Texas grand juries in 1972 by challenging the criminal conviction of Rodrigo Partida for burglary at night with intent to commit rape, a peculiarly phrased felony.

David's argument was that, over a ten-year period, Hidalgo County grand juries had systematically and substantially underrepresented the Mexican American community and were thus constitutionally defective. Put simply, they did not reflect a cross-section of the county. The grand jury that indicted Rodrigo was no different and therefore violated his rights to a fair jury trial and equal protection and led to his unlawful conviction.

At the time of Rodrigo's indictment in 1972, Mexican Americans were almost 80 percent of the Hidalgo County population. Their representation on grand juries by comparison was paltry—half at best, and certainly not a cross-representation of the county.

The Texas Court of Criminal Appeals, not surprisingly, rejected the appeal. David then filed a habeas corpus case in federal court in Brownsville in 1974. A federal habeas corpus action is a collateral attack on a state court conviction, claiming it resulted from a violation of the United States Constitution. If the prisoner's habeas challenge is successful, the federal judge overturns the state court conviction and orders a new trial or dismisses the charges, depending on the nature of the constitutional breach.

The state's response was that, because a Mexican American judge, J. R. Alamía, had appointed the grand jury and that some commissioners and grand jurors over time were Mexican American, albeit underrepresented, there could be no discrimination claim unless the selection of a nonrepresentative grand jury was intentional.

US District Judge Reynaldo Garza agreed and promptly booted the habeas action, as did the appeals court, with hardly a second thought. On appeal from there, the federal case reached the US Supreme Court.

The Supreme Court reversed the lower courts in 1977 and overturned the conviction, ruling that the ten-year history of unrepresentative Hidalgo County grand juries created the presumption of intentional discrimination. That turned the tables and meant the state had to prove that intentional discrimination was not afoot, as opposed to the underlying bias that the historical data indicated.

Judge Alamía was an amicable, pleasant fellow, but he came from, and represented, the establishment. He was, as sociologists frame it, a "border watchdog." The judge was there to protect the power structure, and his being Mexican American helped raise a protective shield to guard privilege against charges of discrimination. Not an unusual tactic in Texas.

The Supreme Court sent back the case for the county to decide if it wanted to pursue it further or dismiss the charges. By the time the case returned, David Hall had assumed the executive director mantle of the recently created Texas Rural Legal Aid.

The county carefully selected a new grand jury and reindicted Rodrigo. Oscar McInnis, the opinionated, bigoted district attorney, personally appeared before the grand jury, urging a new formal accusation. Rodrigo's reindictment demonstrated McInnis's continued sway over grand jury proceedings.

Suddenly, the daunting task of retrying Rodrigo's criminal case fell on this novice lawyer's shoulders, to which McInnis added weight. He postured in the media that the grand jury composition did not make any difference. He publicly opined that a trial jury would convict him once again, despite Rodrigo's protestations of innocence.

The pressure I felt was heavy, scary even. What good would it do to win a Supreme Court case just to have Partida reconvicted? It would make it all seem full of sound and fury, signifying nothing, like a mere legal technicality. If I lost, the power structure would win, and the struggle for reform would be for naught and even ridiculed. Making the pressure that much heavier was knowing deep down how unsharpened my criminal trial skills were.

The trial went forward, and to immense relief the jury quickly acquitted Rodrigo. The case against him was flimsy. He was young, poor, and confused as to why the legal system had caught him up in this drama. As best I could figure out, he happened to be in the vicinity of the crime at the wrong time when the police felt they needed to arrest someone, a Hispanic male.

The victim, whose house in central Edinburg someone allegedly broke into, was a young Anglo woman. She was unable to identify Rodrigo at trial as the culprit and was murky on details overall. The jury resisted the pressure to convict, whipped up by McInnis.

After the jury verdict, David Hall sent a bottle of champagne over to the office. McInnis suddenly developed a bad case of media laryngitis. What hung over me was how close this young man came to serving years in prison for a crime he did not commit, all because of McInnis, himself a racist scoundrel.

McInnis knew he had to serve up a plate with a *mexicano* on it as the main dish, any *mexicano*, for the establishment that kept him in power, especially in a case involving a young Anglo woman. McInnis never denied,

OSCAR MCINNIS, ROGUE DISTRICT ATTORNEY

Oscar McInnis had a ribald and storied life as Hidalgo County's district attorney. The sheriff caught McInnis engineering a brazen plot with a hitman in the jail to kill the former husband of the woman with whom he was having a not-so-discreet, torrid, extramarital affair. McInnis said he would drop the pending charges against the hitman so he could do the job on the outside. That became his downfall.

Ironically, when the man McInnis plotted to kill filed a federal civil rights case against him, McInnis called, asking for help, after years of publicly trashing the South Texas Project, even at a Chamber of Commerce luncheon. Although it was mind-bending that he seemed not to fathom that we would more properly be representing the man who sued him over the murder plot, I took it as a bizarre, backhanded compliment that he thought we did good work on hard cases.

even pro forma, that he practiced the Valley's Anglo-brand racism of the day. He embraced it and spoke its coarse language.

Though McInnis rarely tried jury cases personally as district attorney—he left those to his assistants—he would personally handle a case, even a minor one like public intoxication, against Black defendants, who were few and far between in the Valley.

After the champagne bottle was emptied in victory, our next step was to keep the drive going to overhaul Texas's grand jury system. We continued raising grand jury challenges in individual criminal prosecutions, one case at a time.

The Supreme Court litigation had no practical impact on Hidalgo County other than the judges sometimes telling the grand jury commissioners to try to seat more representative panels than before. But very slight change resulted in the grand jurors' overall demographic complexion.

A few years earlier, I had put myself on the list of attorneys to be appointed at county expense when a poor defendant could not afford to hire a lawyer in a criminal case. The judges would assign me to represent someone every few months. I would then use that case to raise the grand jury issue. I also added the underrepresentation of women to the challenges.

The beauty of a court appointment was that I could hire expert witnesses to prepare the needed statistical proof of underrepresentation and have the county cover the costs (and slightly supplement my meager salary, to my family's benefit).

The judges did not appreciate this arrangement as much as I did. It slowed down the railroad. One judge, obviously an emissary, met me in the second-floor courthouse corridor and, as we overlooked the main staircase, obliquely discussed their conundrum. The judges then removed me from the appointed counsel list but assured me that no retaliation was afoot.

RUNNING AHEAD WITH THE SUPREME COURT WIND AT OUR BACKS

The single-shot, case-by-case grand jury challenges were not doing the job of changing the system locally, let alone for the whole state. Sometimes we could spend a day or two presenting a grand jury challenge in a pretrial hearing, receive the expected adverse ruling from the judge, and then win acquittal at the jury trial, which ended the case in the defendant's favor. Winning a case was certainly good for the client but unhelpful for our grand jury challenges because there would be no appeal on which to pursue the issue and change the system.

One time, we had a three-day hearing in Judge Magus Smith's court. He ruled against the grand jury challenge, of course. At trial, the jury, although finding the young man guilty of transporting sixty pounds of marijuana on foot south of Donna (he was a mule, or courier), gave him a favorable probated sentence, allowing him to return to Mexico. Smith, who deservedly draws unfavorable mention in other parts of this narrative, fiercely chewed out the jurors for the light sentence, even using "wetback" as a racial slur to describe the young man. No appeal in that case either. The client was happy to return to Mexico.

Judge Smith was not known for legal acuity. His loyal court reporter, a lawyer with more legal acumen than Smith, was adept at modifying the trial transcript as he typed up the proceedings to avoid recording any reversible error by Smith that might support an appeal. Sometimes parts of the judge's statements or a witness's testimony simply disappeared wholesale from the trial transcript, but no one could prove their suspicions in the days before recording court hearings was practical or allowed.

Eventually, we hit on the idea of pursuing a federal class action lawsuit, enlisting various Valley groups and leaders as plaintiffs. Our legal theory was that the current system denied Hispanic citizens full participation in self-governance, which included grand jury service, and denigrated their equality rights under the law. The subtext was suppression of Mexican American political participation.

That approach gave us a full-scale assault on the ramparts and short-circuited the tedious, case-by-case process that mired down our momentum, such as it was. It was also a public attack on political structures. A court victory would reinforce the local community groups' organizing actions.

We challenged the overall composition of grand juries in Hidalgo County and neighboring Willacy County, proving a historical trajectory of more than ten years that excluded or significantly underrepresented Mexican Americans, women, young people, and poor individuals.

Mexican Americans, although representing nearly 80 percent of the populace, had less than 40 percent representation historically. Women made up slightly more than half the population but had about 35 percent representation. Any deviance beyond 10 percent raises a presumption of intentional discrimination.

Young people and poor individuals were two groups that had not come up earlier as excluded classes in our grand jury challenges. This was new territory. Using the most up-to-date census data, we defined young people as between ages eighteen and twenty-eight, who made up 16 percent of the total population in each county. Fifty percent and 57 percent of people in Hidalgo and Willacy Counties, respectively, had incomes below the government-designated poverty levels. No members of either group had served on those grand juries for the prior ten years, if ever.

Ultimately, focusing on the Rio Grande Valley was a good tactical move because the discrimination was so stark and statistically unpardonable. Gathering and analyzing the grand jury data was much more manageable than in heavily populated areas like Harris County, even though the same patterns existed there as throughout Texas. A federal court victory in South Texas would reverberate across the Lone Star State and benefit its minority communities and women.

The sociologist and professor Delores Reed-Sanders from Pan American University (now University of Texas Rio Grande Valley) graciously jumped in as an expert witness. Originally from Oklahoma, she was on the socially activist side of the PanAm faculty. She skillfully prepared the statistical analyses from census data and court records to buttress the proof of systemic exclusion and underinclusion. She had done the same for the individual criminal grand jury challenges and shared less-than-gracious views of Judge Smith and DA McInnis.

The probability of random discrimination was so low that it could not be anything but intentional. We all knew this in our hearts, but, like the geographer in *The Little Prince*, we needed to show maps to prove it.

For logistical reasons, we filed separate federal class actions for Hidalgo County and Willacy County in late 1977 and early 1978, respectively, suing the grand jury commissioners in each county and naming our friend Judge Smith in the Hidalgo County litigation (more for poetic justice than legal necessity).

The plaintiffs included two grassroots organizations, Ciudadanos Unidos (Citizens United) de San Juan and Ciudadanos Unidos de Donna, plus twenty-eight activists. The groups and individuals were anxious to get a jump on organizing and assert *mexicano* political power and undo the *patrón* politics that weighed down the community. Some belonged to the Raza Unida political party trying to pry loose the local Democratic Party from the Anglo old guard.

It did not take long for Judge Reynaldo Garza to summarily jettison the two lawsuits just as he had originally thrown out the Rodrigo Partida's case. That the Supreme Court had reversed him did not bother him in the least. Garza was a nice enough judge, and was good on workers' rights, but he had long played ball with the Anglo establishment, as had others of the professional Mexican American elite.

The federal Fifth Circuit Court of Appeals joined the two cases on appeal, as the legal allegations were identical. In January 1980, the appeals court handed down a forceful decision in our favor, strongly affirming our approach to analyzing the discriminatory grand jury system in Texas.

While that appeal was pending, however, the state legislature tried an end run to moot the appeal by amending the grand jury selection statute. It added the requirement that the commissioners "shall, to the extent possible, select grand jurors [whom] the commissioners determine represent a broad cross-section of the population of the county, considering the factors of race, sex, and age."

The appellate judges were singularly underwhelmed, noting the new statute's vagueness, a mere restatement of operative constitutional law that the state should have long been implementing.

THE KEY-MAN SYSTEM BITES THE DUST

The US Supreme Court refused to hear the state's appeal, leaving the Ciudadanos Unidos victory intact. We continued to press our pending litigation and threatened further litigation, adding a fifth class of persons to our claims: Mexican American women. Professor Reed-Sanders proved how this group suffered twofold discrimination (a "double whammy," as she described it), with far less representation than either Mexican Americans or women as separate groups.

A real risk confronted any judge using the key-man system. It jeopardized convictions based on an indictment from an unrepresentative grand jury, with the added ensuing cost of retrying a case, not to mention prosecuting the wrong person and leaving the actual criminal on the streets. The legislature responded by passing a law that kept the key-man system in place but allowed judges the option of selecting grand juries from the

GRAND JURIES REPRESENTATIVE OF HIDALGO COUNTY SHIFT CRIMINAL LAW PRIORITIES

Hidalgo County grand juries that were more representative of the population, according to a study by Professor Reed-Sanders, began moving toward crimes of personal violence, such as sexual abuse and rape, which were often discounted under prior grand jury regimens. Her study reflects the learned literature on this subject across the nation.

I know anecdotally from Rebecca Flores, a member of one of the newly formed grand juries after the Ciudadanos Unidos ruling, that grand jurors called McInnis on the carpet when he tried to take a pass on a rape case. He failed, and they issued an indictment. I'm sure they put Rebecca on the grand jury to forestall any litigation on my part. They obviously didn't know either of us very well.

jury wheel from which trial juries are chosen and are significantly more representative of the community.

After Rodrigo Partida's case and the Ciudadanos Unidos cases (and threats of similar lawsuits in other counties), judges around the state elected to utilize the new jury-wheel route. It was much easier and presented fewer constitutional problems in appeals of criminal convictions.

Others who continued with the key-man system had to carefully monitor the resulting grand juries, often giving grand jury commissioners demographic descriptions of the county ahead of time and written instructions about selecting a cross-section of grand jurors. The writing was emblazoned in large type on the Supreme Court wall, and judges who ignored it did so at their peril.

This issue carried forward from South Texas into my work at the Texas Civil Liberties Union and then into the Texas Civil Rights Project until 2015, when the state legislature finally abolished the key-man system altogether in Texas. Although its final demise was slow to come, the death knell had sounded long before the wooden stake finally found its mark.

TAKEAWAYS: INSPIRING REFORM

The individuals and groups whom we represented in the grand jury cases were impressive and inspiring. They moved forward without hesitation or equivocation: "Let's do it. It needs to happen." They were all in their twenties or thirties. The others referred to the one person in his forties as "the old guy."

All were engaged in one fashion or another at chipping away at the oppressive structures of the Valley's owner class. Each knew the personal risks and possible economic and political reprisals in pursuing the lawsuits. Yet they took up the challenge and changed the grand jury system for the good of the Valley and all Texas. Every one of them continued this leadership journey into futures of promise.

5

FARMWORKERS AND *COLONIAS* ON THE MOVE

Even while the grand jury litigation and McAllen police lawsuits were playing out, the United Farm Workers, the *colonias*, and the larger community stepped up organizing efforts that required protective legal help from the South Texas Project, adding a third dimension to our work.

The lives of farmworkers are more difficult and precarious from what most of us experience: seasonal employment, subminimum wages, poor housing conditions, extreme poverty, lack of education, racism and discrimination, bad and unsafe labor conditions, and inadequate health care.

They are America's essential workers. We depend on them for our livelihoods but have little concern for theirs. Nor are our consciences troubled by the misery to which our society consigns them. We, not they, reap the benefits of their labor.

We should see them not only with the eyes of compassion but also with respect for their contributions, cultural and economic, to our larger communities. They live without any privilege at the bottom of the ladder, but they are as entitled to respect and justice as are each of us.

FARM WORKER ORGANIZING: WILDCAT STRIKES EVERYWHERE

This story picks up in the increasing social and political roiling following the US Supreme Court Texas Ranger case and the Pharr Riot upheaval.

In May 1975, with a great deal of Spanish-language radio and television coverage, the UFW returned to Starr County to begin organizing there again, focusing on the melon harvest, which was at full throttle. The days were so hot that melon picking began at first light, as early as 6 a.m., and ended about 2 p.m., when the blaze of the sun and the humidity became insupportable. The work was hard, the pay low.

Several hundred farmworkers, mostly young men, crossed the bridge each day from Mexico to work on Valley farms, augmenting the number of laborers from the American side. Labor contractors (*troqueros*) would pick them up in trucks and transport them to fields needing workers.

On Memorial Day, which was not a holiday for field laborers, a wildcat strike over low wages erupted at the international bridge near the city of Hidalgo, thirty miles from Starr County.

After milling around at the bridge and becoming increasingly agitated with the low pay and lousy labor conditions in the fields, a group of workers decided to strike. They fanned out to nearby fields to encourage a general stoppage, including at the farm of C. L. Miller, which was within walking distance. Miller's reaction was to shoot at the workers with a shotgun, wounding eleven.

Word of the shooting spread quickly, and it seemed like hell broke loose. The shooting angered men gathered at the bridge. Rebecca was already in Starr County early with the UFW organizers and out of reach when I got a call around 6:45 a.m. about bedlam at the bridge and possible violence.

I was alone at the house with our baby son, Elías. There was no time to quickly find a babysitter at that hour. So I picked him up and headed to the bridge to try to pacify the situation. I had never witnessed so many angry people milling around. Their rage was raw and unpredictable. I feared violence and felt helpless to halt it if something were to happen.

I eventually handed over Elías to a family friend and coworker, who also had come to the bridge in response to the shooting. The next morning, the *McAllen Monitor* ran a front-page photo of me holding him while trying to calm the workers and focus them in a helpful direction. My son, although having no memory of the event, keeps a copy of the photo and has never forgiven me for abandoning him—or so he says.

Wildcat strikes exploded across the upper Valley. Picketers fanned out quickly to fields everywhere, persuading harvesters to walk out of the fields. It was almost a general agricultural strike. At peak, around two thousand workers were on strike.

Othal Brand, originally from Georgia, started one of the Valley's largest agribusinesses, Griffin & Brand, which reached into West Texas. He became mayor of McAllen in 1977.

He carried various unofficial titles, all of which fit like a glove: the Onion King (self-styled), the King of Agribusiness (a label conferred by friend and foe, with different connotations), and the Valley's Last *Patrón* (so named by rising Mexican American leaders and not disputed by Brand).

Brand and the UFW were not friends.

Brand, who owned huge fields all around Hidalgo County, was an obvious target. At one point he became so irate at the pickets that he drove from his office five miles away to a strike site and pulled a pistol on the picketers, charging at them, an event broadcast on *CBS News*. That ratcheted up the situation's dangerous volatility.

The growers beat a path to the courthouse and filed lawsuits left and right against the UFW. We responded with countersuits. Two local Anglo judges (including our old friend Magus Smith), in a political dance trying to resolve the growers' suits and the union's countersuits, called a secret evening meeting at the courthouse with the attorneys involved. Of course, I alerted the press, just to keep everyone honest. The press showed up and waited outside the courthouse. I did not trust the judges. I was outnumbered and did not want to be outflanked. The press being there set a different tenor. The result was positive: each side agreed to dismiss their suits, promising to obey the law. It was good publicity for the union.

The lawsuits often named me as a defendant along with the union to create an ethical conflict so I could not represent the union and so the UFW would have to pay to hire a different lawyer. Attorneys cannot represent themselves and other defendants at the same time, since it might happen that they would arrange a good settlement for themselves at the expense of their clients' interests. The growers' ruse never succeeded. I was able to convince the judges to dismiss me as a defendant or alternatively obtain a signed waiver for ethical purposes from the UFW.

The litigation part was easy compared to responding to the ongoing strikes and the workers' fury at the Miller shooting. I spent a good deal of time for almost two weeks with UFW leaders, trying to calm and redirect the strikers. It was a new and intense activity. None of us had the required training or prior experience. We had to learn as we plodded along.

Wildcat strikes by definition are unorganized, volatile, and undirected. Leadership is amorphous and hard to identify. Individuals have their own agendas. The task becomes one of tamping down any inclination toward violence and property damage—and anything else that would play into the authorities' hands—while supporting the strikers.

It was a fraught dynamic and required careful balancing, a tough tightrope act. We never knew where the next flareup or confrontation would occur. It was chaotic, and the media picked up some ugly scenes at various farms. We sometimes did not know where strikes were going on until the media or law enforcement flagged them.

Sometimes I had to make quick decisions amid a cloud of uncertainty. It was a worrisome time because of the volatility. Everything was decided on the spot, out in the open with the ad hoc strike organizers. The wrong decision could backfire and endanger people. Then we had to sell those decisions to the other workers and get their input, which was difficult with emotions running so high and the adrenaline flowing.

Ultimately, our strategy became one of helping organize targeted protests at different fields. That helped create focus and discipline among the ranks. Another strategy was to organize a peaceful protest march, encouraging nonviolence and justice in the fields. Hundreds of chanting workers and backers walked six-abreast, with UFW flags and placards flying, on a sunny Sunday for eight miles along the highway from the Hidalgo bridge to St. Joseph the Worker Catholic Church in McAllen.

The march wrapped up with speeches and Mass. Having helped organize and lead the peaceful and colorful march, it was gratifying that so many people participated, workers and supporters alike. It was one of those movement moments that showed unity and purpose, and I was honored and proud to be part of it.

The march and the approaching end of the harvest season helped quiet the uprising, as did the growers' temporary wage hike.

A grand jury later declined to indict Miller, which was shocking but not surprising given the composition of grand juries in those days and Oscar McInnis being the district attorney.

MARCH TO THE STARR COUNTY COURTHOUSE

One of the more interesting court hearings was in Rio Grande City in early June 1975 by which growers tried to block UFW picketing through a court-ordered injunction. It was so hot that the hearing began early at 8 a.m. The 1939 courthouse had no air-conditioning, just large ceiling fans slowly churning away in the old-style, second-floor courtroom. Its large windows were thrown open on two sides to allow for some movement of the stifling air. It reminded me of the courtroom in *To Kill a Mockingbird.*

Judge O. P. Carrillo of Duval County notoriety was hearing the case. His jurisdiction covered Starr County as well. Carrillo was already deep in it, trying to escape a quicksand of legal trouble for corruption, but still he was in office. The Texas House of Representatives would impeach him two months later, only the third impeachment since the 1876 Texas Constitution took effect.

As we started the hearing, a sudden and loud commotion outside disrupted the proceedings. Everyone, including the judge, darted to the open windows to see what was happening. Two hundred farm laborers with UFW flags were chanting and marching up the middle of the treelined avenue that ascended toward the courthouse, which sits atop a slight hill.

The judge called a recess immediately and summoned the lawyers to his chambers. The gist of his comments: "What can we do to make everyone happy?" We agreed to adjourn the hearing and see if settling the case was possible.

I was the last to leave the judge's chambers. On the way out, he called me back. I was a new lawyer at that point and nervous about the danger of an ex parte discussion with the judge (that is, a one-on-one conversation with a judge without any other party in attendance), which is considered unethical in most circumstances.

We were standing, facing each other, and he said, "You don't worry. I am on your side." He obviously was trying to gin up grassroots support in light of his legal predicament. This felt shady to me, weaselly even. My response was vaguely noncommittal, and I quickly excused myself. I did not want to have a conversation with him, of all people, even in what might be appropriate circumstances. It was unnerving, even today when I recall this conversation.

We settled the case with a typical, noncontroversial agreement: everybody would abide by the law. Such settlements were good for farmworkers because it meant things were changing. The growers could no longer waltz into court and dictate to the judge what they wanted. Judges and growers just wanted to save face a bit. But judges also had one eye on the increasingly *mexicano* electorate. And the UFW could continue organizing without fear. These injunction hearings were well attended by the media, which had the benefit of giving the union positive publicity.

The irony was not lost on anyone that eight years earlier, when melon harvesters and backers demonstrated at the same courthouse, the Texas Rangers violently dispersed them. This time, however, not a *rinche* was in sight.

STRIKES MOVE TO WEST TEXAS

After the 1975 melon season wrapped up in the Valley, UFW organizers moved to West Texas for the melon harvest there. Their first stop was in the Big Bend around Presidio, across the Rio Grande from Ojinaga, Mexico. Othal Brand owned fields there, as well—a tantalizing prospect for the union.

Surrounded by mountains and plateaus, this ample area is a fertile floodplain at the confluence with Rio Conchos, which flows into the Rio Grande from Mexico. Presidio is economically impoverished yet rich in history, including early colonization and the populist hero Pancho Villa. In 1975, the unincorporated town held about 1,800 people. Until climate change set in, it was one of the hottest areas in Texas. Its climate was desert-dry.

COUNTY SHERIFF? MORE LIKE A CROOK AND DRUG SMUGGLER

In contrast to Presidio County Sheriff Rick Thompson's purported dedication to law and order, he was arrested a few years after the 1975 Presidio strike for smuggling $48 million worth of pure cocaine (2,400 pounds) across the border near Presidio, pocketing a cool million bucks for his own pocket. He pleaded guilty, receiving a thirty-year sentence.

His official portrait still hangs on the courthouse wall, right between his predecessors and his successors. Until his arrest for drug trafficking, the corrupt sheriff had been an iconic West Texas symbol of the War on Drugs, sending others off to prison. How much smuggling he got away with before his arrest is unknown. Rumors were already swirling at the time of the strike.

Most melon pickers working Presidio came from Ojinaga every morning and received abysmal pay, often less than a dollar an hour. It didn't take much prompting for a labor strike to set in. Nor did it take long for Brand and his fellow growers to goad Sheriff Rick Thompson of Presidio County to arrest half a dozen union organizers and ferry them off to jail in Marfa, sixty miles away.

Warren Burnett, a legendary West Texas attorney, answered our pleas and made his way from Odessa to help free the arrestees, entering a deal with the sheriff that Burnett would not sue the decrepit old county jail for its unconstitutional conditions if the sheriff agreed to release the prisoners being held for the strike. The sheriff was not willing to go toe-to-toe with one of Texas's famed (and a bit flamboyant) criminal defense and civil liberties lawyers, known for charming juries as he put them in his pocket, whether for a criminal acquittal or a civil monetary award.

For his part, Brand, besides egging on the sheriff to dispense justice, West Texas–style, filed a civil suit over the Presidio strike, claiming the UFW was violating the state's right-to-work law. This was a regressive statute, though a couple provisions could favor the agricultural laborers. One was that a judge could order an election among worker members to determine whether they belonged to and in fact wanted the union.

We petitioned for an election. To Brand's horror, the judge ordered it, whereupon Brand immediately dismissed the suit rather than risk an outcome in the workers' favor. Judges in South Texas, where Brand lived and intimidated others through political muscle, would never countenance our election requests when he sued the UFW.

Melon harvests are short-lived, about a month or so. But the arrests were enough to break the strike. As for the growers, it helped that they took no chances in pursuing matters and raised the pay scale.

During this time, I had managed to finesse a cheap Presidio motel room. The *El Paso Times* reporter Paul Sweeney was on hand to cover the strike, but the doors all slammed in his face. I shared my room as a place to bivouac. That lasted two days until someone discovered we were bunking in Presidio. The motel then unceremoniously evicted us because we were on the strikers' side. I kept room key #7 as a souvenir in my office desk for years, a standard door key affixed to a flat, oblong strip of hard, reddish leather about six inches long.

THE VALLEY UFW REGROUPS

After the summer strikes ended, a disaffected group split off from the UFW and formed their own union, the Texas Farm Workers Union, led by Antonio "Tony" Orendain. This was a painful situation and personally distressing, since we were *padrinos* and godparents to each other's sons and I had worked closely with folks who went off on their own. The decision to fracture the movement also fractured our friendships.

Documents obtained later through the federal Freedom of Information Act raise the question of the involvement of an agent provocateur, a standard secretive government operation to foment dissent and division with infiltrators. This was quite common (and now well-documented) during the civil rights era and the anti–Vietnam War movement, and it was certainly true of the La Raza Unida party in South Texas.

The UFW responded in 1978 by sending Fred Ross, Sr., someone Saul Alinsky schooled and who in turn schooled César Chávez and Dolores Huerta in organizing tactics to get the farm labor movement up and running in California. He was a tall, lanky, balding man with graying hair and glasses; he looked more like a vintage college professor than a renowned community organizer. One of his favorite lines resonated with me: "A good organizer is a social arsonist who goes around setting people on fire." Fred was a badass.

Fred had remarkable stories about organizing. He was a blunt talker. We spent a late evening together in an emergency room when he had a stomach ailment flareup (probably from Tex-Mex cuisine). It was time well spent. Fred invited me to go to California and help organize there. I was honored by the invitation but demurred. I was committed to the Valley and Texas.

Fred trained Rebecca and the Texas UFW members in the art of house meetings and organizing UFW committees in the *colonias*. Fred's training went on for several weeks and turned the UFW into a South Texas powerhouse. Rebecca took the lead in setting up the house meeting program, which grew into *colonia* support committees.

Family was important in organizing and continues to be. In the house meetings that Rebecca led, she would later take our baby daughter, Sara, in one of those plastic seats and put Sara in the middle of a table. People took turns holding the cooing (usually) infant. The bond of family tied her with the workers and let them see that farmwork organizing belonged to everybody. We always took our kids to picket lines, union meetings, and other activities, and farmworkers began to do the same. That's how the young ones learn organizing. We had only three kids. Many of the women beginning to organize had more (six children would not be unusual), yet they joined in the movement.

The house meetings helped farmworkers find their voices. As Lalo García, who became one of the faces of the union, once told Rebecca: "Before I became involved with the union, I never said more than two words." People would smile when he told that story because he became known as quite a talker, in a good sense. And he took his time in telling a story!

Many farmworkers, men and women, came into their own as leaders during this time. Josefa García, for example, emerged from house meetings north of Mission as head of the Alton UFW organizing committee. She had fourteen kids. She would get up at 4 a.m. to make tortillas for them and, after sending them off to school, go to work the fields. She became such a good, relentless community leader that the city of Alton created a park in her honor when she passed on.

Once organized, the committees began holding annual Sunday Valley-wide conventions in 1979, which I helped coordinate, while Rebecca and the UFW staff did the hard work of preparing the *colonia* delegations. For most of the workers, especially at the beginning, this was their first time participating in a convention and having a voice.

The convocations adopted legislative and organizing priorities and turned themselves into a political force, such that Ann Richards (while state treasurer), Lieutenant Governor Bill Hobby, Agriculture Commissioner Jim Hightower, and all stripes of politicians attended at various times.

César would come for the conventions and talk. He was a sincere and passionate plain speaker. He charmed the delegates with jokes and stories that had deeper meaning and were parable-like. They were important ways of conveying ideas about organizing. The people loved him. They lined up to speak with him and get his autograph on their UFW flags. He was humble and respectful of everyone who spoke with him and listened to them. And he was charismatic. César liked coming to South Texas because it was still "Mexican," as he said, and people spoke only Spanish, unlike in California, where more acculturation was underway.

The conventions were serious and festive. People came dressed in their finest. Workers performed *conjunto* music and painted colorful, full-size canvas murals as podium backdrops; some murals would later hang in the farmworker center. The workers would escort special guests to the stage with a phalanx waving red-white-and-black UFW flags as delegates cheered and chanted. The politicians loved it and would trip over each other to have a photo taken with César.

The most compelling part of the convocations was watching the workers feel empowered for the first time in their lives, making decisions and voting about what they would do together in a concerted effort until the next convention. They had never felt lifted up before. It was as moving for us to witness as it was for them to do. The hands raised to vote were hands gnarled and calloused by years of hard work in the fields. Rebecca often said photographs of them voting were the best pictures in the world. The people were moving from the fields into politics and grassroots community organizing.

UTILIZING LEVEES AND IRRIGATION CANALS

One convention strategy was to begin a series of targeted strikes at various onion fields under harvest as a way of spiking wages in the area by encouraging the workers to walk off the job for the day. The hope was that this would galvanize into a larger organizing effort.

The Rio Grande Valley is a broad subtropical delta, not a valley in the traditional sense. A tapestry of two thousand miles of canals and three hundred levees crisscrosses the Valley to control the flow of water during flooding seasons and to provide irrigation water from the Rio Grande. On sunny afternoons, the canals reflect a blue, glistening patchwork to airline passengers flying above. The cement canals generally are V-shaped with earthen berms on the sides.

The canals and levees, raised above ground by as much as four feet and accessible by motor vehicles, meander deep into the agricultural fields. The UFW took the position that the levees were public property and therefore accessible to everybody, and indeed typically they were.

Whenever union organizers showed up at a field to encourage people to leave their jobs that day for higher pay, the growers would move the harvesters farther back into the fields away from the public roads. The UFW folks would then use the levees and canals to follow the harvesters and get within shouting distance to encourage them to walk out.

WERE THE BIRDS REALLY DISTURBED OR JUST AMUSED?

The levees were not always safe organizing spaces for UFW folks. One levee ran alongside a federal wildlife refuge, separating it from the fields. Government agents arrested two UFW pickets and charged them with disturbing the birds there.

I was looking forward to the trial to see how the government would prove that the union folks had disturbed the birds. I had cross-examined several turkeys by that time (usually in uniform), but never a protected wildlife bird. Alas, the feds dropped the charges. Perhaps they were snowbirds and had returned home and were unavailable.

The growers always called in sheriff's deputies to get the union folks off the levees and canals. But the public right-of-access argument befuddled them, and they never did much other than just hang around to make sure everyone kept the peace.

The union had some success with the targeted strike strategy. It raised wages wherever organizing activity was afoot, but it was difficult to sustain and did not lead to labor contracts. Farmworkers understood the tenuousness of their jobs. A vast supply of laborers was available a few miles south in Mexico to replace anyone who went on strike. Some studies posit that three replacement workers were standing in line for each one already in the field.

Without legal protection and a collective bargaining mechanism, it was self-destructive for field laborers to give up their day jobs to form a union. And the UFW did not have the resources to sustain long-term strikes. Nor was there any chance on earth that an antiunion state like Texas would pass a collective bargaining law for agricultural laborers, as California had done.

MEANWHILE . . . SAN ANTONIO

While organizing was moving forward in the Valley, César was traveling to other parts of Texas, raising awareness and support for the UFW mission. That led to a 1979 visit to San Antonio. Before he arrived, the KBUC radio personalities Ricci Ware and Judd Ashmore began accusing César on the air of being a communist.

Calling someone a communist under Texas law is per se libel and slander, which means there is no defense if the person is not one. Strict liability, in other words. César asked me to sue Ware, Ashmore, and KBUC, even though they were a good distance from the South Texas Project.

What's more, such a lawsuit would fall outside the scope of the ACLU's traditional First Amendment position that the media should generally be protected from suits by public figures, as César was. Litigation stifled the free exchange of ideas and opinion. I knew I could prove the offending duo's comments were malicious and false and enjoyed no First Amendment protection, but I was skating on the edge in the ACLU's eyes. It was not the kind of lawsuit the ACLU would ever pursue.

I based my decision on the damage the *Ricci & Judd Show* did and would do in the Alamo City area because the two on-air personalities were popular and San Antonio was firmly anchored to the military, including veterans and residents employed at nearby bases. "Communist" was more than a dirty word to them.

This led to a delicate balancing act: how to bolster community organizing when others holding our purse strings would counsel passing on handling this litigation. But I knew where I would end up. I did get pushback from some board members of the Texas Civil Liberties Union. This was one of those tough decisions.

KBUC settled after we lined up Mayor Henry Cisneros and Archbishop Patrick Flores as character witnesses for César at trial. The station sent a $12,000 check to the UFW.

I did have the good fortune to spend a couple hours with César on the San Antonio River Walk before his deposition in the KBUC case. A few people recognized him and stopped to say hello. Our conversation covered a host of topics, particularly organizing. I was also lucky to travel with him at other times when he was in Texas, as did Rebecca.

César never finished school. He quit the seventh grade to work the fields and help support his family, but he was bright and a quick learner. He was also a voracious reader and an eclectic one at that. He always traveled with books on different topics to read during downtimes. He had a passion for learning. I remember a book he was reading about a farm co-op in Spain, which he eventually went to visit. He was interested in pursuing agriculture in a more community-focused way and less as a capitalist agribusiness.

He remained passionate about education and helped take on the struggle at the University of Texas to initiate a program to enhance student diversity and minority opportunities. Rebecca reminded me, while I was writing this, that César remained skeptical of the quality of education and its use as a tool by majority society to mold young minds rather than to boost critical thinking and broader learning.

César was right. That struggle continues to this day as conservative state governments create restrictive curricula and censor books and other aspects of student education. It seems that those with power do everything they can to keep the rest of us in check, even to the extent of rewriting history and denying cultural pluralism. Talking with César was always an eye-opener in social and political thought.

THE 1982 MARCH ACROSS THE VALLEY WITH CÉSAR CHÁVEZ TO RAISE WAGES

The farmworker delegates at their 1982 annual convention, wrestling with chronic low wages in El Valle de Lágrimas, voted to accept César's proposal that they organize a protest march clear across the Valley. Marches were a hallmark UFW strategy. They generated energy, support, and publicity and pulled people into the organizing effort.

Enforcement of the $3.35/hour federal minimum wage was as abysmal as the wage itself. Only two federal agents covered South Texas to ensure compliance. Just the four counties of the Rio Grande Valley alone cover 4,244 square miles. They also had to enforce other federal laws such as the OSHA work safety statute. They were short on staff and overburdened, which meant growers could get away with paying less. Our survey before the march showed that citrus harvesters were averaging a paltry $2.45/hour. Vegetable harvesters were barely earning $2.90/hour.

The five-day march began simultaneously from two points, east and west, Brownsville and Rio Grande City. César alternated days leading the two branches of the march, each fifty-five miles long. About two hundred and fifty people marched all the way from each city. More than two thousand walked part of the way under the hot Valley sun as the march passed through their communities. César was their hero, and they came to see him and be with him and talk with him. People offered all kinds of food, often tacos, and cool drinks and provided overnight accommodations in their own homes for marchers.

The march joined in central San Juan on Sunday morning, March 21. Led by mariachis and *charros* on horseback, we proceeded slowly north to the large grass expanse behind the Shrine of la Virgen de San Juan for the concluding rally where people basked in the Valley sun and humidity. The festive rally lasted about two hours. César, of course, was the draw and the highlight. We showed the people and the press more than three hundred sworn minimum wage complaints against growers that organizers gathered during the march. We sent them to the US Department of Labor the next day.

It's fair to say that the march and rally helped hike wages for the spring harvests. The growers were watching. It's equally fair to say that the effort was no panacea to fix the chronically low wages. Only union contracts can effectively address that injustice.

PULLING THE PORTA-POTTY

We had just begun the March Across the Valley with César to raise wages when one of our volunteer law interns showed up from a northeastern Ivy League school. Some of the organizing for the march fell on my shoulders, a mix of community lawyering and organizing. Since everyone else already had a role in the march, I assigned him to driving the pickup that was pulling the porta-potty at the rear. We needed one for obvious reasons and to protect our First Amendment right to walk on the highway without running afoul of any health codes.

At day's end, he told me, "I didn't travel all the way here just to drag along an outhouse. I came to do law stuff." That led to a discussion about attorney elitism and how lawyers need to work with, and be a part of, the community. He didn't seem convinced but was a yeoman about it for the next two days until the march ended. He had plenty of legal work to keep him more than busy afterward.

But the march and rally gave impetus to the organizing effort and demonstrated widespread support for the UFW and its vigor for seeking justice. A spirit of joy, solidarity, peace, and determination enveloped the five days of marching and the rally. And then, buoyed by it all, everyone returned to the daily grind of on-the-ground organizing.

It was an honor to be part of this celebratory event and to see how well the hard toil of organizing was slowly succeeding. Like everyone else, I also knew that the next morning we would return to the hard task of keeping progress alive and growing. But getting charged up was good for the spirit. The touch of solidarity is powerful.

A REMNANT OF SOUTHERN SLAVERY: ABOLISHING *EL CORTITO*

Chapter 6 will detail the distinctive trifecta of major organizing and litigation victories for farm laborers. In addition to those victories, the UFW scored two important successes through intense community and political action and a third through a lawsuit.

The first was outlawing use of *el cortito* ("the short one"), the short-handled hoe that was backbreaking, a cruel holdover from the slave labor era. The idea was to keep people stooped over to make sure they were busy weeding and thinning crops. If they stood to stretch, the assumption was that they were not working hard enough.

The hoe is only twenty-four inches long. Bending and stooping all day with it often led to debilitating back injuries. The growers' purpose was inhumane: to extract maximum labor from people, health be damned. The California Supreme Court banned it in 1975 as an "unsafe hand tool."

The Texas state legislature banned *el cortito* in 1979. After this victory, some growers, ever conniving and heartless, switched to forcing workers to use knives in place of *el cortito*. The legislature banned that practice, too, in 1987, with little opposition, thanks to the dogged efforts of one state representative, Lena Guerrero, herself a former migrant laborer.

Governor Bill Clements, however, vetoed the bill, stating that, since farm laborers had workers' compensation, they could claim against that benefit should back injuries develop. Not only did Clements misrepresent the law; he was about as callous as one could imagine. He had no answer, of course, to what kind of job an agricultural laborer could later perform once sustaining a persistent back injury from bending over and using a knife.

The workers shot back and created the annual Golden Short-Handled Award that they would give out at every convention to a particularly deserving person. It was an actual short-handled hoe painted gold. Clements was the first recipient. César gave it out. He loved it. It fit into his sense of levity during hard times.

BRINGING TOILETS AND DRINKING WATER TO THE FIELDS

One would not imagine that in 1983 toilets and drinking water would be a rarity for field laborers. They were commonplace and required in all workspaces except agriculture.

Two scenarios can be conjured up in the imagination.

First, what is it like to do fieldwork under the scorching Texas sun without drinking water? And what is the resulting damage to the body?

Second, how does a field laborer handle the call of nature when no porta-potty is nearby, perhaps with a crew of fifty men and women working all around? It was not unusual for women to form a circle so their colleague could attend to her needs. Apart from the personal embarrassment and indignity, it meant that all the women lost valuable pay time.

As is unfortunately typical, agribusiness would not do the right thing until compelled. The UFW put pressure on the Texas Department of Health to adopt field sanitation and health rules, which it did in 1983.

One of the UFW's pressure points was the suggestion of a national boycott of Texas fresh vegetables and fruit that "might be contaminated by human waste." The reader can imagine another, less elegant slogan that floated around.

A LAWSUIT VICTORY: FLIPPING THE ANTI-UNION RIGHT-TO-WORK LAW ON ITS HEAD

Half the states, including Texas, have antiunion right-to-work laws. Among other things, these prevent unions from charging dues from everyone benefiting from a labor contract. In other words, non-union workers can avoid paying dues and free-ride on others who do pay. This undercuts the solidarity needed for organizing. The Texas law was drafted so broadly that it probably did not reflect the authors' original intent: any person "cannot be denied employment because of membership or non-membership in a labor union or other labor organization."

María Guadalupe Vásquez helped make good use of the antiunion law to strengthen UFW organizing, winning a victory in the Supreme Court of Texas. The irony was as sweet as the nine justices' unanimous decision.

Ms. Vásquez was a regular field laborer with Bannworths, Inc., for nine years, harvesting different crops in Starr and Hidalgo Counties during various seasons. She did manual labor five to six days per week for up to ten hours per day at minimum wage during the harvest season. She was likely in her early forties. Her hard work gave her the appearance of physical trimness.

In January 1982, Ms. Vásquez stopped in at the UFW Starr County office, seeking help in obtaining permanent resident status in the United States. She eventually became an active UFW member and began complaining about revolting sanitation issues at Bannworths fields; all employees had to share a common drinking cup, and the porta-potties were filthy and failed minimum standards set by the Texas health commissioner.

As a result of a UFW complaint, two health sanitation engineers showed up at a Bannworths field where Ms. Vasquez's crew was harvesting to inspect the porta-potties. Not surprisingly, they were disgusting. Later that day, Bannworths summarily fired her.

We helped her bring a lawsuit for lost wages and sought a court order that Bannworths comply with the right-to-work law and reemploy her. A jury found that Bannworths had fired her because of her union membership and her porta-potty complaints. The jurors awarded her $3,000 in lost wages and found that Bannworths did not rehire Mrs. Vasquez because of her union membership.

The trial judge issued an order against Bannworths but fell short of remedying the harm recognized by the jury. He ordered Bannworths not to discriminate against Ms. Vásquez, if the company should rehire her, but did not order Bannworths to reinstate her. It was half a loaf of bread or even less. The chances of the company voluntarily reemploying her were zero.

The intermediate court of appeals sided with the trial judge, but the Texas high court ordered Bannworths to rehire her. Her victory was complete. No more total antiunion impunity for agribusiness.

MCALLEN'S INFAMOUS MAYOR AND ONION KING

Othal Brand wore two hats, sometimes both at once: mayor and behemoth agribusiness owner. Not only did he display a bullying character, his physical size accentuated his aggressive nature. He was taller than six feet, solidly built, with thick white hair, horn-rimmed glasses, and a loud voice. There was at least one reported incident of fisticuffs with a fellow school board member with whom he served earlier.

It's worth mentioning that Brand once tried to jump security screening with a gun at the small McAllen airport because "he was mayor" and, when unsuccessful, browbeat security officers. A ruckus generally followed in Brand's trail. Nor was he above using condescending racial and ethnic epithets.

As the self-styled "Onion King," Brand had four UFW protesters, including Rebecca, arrested for trespassing on his property when they were there to organize. He had them fenced in at the entranceway to his property so they could not leave after being told to do so. I went to the county jail to bail them out and complained vociferously when I found out the jailers had strip-searched them.

Someone then swore out a warrant against me for obstructing justice or something similar. The authorities kept it quiet until they could spring their trap. A few days later, as I left the courtroom after a hearing on another farm labor case, sheriff's deputies grabbed me and spirited me down a side stairwell, hoping to avoid any commotion by the UFW folks who had also been at the hearing.

The arrest did not go unnoticed. A group of people, instigated by Rebecca, who was there, followed the deputies, loudly chanting "Free Jimmy Chuck," using a humorous nickname my brother had conferred on me for my given name, James Charles. I did not like it.

It was a politically dicey situation. The deputies had to drive around the county to three different justices of the peace before they found one willing to charge me and set a bond until trial. The others refused, not wanting to upset any farmworker voters. It was amusing theater. District Attorney Oscar McInnis dropped the charges after I offered not to sue as a quid pro quo.

When the trespassing trial eventually came along, a jury in the Justice of the Peace court in Mission acquitted the protesters. That was a fun trial, since the court was in a poor, farmworker area of the county. We failed later, however, to have Brand criminally convicted of false imprisonment. Justice of the Peace Arturo Leal refused as long as he could to accept a criminal complaint against Brand. He did so only after a daylong sit-in protest inside his courtroom by Rebecca and the organizers Brand had ordered penned in on his property. They filed false imprisonment charges against the Onion King.

Brand did not dare risk a jury that would be all Mexican American and probably include farmworkers. He read the judge correctly and opted for a nonjury trial. The judge acquitted Brand even though his own field foreman, named "Red," testified that Brand gave the order to lock the fence and detain the UFW organizers on his property. Leal played the game. We filed a civil suit against Brand, and he settled with the four organizers for $10,000.

There were other criminal jury trials of UFW picketers for trespassing and the like. We always won. The UFW people loved the trials because they could use their testimony on the witness stand to educate the jury, judge, and court personnel about *La Causa* ("The Cause"). Such trials were fun in a way, as there was no chance of an adverse outcome, and we played them to the hilt.

LUPE ON THE SCENE

Given the existential realities on the ground, the union began to focus on providing direct services, political organizing, and community action, which eventually, in 2003, came under the wing of the UFW's related nonprofit organization, La Unión del Pueblo Entero (translation: "The Union of All the People" or "The Union of the Entire Community"; known by its acronym "LUPE").

TCRP often worked closely with LUPE, continuing to do so after our South Texas office constructed its own building in 2011 and moved from the UFW premises to nearby North Alamo.

Juanita Valdez-Cox became the valiant and unflagging leader of LUPE until retiring in 2023. LUPE had phenomenal successes in political and community organizing. LUPE also provided services related to housing construction and benefits during catastrophic crises (such as hurricanes and the COVID-19 pandemic).

LUPE evolved into a well-heeded voice for farm laborers because it could organize a crowd of people behind its voice at any given meeting or event when necessary. LUPE steadfastly saw to it that government agencies strictly enforced hard-won field sanitary regulations and right-to-know pesticide regulations.

The South Texas Project's goal was to struggle with, march with, picket with, litigate with, and prop up people seeking to organize themselves for justice. The years of organizing and litigating paid off, made the community better, and lifted the dignity of farmworkers and people in the *colonias*. It was an honor to be in that movement, to be part of *La Causa*.

TAKEAWAYS ON LOSING A LEGEND: *¡ADELANTE!*

When César Chávez died suddenly in 1993, Judge Mario Ramírez from the Valley, before whom we had litigated some important cases, called me immediately. We had been occasional drinking buddies before Mario became a judge in 1980 (he retired in 2024). It wasn't just to express personal sympathy, which he did, but to mourn our loss and recall the impact of what we had all done together because of César, changing the lives of farmworkers and many other people in Texas. We commiserated about what our hopes and goals were to be going forward. I am certain many others had the same conversation.

A group of us from Texas joined 35,000 people marching in César's three-mile-long funeral procession from Delano to the UFW's Forty Acres, as we called the compound. It was "the working people's state funeral," as the *Los Angeles Times* put it. He is sorely missed; his legacy continues to this day in the hearts of those whose causes he championed.

6

THE TEXAS ERA COMES TO THE RESCUE OF FARMWORKERS AND MINORITY VOTERS

A new legal and organizing strategy emerged amid the other ongoing activities described in chapter 5 and yielded the three major farmworker victories. This epic effort drew considerable public attention and radically amplified farmworkers' political *palanca* (leverage). It involved dogged politicking, a few friends in high places, and a wing-and-a-prayer lawsuit. It all flowed together like streams converging to create a river.

THE STRUGGLE FOR EQUAL EMPLOYMENT RIGHTS FOR INJURED FARM LABORERS

In 1978, when field organizing stepped up and the United Farm Workers began annual conventions, workers at *colonia* house meetings turned their attention toward establishing UFW priorities.

One of the first that emerged from the meetings and surfaced at the first convocation in January 1979 was obtaining workers' compensation for field laborers injured or killed at their jobs. That objective resonated deeply and became the prime issue around which union members began political organizing.

The quest started with organizing efforts directed toward the 1979 and 1981 legislatures to change the law and end the discrimination against agricultural employees. The challenge for the South Texas Project was finding a successful legal approach to further the cause. A lawsuit was necessary to spur things along. Legislators are more receptive to justice when facing lawsuits pointed in their direction. How all this came about is extraordinary in retrospect.

Workers' Compensation and Agricultural Laborers' Discriminatory Exclusion

Texas has about 360,000 seasonal and migrant farm laborers. The legislature had excluded them from workers' comp benefits since 1914, when the law first passed. Even though agriculture is the state's first or second most dangerous occupation, depending on the season (alternating with construction), the law denied them relief if injured or killed on the job.

Data from the US Bureau of Labor Statistics shows the agriculture industry is consistently at the highest risk for occupational injuries and fatalities. In 1985, while our litigation was going on, there were 20.6 deaths per 100,000 agricultural workers. There has been slight improvement over the years because of increased regulation, but the rate is still quite high. For nonfatal injuries, the average is about 307 injuries involving days away from work per 10,000 agricultural laborers.

Repetitive bending over in fields for days at a time to harvest row crops and lifting heavy bags cause muscle and skeletal injuries. Farm equipment such as knives, machetes, and makeshift ladders for tree harvesting (citrus and cherries, for example) are hazardous. Nor does Texas's baking sun show mercy. Exposure to pesticides, which growers use to blanket crops, can cause long-term respiratory ailments and cancer. Overexertion, falls, and being struck by objects are other causes of injury.

Added to this is that people living in poverty tend not to seek medical attention until sometimes it is too late. Stopgap emergency room treatment is the norm, not office visits. Migrating to unfamiliar areas for jobs, along with language barriers, likewise discourage workers from pursuing timely medical care, with exacerbating consequences.

The workers' comp law in effect at the time of our legislative offensive required an employer to provide medical coverage and time-lost payments for job-related injuries. It also compensated for death and permanent disabilities. The law stripped an employer who chose not to provide coverage of protection from personal injury lawsuits for job-related injuries, which, if severe enough, could result in enormous jury verdicts and attorney costs.

The law was a trade-off. Workers had immediate relief for injuries suffered on the job, and employers would have protection from prolonged litigation and the risk of sizeable jury awards. Since most injuries are not extremely damaging, workers would have quick payment for medical expenses and lost time through a state agency, the Industrial Accident

Board. Typical of most Texas laws, it was not a great mechanism, but it was far better than nothing.

Being excluded from the law meant that injured farm laborers had to depend on local charity and whatever meager government benefits they could eke out. That, of course, was a double-whammy for already impoverished Hispanic communities. Not only did the communities lose the economic benefit of a productive worker; they had to help support injured individuals and their families. Resources were sparse and never adequate.

Genoveva Puga's Advocacy for Her Deceased Son's Family Becomes a Life's Journey

The possibility of taking legal action simultaneously with political organizing came into sharper focus when Genoveva Puga appeared at the UFW office before the 1979 convention, wanting to sue Donna Fruit Company over the 1977 death of her son Juan Torrez in one of its citrus orchards.

Juan, in his early twenties, was operating a forklift to raise a half-ton wooden bin full of harvested oranges. The machine malfunctioned. While Juan was trying to adjust the forklift, the bin of oranges fell on top of him, crushing him to death. Because no one found his body in the orchard for six hours, no one knows whether his death was sudden or long and excruciatingly painful. This uncertainty plagued Genoveva as a mother.

He left behind a young wife and two small children. Genoveva was migrating to Ohio at the time and didn't learn of his death right away. By the time she returned home, Juan had been buried, but the location of his final resting place was not entirely clear. After a long search, she finally found her son in a barely marked pauper's grave.

As part of covering the UFW campaign for workers' compensation, the *Brownsville Herald* printed a haunting and heartrending front-page photo of Genoveva, weeping and praying at Juan's burial place in the overgrown, weed-covered county cemetery.

Genoveva tried to claim workers' compensation for Juan's family, but Donna Fruit had no coverage, which was typical of Valley growers. We then tried a collateral wrongful death lawsuit, which the trial and appellate courts dismissed. The Supreme Court of Texas ruled in Genoveva's favor in 1982, however, and gave her the opening she needed to challenge in court Donna Fruit's negligence and defective farm equipment for Juan's death. Donna Fruit then settled with financial compensation for Juan's family, essentially what the company would have paid under workers' compensation.

While Genoveva's case was a victory, it was five years in coming and did not provide the speedy remedy for agricultural injuries and death that the workers' comp law did through the Industrial Accident Board. As with our grand jury litigation, a case-by-case approach would not resolve the exclusion of agricultural laborers as a group from the law. Such litigation, because it was expensive and prolonged and catch-as-catch-can, would not be a feasible way to compensate workers with nonfatal injuries.

Nor was Genoveva content with securing financial assistance for her deceased son's family. She pushed on for justice for all her coworkers and became fiercely committed to changing the compensation law. She was a heaven-sent angel.

The Legislature: No Friend of Agricultural Laborers

After unsuccessful attempts in the 1979 and 1981 legislatures, the 1983 legislature was on the verge of extending workers' compensation to agricultural laborers. Over four years, the UFW had built solid backing around the state for the law. Urban legislators, church leaders, and labor unions rallied to the cause.

Farmworkers did the legwork in the legislature, testifying on the record and buttonholing lawmakers. The politicking involved sacrifice for them.

MEETING EMMA TENAYUCA

It was an honor to run into Emma Tenayuca at a legislative strategy session around passing workers' comp. She was a labor leader, civil rights activist, and educator.

She had great respect from people for leading the 1938 San Antonio pecan-shellers strike in which 12,000 Mexican American women struck for higher wages. People called her "La Pasionaria de Texas" because of her passion for worker justice.

Emma was a small woman with a fierce commitment to justice. She reminded me of the women farmworkers who were courageously helping lead the Texas movement. Their organizing was part of Emma's legacy.

They gave up scarce earning opportunities to undertake more than one lobbying venture to Austin. They had no fancy lobbying firm to bankroll the effort. They ate out of their cars and slept on supporters' couches. They never uttered a word of complaint or discouragement. Just gritty determination.

The workers dressed as nicely as they could when meeting legislators, not in the shiny finery of professional lobbyists but as decent, hard-working people. Legislators got to shake hands with the workers, whose hands were hardened by labor in the fields, men and women alike. This was something the former US Senator Bob Krueger spoke about during his reelection campaign: everybody's hands he shook were rough and calloused. That profoundly moved him.

The workers also showed creativity. One year, for example, they passed out onions to legislators with a toothpick stuck in the top bearing a small sign in favor of the workers' comp legislation. The next session it was an avocado. Not a fancy gift, but it made the point.

Genoveva Puga was a stalwart in the effort. A small grandmother with a disarming smile, she was omnipresent, a powerhouse at that. She and the others told their stories with such conviction and dignity that even opponents had to listen with respect.

On the last day of the 1983 legislature, the new workers' comp law was on the brink of passage, needing only a final vote in the state house; the state senate had already voted in favor. We were all sitting on edge in the balcony, palpably nervous, watching the house passing laws while holding our collective breath.

With but a few minutes to go before midnight, when the house had to adjourn under the terms of the state constitution, Speaker of the House Gib Lewis suddenly blocked a vote on the compensation bill over legislators' shouts. He then summarily adjourned the legislature sine die, which meant that the regular session was over, finished.

Pandemonium broke out through the Capitol Building at Lewis's heavy hand, something I had never seen in my years of legislative efforts. Governor Mark White immediately rose to the occasion and called a special legislative session within days. The special session resulted in the creation of the governor, lieutenant governor, and Speaker's Joint Committee on Farm Worker Insurance to fashion a compensation law for farm laborers. Lieutenant Governor Bill Hobby helped broker this arrangement. It turned out to be an adroit political move.

The UFW appointed me to the committee as its representative. Grower and rancher interests, large and small, also had representation, including the Texas Farm Bureau and Texas Farmers Union. The former legislator Tony Korioth was the chair. Other members included sitting legislators.

Even though the governor's actions seemed promising, no one on our side wanted to leave any stone unturned, especially given our prior experiences at the legislature. Three burns on the hot stove were enough. The decision was to move ahead with litigation to hold a meaningful threat over a fickle and betraying legislature. Even though the governor seemed friendly to our side, a lawsuit would help keep him in line and give him ammunition if needed.

But how to engineer a successful lawsuit? Our options were narrow. A federal court approach was out of the picture. Federal judges had decided other cases that such agriculture employee exclusions did not violate the US Constitution. They chose not to look at the exclusions as racially or ethnically discriminatory.

Did we dare risk a lawsuit in the conservative Texas legal system? The last thing we could afford was to lose the case. Defeat would play into the legislature's hand, and we would be through—a devastating rout. We were in a dangerous strategic situation.

We grimaced and rolled the dice on a novel and risky legal theory: the Texas Equal Rights Amendment. The trial judge let us run the table.

Using the Texas Equal Rights Amendment

Yes, Texas has an Equal Rights Amendment, believe it or not, and it's very broad. People are sometimes stunned hearing this news, especially considering the state's white male top leaders, who for years seemed hellbent on anchoring the state in a past era.

It happened in 1972. Texas voters, showing an old populist streak that sometimes pops up as one of their better angels, by a four-to-one margin, adopted a state ERA: "Equality under the law shall not be denied or abridged because of sex, race, color, creed, or national origin." It was astonishing given Texas's clouded history.

The Texas ERA is right up front at the beginning of the state constitution's Bill of Rights. By its terms, the Texas ERA is "self-operative," which means it has its own teeth. It does not depend on the state legislature for enforcement power.

Until our case in 1983, the courts had ruled on only a handful of ERA lawsuits, all involving sex discrimination. None addressed race or ethnic discrimination.

One of the creative legal strategies we developed was to utilize the Texas Bill of Rights to expand state constitutional protections to a greater extent than required by the federal Constitution. At the end of the day, we saw no other option but to gamble on the Texas ERA as the vehicle for striking down the exclusion of farm laborers from the workers' comp law.

Our argument was that agricultural employees, as one of the only two labor groups excluded from the law (the other being domestic servants), were uniquely identifiable in Texas by race and ethnicity. The discrimination did not happen by chance. The legislature knew what it was doing when it adopted the law. That being the case, the Texas ERA should come into play to eliminate the discriminatory exclusion. It was a brand-new legal theory, barely off the printer.

Under our theory, because the Texas ERA is more protective than the US Constitution, it broadly banned discrimination. That put the state in a vise: how to explain why it excluded agricultural laborers while feigning not to know their race or ethnicity.

Proving our case was the easy part. Academic studies abounded, and experts came forth voluntarily to testify on behalf of agricultural laborers. They were essential workers on which society depended for sustenance. There was no denying that farm laborers were in need of as much protection, if not more, than most Texas employees. Nor was there any doubt about their racial and ethnic background as a workforce.

The difficult part of the litigation was legitimizing our novel approach under the Texas ERA, but wind filled our sails. Judge Harley Clark, who presided over the lawsuit (it was a bench trial without a jury), accepted the argument ("Let's give it a whirl," he said with an eye toward the appellate courts) and struck down the farmworker exclusion.

The trial went smoothly. We had experts present statistics, which were convincing and undeniable. We also had experts discuss the intersection of poverty, work injury, and medical care. Not having medical care, which would exist under workers' comp, aggravated and prolonged people's injuries and promised dire financial consequences for their families. There were also adverse economic impacts on the Valley overall that stretched whatever charity was available.

The long and short of the testimony was that not having workers' comp available detrimentally damaged the workers, their families, and the larger

SHOWING A LITTLE LEG IN COURT

For the workers' comp trial, one of our star witnesses was Lalo García, a Valley farmworker and father of six. He was such a genial person that he got into an informal conversation with Judge Harley Clark about what it was like to toil in the fields and the injuries that he and others suffered.

Clark, himself an organic gardener, enjoyed comparing notes with Lalo. (Clark, when he was the University of Texas football head cheerleader, originated the famous "Hook 'Em Horns" hand sign.)

Lalo was a serious soul with a pleasant smile. When he needed to speak, he did. Some kind of *espina* (a long thorn or sharp spine) embedded in the dirt of the crop he was hoeing had pierced his shoe, gone into his foot, and badly infected it such that he could not work for two or three months during which time his family suffered for lack of food.

During his dialogue with the judge, Lalo suddenly pulled off his right shoe and sock and put his foot up on the judge's bench to show the scar left from a bad wound that he suffered while working the fields. Every time I saw the court bailiff after that trial, he would reminisce about Lalo putting his bare foot on the judge's bench.

community. The expert witnesses captured the bleakness of the situation and the undeniable oppressive consequence on Hispanics.

The trial painted a classic portrait of race-based discrimination that perpetuated and exacerbated debilitating poverty. The only beneficiaries were growers and agribusinesses, profiting handsomely as they enjoyed profits riding the backs of laborers, the poorest of the poorest. Unjust and immoral.

The testimony of the workers—respectfully relating stories about what it was like to toil in the fields in the conditions that they did and the injuries they and others had suffered—was powerful and vivid.

They talked about back injuries, infections like Lalo's, and muscle strains that kept them from working for weeks, relating how it meant a lack of enough sustenance for their families, maybe just beans and tortillas. How they had to borrow food and funds from relatives and friends, who themselves did not have enough, and how humiliating that was. How they would keep working when injured or return to work in pain because they could not afford to miss time or pay for medical care. How the older they became the more frequent the injuries were. How they never completely recovered from some injuries. How they had to pull kids from school to work the fields so the family could survive.

I could not listen to these personal stories without a deepening outrage and contempt for the injustices. I felt nothing but compassion for people humbly telling their stories in open court. I sometimes felt like standing up and screaming in the courtroom, "What more do we need to prove? How long will this go on?" Sometimes, I just felt like crying. I embraced each witness as they stepped down from the stand.

Their testimony certainly impacted Judge Clark. He paid close attention to the consequences of even short-term injuries, how weeks or months without a job, and paying the consequent medical expenses, severely impacted workers' families. No one questioned the magnified impact of someone suffering a permanently incapacitating disability or death. Genoveva Puga was a witness, of course.

The workers' testimony underscored the injustices under which they lived and labored. They brought a palpable account of a different kind of life, one of grueling poverty, into an urban court three hundred and fifty miles from their homes. Their humble natures and dignity surrounded their words on the witness stand, told through an interpreter.

When the trial finished, and Judge Clark announced that he was declaring the exclusion unconstitutional, Lalo, who did not speak English and was at the counsel table, turned and said, "¿Qué dijo?" (What did he say?). I replied, "Que ganamos" (That we won). Lalo declared, "¡Claro!" (Of course!).

It floored me that Lalo had such faith in the legal system that it would yield justice, particularly in this case. The more I thought about it, though, I realized Lalo was expressing confidence in the ultimate triumph of justice. He was a union organizer and knew justice didn't appear like magic or in a single lawsuit but understood that it duly appeared incrementally, one step at a time.

Witnesses like Lalo and Genoveva, whether testifying in court or at the legislature, impressed people with their down-to-earthness and self-respect.

They were eloquent in their own right and got their message across. Telling their stories was a thousand times more powerful than a sheaf of statistics. They both presented injustice, and one was a living victim of injustice.

The Select Committee Proposes a Compromise Law: A Quandary

After the court victory, the select committee held hearings in Lubbock, Amarillo, Harlingen, and Austin. Rebecca helped make sure that plenty of farmworkers turned out to testify. We wanted the growers and legislators to hear their stories. Church and community leaders also came and offered testimony for the workers.

A majority of the committee eventually drew up a hard-debated compromise, a phased-in law that would bring large employers under the law first and relatively quickly, then smaller ones a little later so they could better prepare for the changes. This was not the immediate blanket coverage we wanted.

The phase-in compromise created a strategic conundrum. In a sense, farmworkers were holding the ace card: the court's verdict. This meant immediate coverage for all agricultural laborers. However, we also faced the uncertainty of what the conservative appellate courts would do to Judge Clark's bold and groundbreaking finding. We were not on solid ground.

An appellate trajectory could take two or three years, during which there would be no coverage. Even if we prevailed in the Supreme Court of Texas, we could end up in the same place as if the phase-in compromise had gone into effect. The quandary: How to protect most farm laborers as soon as possible?

By this point many political leaders were on our side. We were hesitant to squander their goodwill, since we were planning to file two other lawsuits, tackling farm laborers' exclusion from the unemployment benefits law and the right to know about dangerous chemicals in the workplace. We would need their support. Cooperating with them now would bring along their cooperation later.

We accepted the phase-in law as the best and most prudent option, but it was a daunting decision.

The ever-duplicitous Texas Farm Bureau backed out of the negotiated agreement at the last minute, on the eve of a second special session that the governor had called to ratify a new bill. Governor White called everyone on the carpet. He was furious and imparted a blistering takedown of the

Farm Bureau. It was quite enjoyable, a bit perverse, to watch the Farm Bureau, an institutional archenemy, sizzling on the griddle.

The governor's ire muted the opposition, and agricultural laborers came under the workers' compensation law in the 1984 special session following a five-year struggle.

Governor White signed the new law on a searing afternoon in front of assembled farmworkers at the Virgen de San Juan Shrine in San Juan, where the march that César Chávez led for higher wages had culminated three years earlier. Genoveva Puga, immaculately dressed for the occasion, was standing next to the governor, waving her small UFW flag and smiling. Lalo García was there, too . . . "*claro*."

Governor White and I ran into each other about twenty years later at a Houston TCRP event where Congressman Joe Kennedy spoke. We relived the glory, with a few chuckles, at the Farm Bureau's chewing-out, and I got to thank him again for what he did to bend the moral arc a bit more toward justice.

Another interesting facet of that event was how Kennedy entered through the kitchen, as he generally does, to make time to personally thank those doing the hard chores for the guests. An impressive and respectful gesture.

NOTCHING A SECOND TEXAS ERA VICTORY: UNEMPLOYMENT BENEFITS

Once our workers' comp struggle emerged victorious, eyes turned toward unemployment benefits, which the law denied for agricultural workers. These benefits were critical to farm laborers because of the seasonal nature of their work. The 1936 law did not protect them from employment gaps as it did other laborers. The vagaries of climate and farming meant their work was not year-round.

In many regards, they were in a comparable situation as construction workers, who did draw unemployment benefits during the hiatus between jobs or when bad weather struck. The difference is that construction wages were higher and new job prospects typically better.

We used the same one-two punch: the Texas ERA and organizing. Success was quick in coming. Judge Clark also presided over the unemployment benefits case in 1985. The trial started a day late because a snowstorm buried Austin. That delighted the workers who had driven from the Valley to attend the trial. They rarely saw snow, let alone a foot of it.

Judge Clark found in our favor once again. The legislature used the same phase-in model it had adopted for workers' compensation. Victory number two.

In an interesting twist, the state appealed Judge Clark's decision, and it went before the Supreme Court of Texas, which affirmed the decision in 1988 and awarded us attorney fees in the case. It was a splendid ruling on both counts.

Bringing farm laborers under workers' comp and unemployment benefits helped workers and their families. It also lessened the drain on public health agencies, churches, and charities. The same was true as to the expansion of unemployment benefits. Extending employment benefits to agricultural laborers added an estimated $17 million to the South Texas economy within the first few years of the new law becoming effective.

THE THIRD LAWSUIT: THE LEGISLATURE SURRENDERS AND CURBS PESTICIDE USE

Our third target was coverage under the right-to-know law about hazardous chemicals in the agricultural workplace. Life expectancy for agricultural laborers is lower, by as much as twenty-five years, much less than the general population. Part of the reason is pesticide exposure.

Pesticides cause farmworkers more chemical-related illnesses than in any other workforce nationwide. Short-term effects include stinging eyes, rashes, blisters, blindness, nausea, dizziness, and headaches. Coma and death are possible. Long-term impacts such as infertility, neurological disorders, and cancer are also prevalent. Not only are agricultural laborers subjected to these risks; so are residents in *colonia* communities close to fields. They are subject to pesticide drift when growers spray the crops, raising the specter of environmental racism.

Sometimes growers would spray fields even when people were harvesting in them, flying right over the people and dumping the chemicals on top of them. It was an affront to their health and dignity. It was not unusual to see individuals run from the fields when a plane approached. Oftentimes growers would send laborers into the fields right after dousing vegetable and fruit crops, and people had to handpick them when still wet and oily with pesticides.

Given the two prior lawsuits and the fact we once again drew Judge Clark to hear the case, the legislature rolled over and used the same phase-in structure as it had before. In 1986, Texas became the first state to enact a right-to-know pesticide law. Too bad we had to lead the state by the bridle, but we were happy to oblige.

Jim Hightower became agriculture commissioner in 1983. The UFW worked diligently to turn out the vote for him. He was the first commissioner who cared about the "little people," to use his words. The legislature handed him the task of implementing the new right-to-know pesticide regulations for agricultural laborers. He and his staff did superlative work. The startup date was January 1, 1988.

The new regulations required growers to personally provide farmworkers written information in Spanish and English about what chemicals they were applying and when, what the health effects might be, and how to inquire about or report any concerns. There was antiretaliation protection as well for workers insisting on their rights. Information about chemical use was especially important for pregnant workers and those with respiratory ailments.

Hightower's excellent work irked the growers, who widely used dangerous chemicals. McAllen's Othal Brand saw Hightower as his personal archenemy, which Hightower undoubtedly enjoyed. The growers banded together to elect Rick Perry over Hightower in 1990, but the law was already in place, and they had to live with it. The growers also had the legislature pass a law requiring that future candidates for agriculture commissioner be tied to the "business of agriculture" lest any errant populist like Hightower be elected again.

Farmworkers won the three lawsuits consecutively, about two years apart. And 360,000 Texas seasonal and migrant agricultural laborers benefited—and continue to benefit—from their unwavering work and passionate perseverance.

From time to time, people ask: "What's the biggest case you ever did?" I always hope they are asking the question in terms of justice, not money, much of which I neither saw nor wanted. Two other lawsuits might compete for the title, as discussed in other chapters, but the biggest case that won my heart was the trifecta of farmworker lawsuits, woven together by a common thread.

If the only time given to me on earth was for these cases, my life would have a "well-lived" tag on it. As mentioned earlier in the book, "getting proximate" to the community, according to Bryan Stevenson, is the heartbeat of justice work. Getting proximate also makes you family, and you do what you need to do for family.

THE ERA AND TEXAS VOTING RIGHTS: THE VICTORIES MOUNT UP

When it comes to legislative redistricting, getting it right for minority communities is a critical component, and in this context the Texas ERA became a powerful tool we used to protect voting rights. The US Constitution specifically requires redistricting every ten years to account for population redistribution during the prior decade so that each district at all levels of government represents roughly the same number of people.

Gerrymandering is a favorite government sport, the political party in power trying to adjust district boundaries to cement itself in power. Congress passed the Voting Rights Act of 1965 to prevent race-based gerrymandering and to protect minority voting interests. Litigation always arises under the Voting Rights Act when redistricting occurs, and it takes a year or two before the dust settles and the lawsuits conclude.

We joined forces with MALDEF after the 1990 census to litigate redistricting at all political levels—federal, state, and local. We challenged the redistricting plans that the state legislature had drafted, which unsurprisingly were not solicitous of Texas's minority communities. Those plans provided fewer districts from which minority communities could elect their own officials than what statistical analysis called for. The legislature created the districts in such a way to spread out minority communities into white-dominated districts, thereby diluting their voting strength.

We decided to go to state court under the Texas ERA and avoid the federal courts, which generally oversaw redistricting litigation but were becoming more conservative and less solicitous of minority voting rights. That adverse federal trend has only been exacerbated under the conservative United States Supreme Court.

We provided counsel to a broad coalition of community groups and filed the lawsuits in Hidalgo County in the Rio Grande Valley. We wanted to be in a minority area of the state, hoping for greater judicial sensitivity to voting rights in historically disenfranchised communities. My prior Valley experience helped navigate the legal system there.

We were not the only team at this ballgame. Both political parties had litigation teams as well. The Republicans, represented by white lawyers, were at a bit of a disadvantage, something to which they were unaccustomed. The shoe was on the other foot, and they quietly squawked about it.

Hidalgo County District Judge Mario Ramírez accepted our lawsuits and ruled that the legislature's redistricting plans for members of Congress and state legislators violated the Texas ERA because they discriminated against the state's minority communities. The litigation was complicated and time-consuming, and there were appeals. We finally landed before the Supreme Court of Texas, which gave us some blowback, but we still prevailed. The judges didn't like how we had strategically outfoxed the Republicans and the traditional way of litigating this decennial issue, but they could not say so candidly, just obliquely. Nor could they find a way to stop us.

Ultimately we negotiated new state legislative and congressional districts that were more protective of minority voting rights than what the legislature had put forward. We were able to increase the number of districts in which minority communities predominated such that they could elect representatives of their choosing.

There was a certain pleasure hearing some legislators grouse about how "some judge in South Texas" was invalidating their redistricting schemes. Of course, they, the white guys, meant "some *Hispanic* judge in South Texas" in a derogatory way.

INTERLUDE: HOW THE COURTS BECAME BAD FOR COMMON PEOPLE

The chances of success for creative human rights lawyering took a nosedive in the years following our innovative use of the Texas ERA.

In the 1990s, the character of federal and state courts in Texas began to change dramatically and became one-dimensionally conservative. As president, Ronald Reagan introduced the strategy of systematically selecting federal judges for their political ideology, not necessarily legal acumen. Federal judges are unelected, being nominated by the president and approved

A MORE REPRESENTATIVE DEL VALLE SCHOOL BOARD

We also joined hands with MALDEF to use our Texas ERA strategy to break up the at-large election scheme of the Anglo-controlled Del Valle Independent School District school board and establish single-member districts. Del Valle is a predominantly minority community. Our plaintiffs were from Del Valle's African American and Latino communities. We won at trial and on appeal and created more good Texas ERA precedent. After we won single-member districts, locals were finally able to elect their own representative to the school board.

We had hoped to use this strategy more broadly around the state. Unfortunately, as Texas courts have become decidedly less amenable to protecting minority rights, the prospects for fair redistricting litigation these days under the Texas ERA would be dim at best. But it was a potent tool a generation ago and may spring back in coming years.

by the Senate. Reagan bragged about choosing judges who would carry his agenda forward long after he left the planet. Since the president nominates the judges, campaign money is only one step removed from who becomes a federal judge and how it plays out in Texas.

The political operative Karl Rove ran with a similar idea for Texas judges and masterminded a campaign to select judges according to his ideological agenda and to fund their elections. The people he represented had the necessary large sums of money to donate to election campaigns.

The campaign to take hold of the Texas judiciary initially began under a misnomer—"tort reform"—to change Texas tort law through the legislature and the courts.

A "tort" is an old English term for a personal injury. Tort reform, which sounds benevolent enough, was a successful, concerted, conservative effort to change the civil justice system, making it harder for injured people to file lawsuits, limiting the amount of money or compensation they can receive for injuries, reducing damages to punish egregious wrongdoers (punitive damages), and making it more difficult to obtain a jury trial.

Insurance companies and large corporations spearheaded the tort reform movement, which started in the 1970s, and eventually produced a sophisticated media campaign to persuade the public that the civil justice system was corrupt and had adverse effects on the economy. An integral tort reform dynamic in Texas was the effort to "capture the judiciary," that is, to fund the election of like-minded judges. Texas elects its state and local judges, which unfortunately means that huge sums of campaign money play an outsized role in judicial elections at all levels.

The people of Texas originally wanted a judiciary that was elected, strongly independent, and accountable. They put that in the 1876 state constitution. No one had an inkling then of how money would eventually corrupt the system. Indeed, the people drafted the constitution in reaction to banks and corporations, hoping to diminish their power. Money and power still found a way to seep into the system, as they always seem to do, and eviscerated the people's populist instincts. Their crystal ball was not clear enough to foresee that monied interests would take over the judicial selection process and install judges reflecting that ideology.

As this dynamic began to lock into place, winning our cases became exponentially more problematic and started moving us toward mediation. The odds of outright winning, whether at the Supreme Court of Texas or the US Fifth Circuit Court of Appeals, diminished by the year as more rigidly conservative judges took the bench.

Until then, the judges tended to be middle-of the road, moderately conservative, sometimes with a populist streak (in the good sense), and thus we would have a decent chance at winning as our successes demonstrated. We won the farmworker cases, Opal Petty's lawsuit (see chapter 8), the right to privacy (chapter 12), and reinterpretation of the antilabor right-to-work law (chapter 5), for example. Those victories would have been much different under the current judicial lineup.

This all reflected Texas's dramatic shift in a few brief years from the moderate, progressive administrations of Governors Mark White and Ann Richards and in their state office positions before, White as attorney general and Richards as comptroller.

In Texas, if a judge resigns without finishing the elected term, the governor appoints someone else to finish the term. That gives the new judge the advantage of running as an incumbent in the upcoming election. Most of the judges now play this game, resigning early when they decide not to run again for election. This gives the governor inordinate power over the selection of judges.

All this required some fancy dancing by TCRP. We more frequently agreed to mediation in federal cases. Mediation generally worked out well. Although not bringing us as far as a trial might have got us in the old days, we still made good progress. In state court cases, local trial judges and appellate judges in the large cities and in border counties were usually more evenhanded. The difference is that those judges are elected by more diverse constituencies.

TAKEAWAYS: KEEPING UP THE FIGHT

It is fair to say that each year it is a bit more difficult to move civil rights cases forward to a good conclusion. This means we must keep organizing all the more fiercely and appreciate the importance of elections, which dictate who becomes judges.

Perhaps in the future—when and if the judiciary becomes less dogmatically conservative—some of our strategies might offer a blueprint of creative community lawyering. That's my hope.

With César Chávez in 1986 in advance of a screening of "Wrath of Grapes," about the pesticide poisoning of grape workers. (Photo by Alan Pogue, courtesy of UFW)

Baltazar "Don Balta" Saldaña at a protest in McAllen. He was a steadfast United Farm Workers member and organizer from the beginning of the union. (Photo courtesy of George McLemore)

24/SONS OF ZAPATA

"Get Those Melons Through!"

Captain A. Y. Allee, commander of a company of eight Texas Rangers assigned to break the strike during the melon harvest of May - June, 1967. They were asked to come to Starr County by the large growers and the County Sheriff. Several mass arrests of union members resulted from the unilateral intervention of the Rangers on the side of the growers. (Infernophoto--One World)

Notorious Texas Ranger Captain A. Y. Allee took it upon himself to violently break the melon harvester strike at La Casita Farms in Starr County. (Photo courtesy of UFW)

After a federal jury acquitted three McAllen police officers of criminal brutality charges in 1983, we organized a protest at Archer Park in McAllen. (Photo courtesy of George McLemore)

, TEXAS, TUESDAY, MAY 27, 1975 — 15c DAILY – 35c SUNDAY — 686-4343 — 12 PAGES

Farmer Released On Bond after Shooting

By FREDDIE CALDERON

HIDALGO—A Hidalgo farmer was free on bond today after being charged in the shooting of 11 farm workers during a United Farm Workers Demonstration Monday.

The shooting victims suffered superficial wounds from a .12 guage automatic shotgun allegedly fired four times by C. L. Miller, 40.

The shooting took place at 10:30 a.m. at the Texano Ranch about two miles east of the Hidalgo-Reynosa international bridge. At issue today is whether or not the shooting took place on private property or county property.

An unidentified assistant with Miller at the time of the shooting said the demonstrators were stomping through and damaging melon fields and trying to get workers to leave the field. He said they began throwing melons and rocks when Miller drove up. The union claims the incident occurred on a county road.

Miller was arrested by Hidalgo County Sheriff's deputies late Monday afternoon following the issuance of 10 warrants of aggravated assault charges. Justice of the Peace Dario R. Garcia signed the warrants and Miller was arraigned before Justice of the Peace Matias Morin Jr., who set bond at $1,500 on each charge. Miller posted $15,000 in surety bonds and was released late Monday night.

The series of events leading to the shooting incident started early Monday morning when three UFW members posted themselves near the Reynosa-Hidalgo international bridge and, with the aid of a loud speaker, began recruiting support for the UFW's "huelga" (strike) from Mexican green card workers coming into the U.S.

UFW RALLY TRUCK — Shown is a truck, equipped with loud speaker, which was used to muster United Farm Worker support from Mexican laborers coming into the U.S. to work in Valley fields. Shown standing and holding child, is Jim Harrington, UFW attorney. Benigno Pena is shown with microphone in hand. The truck was stopped by Hidalgo County Sheriff's deputies for a routine license check. (Monitor Photo)

According to a UFW count, 3,000 farm workers from Mexico refused to work for Valley growers Monday. About three truck loads of Mexican laborers were taken to Starr County to join in the protest against La Casita Farms.

During bridge picketing, Othal Brand of Griffin and Brand Produce Co., appeared, he said, "To see for myself if there was any violence which was rumored to include overturning of trucks and harrassment of crew leaders." After seeing the bridge rally, he said, "They (the farm workers) are out there just to get publicity."

At one point during the rally, crew leaders offered $2.10 an hour to the laborers, 30 cents more than minimum wage, the UFW said. "Farm workers will not work until they are paid better wages and have better working conditions in the fields with on-going abuse from crewleaders and discretionary employment from the growers," the UFW said.

At about 10 a.m., some 50 UFW supporters marched to the Texano Ranch in an attempt to organize Miller's non-union farm workers, who were picking melons from a field being leased by Miller and Chester Moore from Bill Pate of Hidalgo.

The unidentified assistant with Miller said, "The strikers stomped through our melon fields and began asking the pickers to stop working and join in the strike," he said. "They tried to overturn a truck with Chester Moore still inside and began throwing melons and rocks."

He said Miller arrived in a pick-up and stopped near the protesters. "When they saw us

See SHOOTING, page 3

...banese Sought

...ominating Karami, a former ...remier and political enemy, ...ut bowed to the demands of ...loslem leaders.

Rifai stepped down as head of

Holding my son at the Hidalgo International Bridge near where the grower C. L. Miller shot eleven farm workers. (Photo courtesy of the *McAllen Monitor*)

The organizing conventions in the Rio Grande Valley were always a mix of music, speeches, resolutions, and midday lunch, often led by women from the *colonia* committees. (Photo courtesy of George McLemore)

César Chávez's attendance at the first Texas farm worker organizing convocation in 1979 drew considerable media and political attention. (Photo by Alan Pogue, courtesy of UFW)

The most interesting part of the newly initiated United Farm Workers conventions was listening to the delegates debate resolutions and political endorsements, where personal stories resonated among the delegates, and tables for the delegates helped them feel the importance and seriousness of their work. (Photo courtesy of George McLemore)

With Starr County farm worker María Vásquez (on my immediate left) announcing her lawsuit against Bannworths Farms for refusing to rehire her because of her United Farm Workers membership. This was the first farm labor organizing case under the Texas right-to-work law, which the Texas legislature passed and intended as an anti-union measure. (Photo courtesy of UFW)

Genoveva Puga weeping at the grave of her son who was crushed to death in a farming accident at a citrus orchard. (Photo courtesy of David Hanners)

The workers' compensation trial team with eight farm worker plaintiffs, and my former wife Rebecca Flores, in January 1985. The trial started a day late because of a snowstorm that hit Austin and closed the Travis County courthouse. (Photo courtesy of the author)

Addressing farm worker delegates at the first annual United Farm Workers organizing convocation in the Rio Grande Valley in 1979. (Photo by Alan Pogue, courtesy of UFW)

Political cartoonist Ben Sargent captured the underlying tensions beneath the farm laborers' campaign for workers' compensation. (Courtesy of Ben Sargent)

Governor Mark White in the Rio Grande Valley in 1984 signing the law extending workers' compensation to farm laborers after a five-year lobbying campaign and a successful lawsuit. Genoveva Puga, whose son's death in an Edinburg orchard prompted her activism in the struggle, is at the left, next to the governor, holding high her UFW flag. (Photo courtesy of Gov. Mark White's office)

Opal Petty spent fifty-one years wrongly confined in Texas mental institutions during a period when they were particularly grim and oppressive. (Photo courtesy of Clint Denson)

Attorney Joe Berra at a press conference with representatives of the disability community announcing the filing of lawsuits across the state on the anniversary of the Americans with Disabilities Act, July 26, 2015. (Photo courtesy of TCRP)

A client in our case using the Violence Against Women Act. Having regularized her status in the US, she was visiting her grandmother in Mexico for the first time in eighteen years. (Photo courtesy of TCRP)

A graduation portrait of Debbie Rowinsky's daughters, Jessica and Jaqulynn. Debbie led a struggle against Bryan Independent School District over the sexual harassment of her daughters and other young women. (Photo courtesy of Jaqulynn Naumann)

Leaving the capitol after a press conference with my grandson, a successful plaintiff at the age of eleven months. (Photo courtesy of the author)

With a group of elementary students at a former Hizmet school in Antalya, Türkiye. (Photo courtesy of the author)

With Dolores Huerta at the LBJ School of Public Affairs, where she spoke passionately about Hispanic Heritage Month in 2023. (Photo courtesy of the author)

7

UNTETHERING FROM THE TEXAS CIVIL LIBERTIES UNION

Birth of the Texas Civil Rights Project

While farm laborers' drive for workers' compensation, unemployment benefits, and pesticide protection was underway, I took a related job and moved to Austin. That journey eventually led to founding the Texas Civil Rights Project.

Twice during my South Texas sojourn, the legal director's position at the Texas Civil Liberties Union (TCLU) opened in my direction. I demurred on the first offer but accepted the second and started work in Austin ten years after showing up at the UFW center in San Juan.

My plan had been to always stay in the Valley. That led to my balking at the first offer. The second time around, two years later, I looked at the position with different eyes—as a golden chance to do statewide what the South Texas Project was doing regionally.

Still, we had planted roots deep in the Valley and made many friends and movement colleagues. Leaving felt almost like betraying the farmworker community where I had promised to stay. The Irish guilt did a number and slowed down the decision process.

Besides the appealing prospect of Texas-wide legal work, there was the tug of our three kids as young or about-to-be schoolers. As wonderful as the Valley's teachers were, educational opportunities in Austin shined more brightly. That is partly a function of Texas's messed-up school financing system. Bishop John Fitzpatrick of Brownsville, whom I respected, had supported our undertakings against criticism from the established powers; he sent a "do it" note to take the Austin job and spread out the work to all Texas.

Moving from the Valley was very painful, leaving Lalo, Genoveva, and all the many others. But as with relatives, whenever we gathered afterward,

A FREE MOVE TO AUSTIN?

When the news came out that we were relocating to Austin, our nemesis and antagonist Othal Brand publicly said he would pay our moving costs to make sure we left the Valley.

Since I never knew Brand to have a sense of humor, I suspected he was at least somewhat serious and relieved. For my part, I took his comment as an oblique (and unintended) admission that we were doing a good job. As he would learn, distance didn't make much difference. The South Texas Project and LUPE continued to keep him busy.

it seemed like yesterday. What an honor to live, strive, mourn, and celebrate with the farmworker family and to be their brother in justice-seeking. Another Irish proverb fits here: "Under the shelter of each other, people survive."

And so it happened on Memorial Day weekend 1983 that we packed up the Hertz moving truck and drove away from our home on East Boone Street in Pharr with the help of friends. It was a hot, six-hour drive to Austin, lugging assorted house furniture, boxes of law books, and three impatient kids. Our staff attorney Richard Flores became the new director for the South Texas Project.

We arrived in Austin just in time to make it over to the Capitol Building and watch the legislature in late-night session vote down the proposed workers' compensation bill once again, albeit more narrowly, and the raucousness that followed, as described in chapter 6.

The first five years as TCLU's legal director flowed along placidly. I brought the farmworker cases from the Valley with me to a safe harbor, and we racked up other eye-catching legal victories.

There were four of us: the executive director, his assistant, my legal assistant, and myself. We officed with the *Texas Observer* in an imposing 1900s downtown corner yellow brick house on Judges Hill. The first floor of the two-story house was spacious, ornate, high-ceilinged, and airy. Both floors had large built-in front porches. We occupied three of the second-floor rooms. Mine had no window and might have been a large back storage room in its earlier history.

In 1985, TCLU's well-respected executive director, John Duncan, retired. A series of organizational financial decisions under his successor, including taking over fiscal responsibility for the South Texas Project, depleted funds and moved TCLU to the red side of the ledger. Not long afterward, a new executive director took the helm of the wobbly ship.

Philosophical differences began to simmer. Although my litigation track record was quite good, some TCLU board members (many of whom were academics) seemed less than pleased with the emphasis on drawing lawsuits from the community. They did not pinpoint any specifics, but the undercurrent was palpable. To this day, my understanding of what was driving them is speculative at best. Nor do I know if KBUC's slander lawsuit affected their thinking.

It began to come to a head in early 1990, when the board fired the executive director and his assistant for financial reasons, leaving legal assistant Fara Sloan and me to run the entire shop and cover all four jobs. We did an emergency mail appeal and raised close to $50,000—one of TCLU's most successful appeals. Fortune also smiled at the time, and we landed $120,000 in grant money for the South Texas Project.

Fara came to us directly out of the army at Fort Hood (now Fort Cavazos) and over time became a remarkable civil rights advocate, a fascinating and welcome character development. There had been internal resistance to my hiring someone from the military, but her credentials were excellent. She was affable, and TCLU was bereft of diversity. We are good friends to this day.

Fara and I viewed all this ominously and decided the time was at hand to join a union for job protection, and so we enlisted the Communications Workers of America as our representative. That upset the board of directors, even though a couple members themselves belonged to teacher unions.

Fara took leave to have her first baby, and the board summarily fired me on a Saturday morning without warning or discussion, just as I was getting ready to take the kids camping at Inks Lake State Park in Burnet. That ruined our trip, and we had to unpack the tents and gear from the car. The kids were not happy, and I was suddenly wondering about the future and caring for them. Getting hit with shock and apprehension at the same time was not a pleasant experience.

This sudden course of events caused considerable community stir and opposition. To make matters more bizarre, the board announced it was dismissing me for "incompetence and ineffectiveness," almost in the same breath lauding my professional performance as "impeccable and impressive"—"one of the best civil liberties lawyers in the nation." They denied, sort of, that they were retaliating for our forming a union—such retaliation being against the law.

Ironically, while this commotion was astir, I was on a plane to Philadelphia to receive the Judge John Minor Wisdom Public Service and Professionalism Award at the American Bar Association convention. It was the first time the ABA gave this award.

The year before, I was corecipient of the national Trial Lawyer of the Year Award from Trial Lawyers for Public Justice (now Public Justice). This is not about any horn-tooting, heaven forbid. I am acutely aware of my deficiencies (as are others—it's a shared experience), but I offer this to underline the incongruous and strangely weird existential predicament.

After a bit of maneuvering, we ended up in a long Saturday night mediation during which the opportunity presented itself to part ways and form a new civil rights program. Just as moving to Austin and TCLU in 1983 was an opportunity to spread wings statewide, so too was this new organization a once-in-a-lifetime chance to do some real wing-spreading in a direction that TCLU was not heading. Good fortune opened a door and, smiling, beckoned.

The idea was to set up a community-based civil rights project under the auspices of Oficina Legal del Pueblo Unido, Inc., a tax-exempt nonprofit grassroots foundation I helped set up years earlier in South Texas and with which I still had ties. Oficina Legal gave the nascent Texas Civil Rights Project an immediate launching pad.

TCRP officially kicked off Sunday morning, September 23, 1990. It was an auspicious day, indeed. Fara's baby, Maya, arrived that same Sunday.

Part of the settlement involved giving TCRP the law books and $80,000 in startup funds. Since TCLU no longer had a legal staff, I kept the twenty or so lawsuits on which I was working and agreed to take over the South Texas Project, which TCLU wanted to cut loose.

The dustup settled fairly easily within the community. No public acrimonies were aired between TCRP and the ACLU side. Many folks helped both. TCRP was a homegrown organization that concentrated on lawsuits, and that attracted backing. It was amazing how things always came together and how many friends and allies shored us up. That list grew ever longer by the year.

As the coming years would prove, the creation of TCRP benefited Texas. No doubt about it.

Looking at everything that happened at the launch of TCRP, it seems rosy in retrospect; but I must confess to severe anxiety at the time, especially as to how to make TCRP fly with new wings, raise funds, and support our family. It was more than a bit fearsome to suddenly be out on my own, but I gritted my teeth and wrapped my arms around the unknown. There were months, if not years, of sleepless nights, both worrying and working, learning to walk that path with steady feet.

AFTER THE SEPARATION

Through Rebecca's help, we quickly found rent-free space in the Peace Building, where she was already officing for her UFW work. It was a small, two-story, iconic, red-brick corner structure on Congress Avenue in downtown Austin. Built in 1900, it had once served as a hotel of mixed repute and a train stop. The railroad tracks, since filled in with concrete, were still visible along adjacent Third Street.

Genevieve Vaughn, a philanthropist hailing from a Corpus Christi oil and gas family, owned the building under the aegis of the Foundation for a Compassionate Society. She provided rent-free space to small community groups. We landed on our feet and sped off running.

We officed on the second floor and shared 1,600 square feet of open space with three other organizations, including the UFW. Bookshelves and cabinets served as office dividers. The ceilings were high, as were the windows in beautiful old wooden frames. My desk faced west, against the window, with a pleasant view of Austin's Violet Crown.

When Fara returned from maternity leave, TCLU terminated her via fax. She then came to work with TCRP, living on unemployment benefits. I helped support my family with part-time teaching at the University of Texas School of Law. We survived that way until January 1991, when the Texas Equal Access to Justice Foundation (TEAJF) offered a lifeline.

TEAJF managed the state supreme court's Interest on Lawyers' Trust Accounts (IOLTA) program and added us to its list of nonprofit recip-

CUB SCOUTS BOO THE GOVERNOR

The Peace Building was part of a block of buildings, including the famed and frequented Las Manitas restaurant. One time, the two sisters who owned and ran the restaurant and were my friends, gave permission to take the Cub Scout Pack (I was the Scoutmaster) up on their flat roof to watch a Saturday morning parade on Congress Avenue. I believe it was a July 4 parade.

The day was sunny and the weather mild, almost balmy. At some point, the Republican governor at the time, Bill Clements, rode past in an open-air car; without any instigation on my part, the Scouts started booing him. I'll never forget the astonishment on his face when he looked up and saw a group of young Cub Scouts in their blue uniforms with yellow neckerchiefs booing him, while I tried to quiet them down (I really did).

I guess this said something about the politics of the boys' parents. We did have a discussion on civility (i.e., not to wear their uniforms when booing the governor).

ients. The IOLTA program gathers the interest on trust accounts that lawyers hold and then distributes those funds to legal organizations that serve low-income people. We started off with a modest $80,000 grant and increased it every year thereafter.

Not everyone was happy with our being on the TEAJF roster. Senator John Cornyn, who was on the Supreme Court of Texas at the time, ordered an investigation into how we were spending the funds, hoping, I am sure, to defund us should anything turn up askew. Low-profile legal aid cases were acceptable, but high-profile lawsuits (our specialty) were suspect. Political undercurrents were detectable.

However, we ran a tight ship and sailed through the investigation. TEAJF's backing was critical. Other probers later followed Cornyn's game plan. TEAJF parried the queries, and we stuck to our work of serving poor Texans. Despite our parsimonious budget, we produced admirable results.

We were profoundly grateful to TEAJF board members, especially to Dick Tate and Executive Director Betty Ballí Torres, for twenty-five years of staunch support and for floating the rescue raft at TCRP's beginning.

SHAMELESSLY USING CHILD LABOR

I must admit to fund-raising by child labor in TCRP's early days, bribing my three young kids with pizza to do folding, envelope-licking, and sorting for financial appeal mailouts that lined the kitchen floor from the far end to the stove.

No lasting harm or trauma seems to have occurred from their conscription. They've all turned out well, and I have the characteristic father's pride in them.

We did our absolute best to honor their faith in us to diligently serve those in need. TEAJF became the Texas Access to Justice Foundation.

In time, I began to supplement our budget with part-time employment at Advocacy Inc., for a few years, as I describe in chapter 8, and continued teaching a UT Law seminar. I also penned a twice-monthly column for *Texas Lawyer* for seven years. This and the ever-increasing TEAJF funds provided enough to eventually bring on board two other lawyers and a paralegal at modest salaries.

Our first fund-raising event was at a nightclub next to the Peace Building around Halloween. Molly Ivins, the famed Texas writer and political humorist, came dressed as "white trash," wrapped in large black garbage bags with all sorts of discarded junk dangling from various parts of her body. Thereafter, we began our annual Texas Bill of Rights Dinner.

We stayed in the Peace Building until Genevieve sold it in 1996. We then purchased a small house in East Austin, the African American side of town, on, appropriately enough, Martin Luther King Jr. Boulevard.

Local community architects, Eddie and Letty McGarrahan, helped build out the facility. Artist Robert Andrada painted a large, colorful mural at the outside entrance, depicting Dr. King, César Chávez, Mahatma Gandhi, and Jane Addams (founder of the Chicago Settlement House), with two small vignettes: a silhouetted protest line, and a Native American eagle symbolically soaring over the Mount Rushmore presidents.

A poignant quote from Senator Robert Kennedy's 1966 Day of Affirmation Address in Cape Town, South Africa, ran along the bottom, beautifully lettered: "Those with the courage to enter the moral conflict will find themselves with companions in every corner of the globe." I had the entire quote from which this excerpt came taped to the back of my attorney bar card for most of my career and often used it as a conclusion for speeches:

> Few men are willing to brave the disapproval of their fellows, the censure of their colleagues, the wrath of their society. Moral courage is a rarer commodity than bravery in battle or great intelligence. Yet it is the one essential, vital quality for those who seek to change the world which yields most painfully to change. . . . I believe that in this generation those with the courage to enter the conflict will find themselves with companions in every corner of the world.

It was a good reminder to TCRP (and me) of what we needed to live up to, and it was an honor to find myself meeting so many moral companions throughout my career.

We eventually outgrew the house and in 2002 found a vacant old mechanics garage in the Montopolis Mexican American community that the Beaumont attorney Wayne Reaud purchased for us. The same local architects who built out our MLK Boulevard location did an excellent job converting the garage into offices.

The move provided a great fund-raising opportunity. A donors' wall decorated the entrance lobby with a handcrafted terra cotta tile for each donor, sized according to the amount of contribution. (We used the tile idea for our South Texas and El Paso offices as they came on line.)

We eventually collected thirty-nine donor plaques of varying sizes and different messages. My two favorite tiles were "Lousy golfer, Good lawyer" and the tongue-in-cheek one from Chuck Herring. "Chuck, Ginny, and Othal [Brand]"—"Honoring Jim." I bought tiles in memory of my grandmother and my parents.

Wayne had the building named in honor of the legendary Michael Tigar, a longtime TCRP friend. Molly Ivins, Travis County Judge Sam Biscoe, and other luminaries spoke at the 2003 dedication at which we planted a "human rights" oak tree in the backyard. Our Montopolis neighbors joined us, and mariachis livened up the dedication, which we set for the César Chávez memorial holiday.

The mural from the MLK Boulevard office went into the conference room and became an apt backdrop for innumerable press conferences. Reverend Frank Sabbaté sculpted a bust of César Chávez; a group of Rio

Grande Valley judges picked up the cost of the materials. The local artist Meeta Morrison added a mural for the lobby, and Stephanie Distefano created an outside sculpture.

As to our other offices, TCRP was able to find capital funds from foundations and individuals to purchase and build out offices in El Paso and South Texas. The Houston NAACP allowed us rent-free use of a small house it owned next to its office. This was not just a financial blessing; it gave us roots in the Houston minority community. In Dallas and Odessa, other nonprofits let us share space for modest rent. We always tried to locate our offices where the people were—"getting proximate."

My lodestar principle as a civil rights lawyer was to take direction and guidance from the community, to never litigate in a vacuum with my own priorities. As Michelle Alexander writes in *The New Jim Crow: Mass Incarceration in the Age of Colorblindness:* "With all deliberate speed, civil rights organizations became 'professionalized' and increasingly disconnected from the communities they claimed to represent." TCRP, by practice and philosophy, resisted that professionalization and "disconnectization." Our goal was to connect increasingly with the community that needed our help. It's fair to say that we accomplished that aspiration.

ELIZABETH GOHAR: DISENFRANCHISED AT THE BEGINNING AND END OF HER LIFE

A voting rights case that graced me with one of my most emotional career moments is an appropriate conclusion for this chapter because it represented everything TCRP would strive to be about. In mid-2014, I had the honor of taking Elizabeth Gohar's deposition for a federal case in Corpus Christi, where litigation was underway challenging Texas's repressive 2011 voter ID law.

The law required voters to have a specific state-issued identification card, no matter how many years they had been a voter and no matter how many other kinds of valid identification they possessed. The law was burdensome and operated like a poll tax from the era of segregation. It impeded people from voting rather than encouraging them. The federal judge eventually voided the law as disenfranchising elderly individuals, poor people, and citizens of color.

Mrs. Gohar testified by videotaped deposition in Austin because traveling to Corpus Christi to appear in person was too difficult given her advanced age. She was amazing and became a star witness in the lawsuit, exemplifying everything the case was about.

Mrs. Gohar, an elderly, petite African American woman well into her seventies, had moved to Austin from Louisiana to live out her remaining years with her daughter. She had retired from a life working in an elementary school cafeteria.

However, she was unable to vote in Texas because she did not have, and could not get, a Texas ID to vote. Her Louisiana ID was not good enough. She did not qualify for a Texas ID because the midwife who had delivered her in rural Louisiana had miswritten her name on the birth certificate so as to not line up exactly with what Texas demanded. Her parents had used a local midwife because the segregation era kept them from using the hospital, just as it had denied them decent educations. To vote in Texas, she would have to hire a lawyer back in the Pelican State to correct her birth certificate, assuming that was even possible given how more than seventy years had elapsed.

Mrs. Gohar came to the deposition impeccably dressed and coiffured. Unlike other witnesses in similar situations, she was not nervous. She bore a convicted sense of the mission of her testimony. She had pride in doing her part for the arc of justice.

Mrs. Gohar's words were deeply moving. She had voted in every election upon becoming eligible out of respect for the civil rights movement and for all the people who had fought, suffered, and died to make sure she could vote. She showed up in person at the polls in every election for that reason: to make a statement of honor and respect.

The eloquence of her words came not in response to questions from me but in calmly parrying with the state Assistant Attorney General. Here was an elderly African American woman addressing a young white guy who did not want her to vote, relaying her life story and that of her community. The injustice of it all seemed too profound for him to grasp. Maybe he, like the others, didn't want to—or maybe he didn't give a damn.

Voting, Mrs. Gohar said, was a "celebratory moment" each time she cast a ballot. She had never missed an election in her life. Her dignity and grace sent muffled emotion throughout the courtroom when her video deposition played. Her testimony dramatized how the statute operated against upstanding citizens and hard workers in the autumn of their lives.

No one missed the irony that she had been disenfranchised both at the beginning of her life and at the end.

Our side won at trial and on appeal. However, the US Supreme Court left the law in place until after the upcoming election. It was a quintessential Catch-22 ruling that Joseph Heller would have grabbed on to: "Sure, the law unconstitutionally keeps people from voting, but we'll go ahead and let it happen anyhow. Just don't do it again."

So much for Mrs. Gohar's rights and those like her. Justice delayed is justice denied. As the Maryland Governor Wes Moore has put it, she understood the brokenness of this country but still showed up.

It was as moving for me to watch her in person as it was for the judge and others later to see her by video in the Corpus Christi courtroom. Mrs. Gohar, as she sat there, was for me what the civil rights struggle was all about—and what TCRP had been all about. I felt honored or, as she would say with a slight smile, "blessed."

TAKEAWAYS: THE LEGACY OF VOTING RIGHTS

Untethering from the Texas Civil Liberties Union, to which I had committed a portion of my life, was fraught with uncertainty at first. It was hard to understand the logic behind the separation given our success; but soon we landed on our feet, thanks to the people closest to me professionally and the allies we could count on in the community.

Voting rights became an important part of our work going forward. And no one personified that more than Elizabeth Gohar. She was brave—braver than any of the bureaucrats trying to take her vote away. More than anyone, Mrs. Gohar symbolized the legacy of the voting rights struggle in Texas.

8

CONVINCING TEXAS BUSINESSES AND GOVERNMENT TO RESPECT PEOPLE WITH DISABILITIES

Bolstering the disability community's organizing efforts was one of TCRP's signature strategic programs and extended over my entire tenure there. Some of our most impactful litigation came out of our close relationship with these tenacious and faithful advocates. It was work that got a head start with the Opal Petty case while I was at TCLU and carried over, augmented by passage of the Americans with Disabilities Act.

Back in the early 1970s, when I was in law school, there was nary a mention of disability rights. Nothing in the curriculum. Nor were protective laws in place as there are now. It is remarkable today to think back on how disability rights came onto the horizon and became a major TCRP focus along with our other work. This is testimony to the evolving nature of human rights in society.

OPAL PETTY: WRONGLY JAILED FOR FIFTY-ONE YEARS

My rite of initiation into the civil rights struggle on behalf of the disability community began with a case that took on enormous importance for people wrongly confined to Texas's state hospitals for people with mental illness and state schools for those with intellectual or developmental disabilities.

Opal Petty, a short, kind, and portly woman, who looked like anyone's grandmother, with a flair for fancy hats, became the protagonist of this story; more accurately, Linda Kauffman, Opal's niece by marriage, became the protagonist on her behalf. Her lawsuit rocked Texas's mental health system, something long overdue by decades.

The case had one of those sad, you-can't-make-this-up origins. Linda and her family had journeyed from their home in San Angelo to a family reunion around Amarillo, during which she overheard hushed comments about "Aunt Opal in a mental hospital."

Linda, not one to let things go, gleaned enough information to learn that Opal was somewhere in a state facility and had been there a good number of years—fifty-one as it turned out. Linda decided to find Opal because she felt something fishy was afoot, especially since her husband, Clint Denson, had never heard much of his aunt. It was a well-kept secret among the family elders. Since Opal was family, Linda wanted to find her, learn her story, and go from there.

Back in San Angelo, Linda began the task of what she thought would involve possibly telephoning every state hospital and state school in Texas. She started first with the nearby San Angelo State School in Carlsbad. Lo and behold, Opal was there, just seventeen miles away.

Opal, in fact, had resided there fourteen years, unbeknownst to Linda and Clint. Austin State Hospital had transferred her there. She had spent thirty-seven years at the facility until it finally acknowledged she was not mentally ill. The hospital did not know what to do with Opal after all those years. So they shipped her off to a state school for people with developmental disabilities.

Linda was outraged when she learned Opal's history and reached out for legal help. Deborah Hiser, an able attorney with Advocacy Inc. (now Disability Rights Texas), responded to our call for assistance and helped organize a lawsuit, claiming that the state had wrongly confined Opal all her life. If anything, she should have been hospitalized only very briefly.

Apparently, as a sixteen-year-old teenager, Opal suffered a psychotic episode of depression. She wanted to go dancing and participate in typical teenage girl activities, but her parents forbade her. She began acting out and even tried digging a grave in the front yard. This greatly grieved and worried her father, a fundamentalist Baptist deacon in small-town Goldthwaite.

He didn't know how to deal with Opal when prayer sessions on the front porch over her failed. So in 1934 he put her in the family vehicle and drove over to the Austin State Hospital, a hundred miles away, and left her there. He died a few years afterward.

From the get-go, Opal's family did little to stay in touch with her or inquire about bringing her home. Nor did hospital administrators reach out to anyone in the family in Goldthwaite except in the most occasional, perfunctory manner. They knew she had an aunt (her father's sister) who lived within short walking distance of the hospital but made no effort to contact her.

We couldn't make any headway with her older sister, whom we visited near Amarillo, about what had happened, but we were able to unite Opal with one of her teenage friends, who had later become county clerk. They had a joyous reunion, running toward each other. Her friend said she and the others who palled around with Opal were surprised when she was suddenly taken away and never understood why.

Our psychiatrist expert, Dr. Jeffrey Nelson, testified that Opal would have recovered from her episodic event within weeks of her admission, after which the hospital should have released her. Instead, the state kept her wrongly confined, causing her to suffer from what he called "institutionalization syndrome" such that, when she finally was released five decades later, she had not become appropriately socialized as would typically happen in daily outside life. She had adopted the ways of living to which she had been subjected while in confinement. The state irreparably harmed her.

Historical records and photographs from Opal's almost four decades in the hospital showed abhorrent conditions. The hospital was performing lobotomies. Electric shock treatment was commonplace. Large numbers of patients were sleeping on concrete floors or in dorm settings with multiple beds in large single rooms. Burial was often in anonymous graves in an unmarked cemetery six blocks north of the hospital.

This was involuntary confinement, not rehabilitative care. The state so poorly funded the hospital that patients had to take care of each other for lack of staff. Conditions were horrible enough that Governor Alan Shivers felt compelled to initiate reforms, although inadequate. Try to imagine a teenage girl in this horrific situation among adults with serious mental illness.

Our best guess from staff interviews as to why the hospital never tried to release Opal was that she was such a good help with doing laundry (for thirty-five years she did so, eventually earning $2/week), a docile person who made no waves. The hospital had an incentive to keep her there: sheer unpardonable exploitation.

We went with Linda to visit Opal at the Carlsbad facility. It was depressing, one of those cinder-block buildings, painted an institutional, monochromatic light blue. Calling it a "school" was a euphemism that belied its grim reality. It didn't take long for Linda to bring Opal home when the school told her Opal wasn't capable of independent living, an oblique, appalling admission of what the state had done to her.

When Linda picked up Opal in 1985 from the "school," they stopped to buy groceries on the way to the house. Her first time in a store since 1934, Opal gleefully ran up and down the aisles of the produce section. She had never been surrounded by so much color in her life, and it delighted her. That incident says it all in its own way.

The next time I met Opal was when Linda brought her by the house the evening before a court hearing. Seeing Opal as she walked into our family room and then speaking with her weighed down my soul with compassion and anger. The state had stolen her life, denied her a family, and never even helped celebrate her birthday for a half-century (something that grieved Opal). A tragic case, living pathos. Those feelings churned up in me every time I saw Opal.

The sadness became heavier, and the anger deeper, when considering the many others like her, those whose lives the state had heartlessly wrecked, a number likely in the thousands. They had no Linda Kauffman in their families to rail against the suffering imposed on them.

Partnering with Advocacy, we filed a wrongful confinement lawsuit in 1987, both as an individual damages action for Opal and as a class action for all others wrongly confined in state hospitals and schools.

Travis County District Judge Harley Clark presided over the case and divided it into two phases. First would be a jury trial on personal damages for Opal. How the jury ruled in Opal's case would give him guidance as to how to rule in the class action for others wrongly confined.

Opal could play the piano, though not well. She had been learning as a young girl, but there it stopped. As part of our jury argument, cocounsel Debbie Hiser showed a video of Opal playing "America the Beautiful" after her release a half-century later. A truly poignant moment, bringing tears to jurors and people in the courtroom.

We tried the case over five weeks, and the jury deliberated for three weeks. The jury initially could not reach a vote of ten people in Opal's favor, which we needed for a winning verdict. They were stuck at nine to three for a good while. Eventually, the jury found in our favor on a negligence claim and against us on the constitutional claims, awarding a total of $505,000.

In other words, the jury blamed the state but not the individual actors. The jurors felt that those mostly culpable had long since departed the earth and that the burden should not fall on their successors. The law precluded them from knowing that the state would have covered any judgment against individual actors. They crafted a compromise verdict to provide some kind of relief.

Unfortunately, state law at the time limited recovery to $250,000; Judge Clark regrettably reduced the verdict accordingly. That averaged out to $5,000/year for Opal's wrongful confinement, a pitiful sum. The recovery limit was not good news to the jurors when they learned about it. Nor were they happy not knowing about the employee reimbursement issue. With accrued interest, the judgment totaled about $350,000 after the appeals wound down.

In 1992, the Supreme Court of Texas allowed the judgment to stand. The victory resonated like a thunderclap across the state's mental health

JURORS HAVING FUN, PARADING AROUND

Something that puzzled us during the jury's three weeks of deliberation in the Opal Petty case, which the jurors clarified after trial, was why they sent so many questions to the judge. It seemed like one every day. If jurors send a written question to a judge asking for guidance, the attorneys can present a short argument to the jury about how to apply the judge's response. This we dutifully did. But their questions seemed all over the place, showing no train of thought.

The jurors told us they did it when they were getting bored or needed a break when their deliberations hit a tough spot. They enjoyed listening to the lawyers argue, and the distraction would fill a couple hours of their time.

We also wondered why there was so much loud laughter during deliberations. We could hear it in the courtroom. It turned out that the jurors disliked opposing counsel from the Attorney General's office and sometimes spent time mimicking that attorney, parading around the jury room table, gleefully imitating the lawyer's peculiarities during trial.

system. After the damages issue was resolved in Opal's favor, the state settled the class action and agreed to immediately review everyone's case in state hospitals and state schools and thereafter conduct an annual evaluation as to whether there was legal justification to continue a person's confinement or if the individual should be released. The legislature changed the law accordingly.

At the time of Opal's lawsuit, more than 9,000 patients were confined to the state's eight mental health hospitals, with about 6,000 people remaining in its thirteen state schools, which the state renamed "living centers." This case impacted a considerable number of people then in custody and for years to come.

I do not remember exactly how many people the state eventually released from confinement because of the patient reviews, but it was a surprisingly large number, a few hundred. What was depressing was that individuals had become institutionalized like Opal and so could not live by themselves. Others were elderly and had no surviving family members who could attend to them. These folks had to remain confined. The state robbed them of their lives, as it did with Opal.

True to form, no representative of the state ever expressed an ounce of remorse or uttered a word of apology. Sometimes it's hard melting frozen hearts.

Once the state paid the judgment, Linda took Opal on a train ride to Disneyland with family and friends. Opal then built a small house next to Linda and Clint on their property and lived there happily for almost twenty years. She shot hoops outdoors with her grandnephew Johnathon until he left home.

Her family buried her with six dolls that she had cared for since confinement—the children she never had. Without her late-discovered family, the desolate unmarked state hospital cemetery in Austin might have been her final resting place, as it was for many who were locked up with her, just a few blocks north of where the state once forced her to live.

The legacy of Opal's case was such that, when she died, the *New York Times*, the *Los Angeles Times*, and other newspapers around the country published her obituary.

Linda Kauffman and her husband, Clint, are the heroes of this sad saga, turned partially victorious. Linda was one of those archetypical tough, but compassionate, West Texas women.

The Christmas tree sketch that Opal, Linda, Clint, and Johnathon created and sent still decorates my wall decades later. The drawing shows the rays of the late afternoon sun shining through from the back of the green tree. Symbolic, it seems.

THE AMERICANS WITH DISABILITIES ACT

Just as Opal's case was wrapping up, the Americans with Disabilities Act (ADA) was coming into force, signed by President George H. W. Bush on July 26, 1990, after decades of intense organizing by the disability community and allies. The ADA became law two months before TCRP started up and dovetailed with our overall goal of effecting structural change and sustaining community organizing.

The ADA requires all government and private facilities and programs to be as accessible as possible to persons with physical or intellectual disabilities, which includes mental illness. The ADA enjoys broad public support because disabilities cut across race, ethnicity, sex, age, religious belief, political philosophy, and economic or social class. Indeed, the longer an individual or a family member lives, the more likely they will develop a disability. The Centers for Disease Control and Prevention reports that one in four Americans has a disability, either a physical condition or mental impairment.

Not only are the accidents of birth and infirmities of age at play; so are happenstances and accidents, whether at work, on vacation, at home, or on the highway. Mental illness is a disability issue drawing more and more attention these days. Virtually everyone knows someone who has struggled with long-term or short-term depression. And then there is the ever-increasing suicide rate in our communities, especially among younger folks, which is often related to depression.

My sainted mother (she raised six kids) was a good example. She used to wonder why so many disability parking places were close to the grocery store entrance and were not always taken. This kept her from parking as near to the front door as she wanted. As she got more "decrepit in her old age" (to use her phrase) and increasingly disabled, her complaint shifted toward those who wrongly used the parking spots and displayed no mirror-hanging disability tag or license plate. She understood, and TCRP helped others understand.

A few years after Opal Petty's case and as TCRP revved up, a couple part-time side jobs I took helped kick-start and sustain TCRP's disability rights trajectory. I signed on part-time with Advocacy for three years, helping train lawyers and community members in Texas how to litigate disability cases.

Advocacy was part of the national federally funded Protection and Advocacy (P&A) system for people with disabilities. Each state and territory has a P&A entity to serve its disability communities. Advocacy Inc. is now Disability Rights Texas.

The part-time stint at Advocacy provided health insurance and a salary, which meant less of a drain on TCRP's budget and freed up funds to hire more staff. Another part-time job I took was teaching at the University of Texas School of Law. I taught for twenty-seven years and did my best to help students learn how to creatively approach the law for the community's benefit. The classes and seminars, which dealt with how to litigate civil rights cases in federal and state courts, picked up the reputation of being different than regular pedagogy.

So many pieces fell together in the puzzle of life, all for the ultimate benefit of TCRP and the people we served. Quite amazing.

ANNUAL ADA COMPLIANCE CAMPAIGNS WITH TEXAS'S DISABILITY COMMUNITIES

At Advocacy we fashioned a strategy, which carried over to TCRP, of organizing annual ADA campaigns with disability groups around Texas every July 26, the anniversary of the act's passage. Our strategy was to focus publicly on various government entities and businesses as a way of improving ADA compliance and bringing greater awareness to the cause.

Each campaign involved abundant lawsuits filed that day, which members of the disability community announced with considerable fanfare at a press conference, often strategically staged at an offending, non–ADA compliant location. The message was clear: We're watching, we're suing, and you're next if you don't have your act together.

The press, including Spanish-language and English media, loved the novelty of the campaigns and indulged us. They helped send out the message across the community. This public education component was critical. It was impossible to litigate against everyone who was not ADA compliant. The "you may be next" message, along with targeted in-person encouragement from local disability advocates, helped rally voluntary compliance.

Our goal of enhancing statewide ADA compliance meant we focused on chain stores. For example, there were suits against Diamond Shamrock (now Valero) and Shell gas stations to lower their fuel pumps and make them accessible for customers in wheelchairs. In the past, pumps were perched atop small cement islands, so high that drivers in wheelchairs could not reach the credit card mechanism to activate the pump or utilize the gas nozzle. As a result of our litigation, one gas company after another lowered their pumps.

Another successful effort with great impact around the state, and eventually the country, was convincing the Texas Lottery Commission, after promising potential litigation, to require all retail outlets it licensed (now nearly 20,000) to be ADA accessible to people with mobility disabilities. The ADA held a winning lottery ticket.

Word spread. It required only this "kind and gentle" threat of litigation to motivate the Texas State Parks system to enhance park accessibility throughout the state (bathrooms, picnic tables, and trails, for example).

The Texas organizing strategy was so effective that I was invited to create the National ADA Backup Center, a small federally funded project of the US Department of Justice (DOJ). That sent me, as its part-time director, traveling to twenty-six states and territories over three years to train P&As, attorneys, and disability communities on using the ADA campaign model to fortify compliance with the law. I also wore my TCRP hat on the trips to carry our message of the broader human rights agenda.

The strategy had excellent results. Some P&A campaigns were quite creative, as in the US Virgin Islands, which saw an eight-week campaign. They began each press conference with a rhyming poem by T. Jameel Muhammad, addressing the target ("No Room in the Inn" for hotels, as an example).

TCRP ran with this campaign strategy, too. Each year on July 26 for two decades disability communities and advocates around the state, with TCRP's help, held press conferences with inventive visual exhibits to announce the filing of ADA lawsuits, which we would try to match with the specific ADA anniversary year (fifteen cases on the fifteenth anniversary, for example). The media honeymoon was sweet and lasting.

Often the annual campaigns focused on a specific target. One year it was access to government buildings; another it was lack of interpreters at medical facilities, then restaurant access, and so on. Even Austin's famed Sixth Street with its music scene and lively clubs became a bull's-eye. Disability rights folks used the campaigns to show how lack of accessibility blocked them from fully participating in society's benefits and offerings.

The ADA litigation dealing with facility access was quite satisfactory to disability community litigants because we could see the physical results of our toils together whenever we drove around town or across the state. The intent of the ADA became tangible and visible. Not only did the ADA benefit the lives of people with disabilities, it showed the larger community what inclusion looked like and helped attune people to respect and promote inclusivity.

Altogether over twenty-five years TCRP, by collaborating closely with ADAPT of Texas, the Coalition of Texans with Disabilities, Desert ADAPT, Volar of El Paso, and other advocacy disability groups, oversaw more than 550 lawsuits and conducted more than fifty ADA enforcement campaigns throughout Texas.

The disability organizations, especially the ADAPT groups, were leading activists pushing firmly for change—exactly our sort of folks. On March 12, 1990, ADAPT participated in a march of more than a thousand people from the White House to the US Capitol to demand that Congress pass the ADA. When they arrived, fifty-eight of them, including an eight-year-old girl, cast aside their wheelchairs and other mobility aids and crawled up the eighty-three front steps in the fierce sun. The next day, 104 demonstrators were arrested inside the Capitol Rotunda. The elder President Bush signed the ADA into law four months after this "assist" from the "Capitol Crawl." This was but one of ADAPT's many nonviolent direct actions.

As TCRP's disability docket was growing, the courts were weakening (and sometimes just plain eviscerating) the standard federal civil rights laws that for years had been the mechanism to combat discrimination and lack of due process.

The courts undermined civil rights by conjuring up new rules to tolerate officials' misconduct. These included excusing illegal conduct done in "good faith," severely restricting governmental liability for employees' misdeeds, redefining what creates a civil rights violation, and so on. It was death by a thousand cuts or, in this context, dismemberment by a thousand legal decisions.

In some important ways, the ADA helped pick up the slack. The ADA allows no "good faith" excuse. Municipalities and state agencies are liable, even for monetary damages, for the noncompliance of their employees and agents. The ADA permits private individuals and organizations like TCRP to help enforce the law by filing lawsuits, complete with awards of attorney fees, which Congress intended as an incentive mechanism to achieve compliance.

The ADA—one of the strongest civil rights laws that Congress has enacted—became an effective tool to fill in gaps in traditional civil rights laws that the courts were reinterpreting in a more restrictive fashion. It required creative lawyering—and TCRP was up to it.

Some of the major cases drew more attention, and some had important national consequences.

WEST TEXAS SHOWDOWNS: THE EL PASO DISABILITY COMMUNITY'S TRIPLE-HEADER OF VOTING, THEATERS, AND UTEP

Two groundbreaking ADA lawsuits with favorable national consequences came about thanks to the organizing savvy of the El Paso disability community: voting rights for people with visual impairments, and redesigning stadium-style theaters for patrons with mobility disabilities. The Volar Center for Independent Living, Desert ADAPT, and Disabled Ability Resource Environment (DARE), El Paso's three premier community disability rights groups at the time, happily took up the mantle of leadership for the fight.

In the first major litigation, DARE and five voters with visual and mobility impairments got behind a 1994 federal class action lawsuit that had two components. The voters with visual disabilities argued that the county's election system prevented them from voting in secret. They had to tell somebody how to mark their ballot, thereby betraying any confidentiality they wanted to retain. They had no secret ballot like other voters enjoyed. Privacy in election choices can be important for a host of reasons, political and personal. As for the voters with mobility impairments, we pointed out that not all county polling places were physically accessible on election day as the ADA required.

The class action suit also named the Texas secretary of state as a defendant besides the county. The secretary has broad legal duties related to elections in Texas, and we wanted to reach all 254 counties through the lawsuit, not just El Paso County. The secretary was the key to opening that door.

Voting is a government program under the ADA and therefore must reasonably accommodate voters with disabilities. There was no dispute as to that. The question was how to get it done. All that the defendants needed was motivation, which the El Paso disability community happily provided with a swift kick in the behind in the form of federal litigation.

As for physical access at polling sites, the county pledged it would select only those locations that were ADA compliant or, if needed, make them temporarily accessible (with portable wheelchair ramps, for example).

On the secrecy issue, the county agreed to use Braille ballots. They were cumbersome and expensive to create and had to be adapted to each precinct. And fewer than 10 percent of people with sight impairments are Braille users, and there was no way of knowing how many Braille ballots were appropriate for each precinct. Braille ballots did not completely resolve the privacy issue, but they were an improvement.

The lawsuit moved the county to look at other voting technologies. The El Paso case carried national impact because it helped propel use of special voting machines, now commonplace, with an audio function to guide voters with visual impairments. The lawsuit was a big step forward in that national impetus. The lawsuit drew a friend of the court brief (amicus curiae) filed by the US Justice Department supporting our position.

As this case demonstrated, the benefit of the ADA passing when it did is that technology had advanced such that it provided the means in many respects to facilitate ADA compliance. Adapted voting machines for the visually impaired represent a quintessential example.

The one issue that we lost was tagging the Texas secretary of state as a defendant in the ADA litigation. We won the issue at trial but lost on appeal. After the county settled, the only defendant remaining was the secretary, now facing a class action on behalf of voters across Texas with visual and mobility impairments. The secretary refused to settle, even refusing to send notices to all Texas counties that they needed to accommodate voters with visual impairments and make sure polling places were physically accessible.

The judge then entered judgment against the secretary, phasing in different ADA requirements over a three-year period. It was a gentle court order and easy to comply with. Not to be cajoled into doing the right thing, the secretary appealed.

The US Fifth Circuit Court of Appeals ruled in August 1997 and agreed that the ADA applied to local voting jurisdictions and to the secretary. However, the judges ruled that the secretary did not have mandatory control over local jurisdictions such that the ADA would require him to guarantee ADA compliance by county election systems. This was absurd, as Texas law required the secretary of state to certify voting machines used by the counties.

Even the simple suggestion that the secretary send information and guidance to the counties, advising them to implement the ADA, was anathema to the Fifth Circuit. The secretary routinely distributed information and updates to county election officials. Why not add an ADA bulletin?

Sometimes I have referred to the Fifth Circuit as "disingenuous," but I would mark this case as "dissembling." The panel of judges tripped over themselves to manufacture a desired result. The court did not even mention the Justice Department's amicus curiae brief filed on our behalf.

As US District Judge David Briones, who oversaw the trial, observed in his written opinion, the secretary put more taxpayer money into fighting the case than what it would have cost to simply send the notices. The judge pointed out that Texas had the "opportunity to lead the nation into a world of equality for the handicapped and the disabled regarding the most cherished right and greatest responsibility in any democracy." True to form, Texas squandered this golden opportunity.

Despite the secretary's recalcitrance, the case got the message across to Texas counties and the nation: voting systems and polling places must provide for and accommodate voters with visual and physical impairments or face lawsuits. The state legislature also got the message, and on September 1, 1999, Texas became the first state to require that all new balloting systems be fully accessible for voters with physical disabilities. A sweet victory for the disability community.

The second major case was an attempt to ensure disabled individuals were accommodated with appropriate seating in movie theaters, which commonly relegated wheelchair users to the frontmost row. As the voting litigation was winding down, eight El Paso activists with mobility impair-

THE WRITING WASN'T ON THE WALL

The El Paso voting rights trial had a bemusing and instructive episode about our clients with sight impairments, who were sitting behind the counsel table in the public area. The trial moved slowly through the morning. Near lunchtime, we could hear soda cans popping and potato chips crunching behind us where the plaintiffs sat. The judge motioned to the bailiff to put a halt to the eating and drinking. I was conducting direct examination of a witness and could not pay attention to the scenario behind me.

During the lunch recess, our folks got into a polite, apologetic discussion with the bailiff, pointing out that there was no Braille signage or otherwise signaling not to eat and drink in the courtroom. The clients were embarrassed. They were keen on being respectful. They had never been to court before and wanted to honor the rules but didn't know about them.

The bailiff informed the judge of the conversation. When the trial resumed in the afternoon, Judge Briones cordially acknowledged that he and those at the courthouse had learned a lesson about the importance of compliance with disability guidelines for people with visual impairments. He assured the plaintiffs that the courthouse would do better.

We laughed about this incident every time we got together afterward because it was so funny to hear the soda cans popping and chips crunching and the people blissfully oblivious that eating and drinking was not acceptable.

Kudos to the judge for the respectful way in which he handled it all.

ments, along with Volar and Desert ADAPT, took on the new Cinemark USA's Tinseltown stadium-style theater complex in El Paso. Their lawsuit in 1997 contended that eighteen of its twenty theaters were inaccessible to them because their only seating choice was in front of the first row of those theaters, directly facing the large screen. This case also had nationwide impacts.

Stadium-style theaters were becoming the rage. They provide stepped seating that boosts patrons' viewing experience. The elevated seating configuration eliminates the line-of-sight problems that typically occur, for example, when a tall individual sits in front of a shorter customer. Tinseltown's stadium seating, however, relegated wheelchair patrons to seating areas with inferior lines of sight.

The plaintiffs argued that disability seating should be midway in the theater as with high-school football stadiums, where ramps take fans up midway. Sitting right in front of the movie screen, however, did not provide a line of sight comparable to that of nondisabled viewers and could be quite uncomfortable. Moreover, depending on the type of wheelchair and the person's disability, viewing from that close to the screen might be physically problematic. One more hindrance: the sound is louder for front-row viewers as it blasts through the screen.

People typically do not sit in the front row because they must crane their necks to see the screen. Seeing *Titanic* from the front row, for example, as I did because of arriving late, is experiencing only part of the movie—looking up from the ocean at people dining and dancing.

The ADA also requires companion seating for someone accompanying a person with a disability. One of the plaintiffs, Margie Lightbourne-Harbeck, a grandmother in a wheelchair, recounted how she had taken her young granddaughter to a Cinemark theater and had to sit in front of the screen. Her granddaughter did not want to sit with her in the companion seating because the screen was too close. The little girl found a seat nearer to the middle so she could see better. This saddened Margie, who wanted to share the movie with her.

US District Judge Harry Lee Hudspeth ruled for the disability community and ordered Cinemark to modify the eighteen theaters by moving the wheelchair seating location farther back from the screen and higher off the floor and by lowering the screen approximately a foot. It was a benign court order, not particularly onerous for Cinemark.

The judge wrote that "a person seated in the 'wheelchair row' has to lift his or her eyes and/or crane his or her neck at a very uncomfortable angle in order to view the feature on the motion picture screen." Therefore, "the wheelchair-bound patron is denied the full and equal enjoyment of the movie-going experience in these theaters." Tinseltown, the judge noted, confined patrons in wheelchairs to an area with an "average viewing angle [of] above thirty-five degrees, which the plaintiffs' expert witness has properly described as 'well into the discomfort zone.'" The judge called it "headache city."

University of Texas at El Paso student volunteers bolstered the expert report on which the judge grounded his opinion. They did a field study of how patrons filled the Tinseltown movie seats. Not surprisingly, they found that viewers began filling the seats in the middle and then, as more people arrived, filled the seats going up from the middle and then down from the center. No one grabbed seats in the front row.

Enter the US Fifth Circuit on Cinemark's appeal. The court went out of its way to overturn Judge Hudspeth's ruling that Cinemark had to get square with the ADA. Even though the US Department of Justice was with us and helped argue the appeal, the judges ruled contrariwise.

The appellate court agreed that the ADA applied to theater construction but fudged on what "unobstructed line of sight" meant in the ADA regulations. The Justice Department has a congressional mandate to adopt rules implementing the ADA. The stadium-style theater regulations were in progress, and the department had not formally adopted a precise definition of "unobstructed line of sight." The judges zeroed in on that instead of the "comparable lines of sight" ADA requirement. As far as the higher court was concerned, sitting in the front row near the large movie screen at floor level was an unobstructed line of sight, no matter what the experts and theatergoers said.

ADA regulations, whether officially implemented or not, do not limit a court's ability to adapt an accessible remedy for people with disabilities. The judges opted to punt rather than tackle the theater industry. The court waltzed through a contorted dance choreography to attain the desired result. The best guess is that the judges wanted to free Cinemark from the cost of retrofitting its inaccessible theaters.

Nevertheless, our case made the point: the Justice Department adopted the regulations, which are now standard for theaters. It was a victory despite the appellate judges, but it left a sour taste that the court can be so intentionally parsimonious when it comes to the rights of people with disabilities.

Sometimes victories are not total but instead incremental. Sometimes losses are steps to victories. The plaintiffs, being from the disability community, understood this well and continued sporting their "I Survived Tinseltown" t-shirts they made for the trial.

The third home-run lawsuit was another federal action against the University of Texas at El Paso. The complaint laid out a laundry list of facility access and program deficiencies for students with disabilities. The lack of compliance with federal law was stark. A daylong mediation lasting well into the night—close to midnight, in fact—yielded a comprehensive accessibility plan for UTEP's student programs and facilities.

CENTRAL TEXAS

One of TCRP's more iconic ADA lawsuits, this one filed in Austin, sought to remedy inaccessibility issues at the recently remodeled Supreme Court of Texas building. The state had refitted the building in 1996. It housed Texas's two highest courts (the Supreme Court and the Court of Criminal Appeals), the state law library, and the Attorney General's office.

Despite the refurbishing, the building remained mostly inaccessible to people with physical disabilities despite the ADA requirement that, when buildings are remodeled, they must be fully compliant with ADA guidelines. No exceptions.

The remodel in fact made the building less accessible than it had been, which wasn't much to begin with. TCRP filed a federal lawsuit on behalf of an attorney who used a wheelchair. This occurred at the same time that then-Governor George W. Bush appointed Greg Abbott, who himself uses a wheelchair, as a state supreme court judge.

An ironic twist was that the *Austin American-Statesman* published a Sunday front-page article about the fact that a lawyer with a physical disability had to go so far as suing because he couldn't get into the court building. The article featured a photo of the attorney in a suit and tie with a briefcase in a wheelchair at the front door of the court building, unable to enter.

In an interview for the article, Justice Jack Hightower, the supreme court judge in charge of the renovation (and whom Abbott succeeded on the court), stated they had not thought about accessibility while remodeling. That stunning front-page admission drove a settlement of the case within days and a scramble to make the facility accessible.

When the press inquired of Abbott about the lawsuit, he obliquely said he understood why it was filed, an understatement to say the least, as much of the facility and Supreme Court bench itself would have been off limits to him personally.

It is astounding and disappointing that Abbott (the current governor as this book went to press) has been no friend to the disability community. For example, while still on the state supreme court, he once called me about a campaign event in a Houston hotel venue that was physically inaccessible to him. He asked us to remedy that situation, which we did. Afterward, I asked him if he would go public because it would be good public education to point out that this happened to a supreme court justice. He would not. It was only about him and no one else. Nor would he associate with disability groups or align with them for advocacy purposes.

Abbott is characterized, accurately in my view, as a weathervane pointing in the direction of his political base. Abbott has no shortage of political ambition and no depth of moral conscience. His political journey unfolded in tandem with the movement to radically change the Texas courts.

Abbott is in a wheelchair because of a freakish accident. An oak tree fell on him in 1984 when he was jogging in an affluent Houston neighborhood. His financial settlement with the property owner was substantial, guaranteeing a respectable six-figure yearly income for life.

After he was appointed to the Supreme Court of Texas, however,

HONORING THE CONFEDERACY: ANOTHER SUPREME COURT OF TEXAS BLUNDER

Not only did the Supreme Court of Texas stumble badly in refurbishing its building so as to be inaccessible to people with physical disabilities, but it required a joint press conference with state NAACP president Gary Bledsoe in 2000 to shame it into taking down two fancy bronze plaques memorializing the Confederacy.

They were at the marble entrance to the court building. Imagine the "equal justice" message they sent to minority folks. One plaque bore the Confederate battle flag and a quote from Robert E. Lee, praising Texas troops. The other was the Confederacy's Great Seal.

Bledsoe pointedly called them out as "hate symbols . . . an unnecessary stain on our judiciary." The offending plaques provided a good visual—an embarrassing backdrop for the press conference.

Abbott provided one of the votes that took away that type of lawsuit for anybody else who would suffer the same injury. It was fine for him to recover a handsome settlement, but not for others.

NEXT, THE STATE CAPITOL BUILDING

Another Central Texas standoff came after the first remodeling dustup. One might think that lawsuit would have made some headway in educating officials about access issues. But no. In this case it was the Capitol Building itself being refurbished. ADAPT and the Coalition of Texans with Disabilities had to boost their efforts to improve access through a lawsuit. After all, they spent considerable time there lobbying legislators to do what was right by the disability community.

This ADA litigation led to major improvements in physical access inside and outside, in addition to accommodations for people with visual and hearing impairments. Those changes were broad and comprehensive. The lawsuit fit like a glove with the renovation project just then getting underway.

As with the remodeled state supreme court building, the State Preservation Board, which was supervising the refurbishment, had not considered ADA requirements for new features. The litigation helped the board think more clearly, and the board did an excellent job thereafter.

The case was memorable in another way. We were holding a hearing on a late Friday afternoon before US District Judge Sam Sparks, known for his caustic ragging on attorneys arguing in front of him. The state had filed a motion to dismiss the case.

Sparks was in typical form and did not spare me from his verbal arrows. After a while, I finally said: "With all due respect, Judge, I'm too old for this kind of treatment." Everyone in court sucked in their breath. One did not talk back to a judge, much less Judge Sparks. I braced myself. Would my clients have to bail me out of jail for contempt? To my surprise, he backed down but said that he was going to rule against us and dismiss the case.

But over the weekend he reconsidered, read the applicable law, and on Monday morning ruled in our favor on this motion. As noted, we settled the case on good terms.

FRANKLIN JOHNSON AND HIS DOG, ROMNEY, TAKE ON THE SHINER BREWERY AND WIN MORE THAN FREE BEER

Franklin Johnson, who was completely blind, brought us an inspiring case in 1995 as someone who stubbornly sticks up for his rights, wins, and vindicates the rights of thousands of others unknown to him.

The brewery that makes Shiner beers, located north of Yoakum in Shiner, had a strict "no animals" policy for its guided tours of the beermaking facility, tours that wrapped up with free beer and snacks in a hospitality room.

Franklin learned of the policy the hard way. He showed up with his service dog, Romney, for a tour along with a friend and his friend's son. The brewery refused admission to Romney, claiming he was a health hazard. The brewery offered a human guide instead, or he could have a complimentary beer and wait for his friend to finish.

Franklin adamantly declined, citing the ADA and a Texas disability law, which guaranteed service animals entry into business establishments, including places that prepared food and drink.

The brewery was unmoved, and we landed in federal court in Victoria. Franklin did a stirring job testifying, explaining why he had rejected the human escort: his ambition as a blind person was to live on his own, which he had done for a good number of years.

He talked about how blind people care for and build partnerships with their companion dogs, even living and sleeping with them during their mutual training period. Romney was a young, lean, brown-haired German shepherd. This would be Romney's gig until age necessitated his retirement. In a real sense, Franklin testified, he and Romney developed an intimacy in their bonding process. Their special relationship rested on shared dedication, love, and trust.

Franklin credited Romney with performing brilliantly except that Romney didn't have a sense of height and sometimes walked Franklin into an overhanging tree branch. Franklin thought this was quite humorous, as did people in the courtroom. But otherwise, Franklin depended on Romney for guidance and safe passage. Franklin entrusted his life to Romney.

Franklin was of average height, moving into his fifties, and a friendly fellow. He refused any human assistance getting to the witness stand to testify. He wanted to do it himself. He asked me ahead of time to help him count the number of steps so he would know when it came time. Romney sat attentively next to Franklin at the counsel table and kept a watchful eye. He let Franklin walk to the witness stand by himself.

Franklin testified with such dignity about his personal quest to live independently. The judge paid close attention. When he finished, the judge said: "Mr. Johnson, I have been impressed by your testimony. Do you mind if I stand and watch as you walk your way back to the counsel table?"

That stunned me, but it showed the respect that the judge had for Franklin's efforts to live an independent life. That was the only time in my long career that I saw a judge do something like that. Franklin was a living example of what the ADA is all about. We won, and the judge let Romney into the brewery.

The brewery appealed, and we won again. It was an early case under the ADA, and the appellate panel of judges honored Franklin by writing a strong "breakthrough" decision for ADA plaintiffs.

ROMNEY: CLEANER THAN HUMANS

We picked up fascinating facts about service dogs at trial, which discombobulated the brewery witnesses.

The brewery contended, without proof, that guide dogs were dirty and their hair would float through the air and into the beer vats. The fancy word for this is "aerosolizing." Our expert, however, testified that guide dogs are much cleaner than humans—an interesting comment on humans' solipsistic thinking. One reason is that the seeing-impaired person, in building a close relationship with the companion dog, constantly brushes and grooms the dog—morning, evening, and in between. Thus, the odds of Romney's hair polluting the beer was less than the chances of human tourists doing that.

Visitors walking alongside the vats did not wear hairnets over their heads and beards. The brewery had no "clothing required" rules for visitors. Many wore sandals and shorts. Romney was likely cleaner than the human visitors, including the personal guide the brewery wanted to provide.

The case became a gold standard of sorts because of how it analyzed the trial evidence for people with disabilities and how it shifted the burden to the brewery to justify excluding Franklin and Romney.

My personal takeaway was admiration for Franklin and his passion to live on his own. He had such self-respect, almost nobleness, about him. This is exactly the ADA's purpose—for people to live as independently as possible and be part of, and enjoy, their community.

Franklin was such a fighter for his rights that he and Romney came to the appellate oral argument in New Orleans at the majestic Fifth Circuit building. Oral argument is when both sides present their legal briefs in court to a panel of typically three judges, who can ask any questions about the case. Very few clients attend because they need not be present, and there is no witness testimony—everything is based on the trial record. Likewise, the trip can be long and expensive for just a half-hour in front of three judges.

I have often mused as to whether Franklin's appearance had an impact on the judges hearing his appeal, just as it did on the trial judge. Nor do I know if Romney and Franklin took in Bourbon Street and had a few beignets while in New Orleans, but I would wager on it.

LIVE CAPTIONING ON THE JUMBOTRON: SUING THE NBA AND THE SAN ANTONIO SPURS

Another case in which TCRP lost the opening skirmish but helped win the national battle involved San Antonio's hearing-impaired community, many of whom wanted live captioning for pro basketball games at the Alamodome, where the Spurs played their NBA games.

In a case of first impression (the first of its kind), as the federal judge characterized it, Isabel Cortez, along with other avid basketball fans and devoted game attendees with hearing impairments, sued the National Basketball Association, the San Antonio Spurs, and the Alamodome in 1996.

They wanted live captioning on the Alamodome's Jumbotron, the giant video screen hanging from the rafters, so that all the fans could see and read what was broadcasting through the audio system. Our argument rested on the ADA requirement that public and private programs (sports being an example) had to be as accessible as reasonably possible to people with disabilities, and this included anyone experiencing a hearing disability.

The judge dismissed the case against the NBA as a defendant, deciding that the behemoth sports league did not exercise enough actual control over the Spurs games to be jointly liable for not providing captioning, despite the ultra-specific, precisely detailed, thirty-five-page NBA "Facility Standards" contract with the Spurs. The suit went forward against the Spurs and the Alamodome and settled favorably. We did not appeal the decision dismissing the case against the NBA, given how hostile the Fifth Circuit was in this kind of case. We did not want to lose and make any more bad case law than what existed.

The day of reckoning, though, was just around the corner for the NBA. There was no dispute that the ADA required some kind of captioning or accommodation, and the outcome of the next suit in a more favorable court would not be to the NBA's liking. And the change happened. Today, it is taken for granted that arenas provide live captioning for people with hearing disabilities, although all fans benefit. Live captioning now is a

ISABEL CORTEZ, HERO

For nine years until 1999, I taught seminars on disability rights and state constitutional law at St. Mary's University School of Law. For the disability law seminar, Isabel Cortez, who had no hearing since birth, would come and converse with students through a sign-language interpreter. She was humorous, kind, a fierce advocate, and an ardent Spurs fan.

Something I learned from her that should have been self-evident is that each country (and even regions therein) has its own sign language, as with spoken language. She related being at an El Paso conference with Mexican hearing-impaired communities and how, to communicate with each other, they needed to find sign-language interpreters from those countries who spoke both English and Spanish. No easy task.

Isabel moved to Oklahoma, and Texas lost an effective advocate for her colleagues with hearing impairments. Whether she remained a Spurs fan or switched over to the Oklahoma City Thunder NBA team, I do not know. But I would bet her heart stayed with the Spurs.

technological snap. At one time, court reporters were employed to do the job. Not only is captioning easier, but it's less expensive.

The towering, elegant NBA headquarters on New York City's Fifth Avenue, which I visited to review the contract documents, accentuated the NBA's wealth and power and raised the question of why it so adamantly resisted making its games more accessible to fans with hearing disabilities.

THE ADA HELPS IMPROVE THE JUSTICE SYSTEM

Because few lawyers and organizations in Texas take on the state's justice system, TCRP found itself stepping into the void from time to time, digging deep into serious issues that affected people caught up in the criminal justice structures.

A very important issue was jail suicides, which were and continue to be at crisis levels in city and county facilities. The Hogg Foundation posits that about 30 percent of those detainees held in county jails in Texas have at least one serious mental illness. The US Department of Justice lists suicide as the major cause of jail deaths. Most jail suicides should never occur. They typically result from the jailers' negligence, indifference, and callousness. Suicide casts deep pain and often guilt upon surviving family and friends.

Four jail suicide lawsuits came my way, three of them in San Angelo in Tom Green County, over a seven-year span. All involved young men. Each was heart-wrenching and should not have happened. The young men left behind grieving kids, wives, parents, and siblings.

By law a jail is responsible for the well-being of every detained person. When an officer checks someone into a jail, the officer conducts a so-called classification interview to determine whether the detainee is physically or mentally ill, suicidal, or likely to harm himself or others. These factors determine the kind and location of the cell for the detainee.

The classification checklist contains questions and observations about suicidal ideation. A person deemed suicidal is supposed to be placed in a cell under intense, frequent observation and without any item that could be used to inflict self-harm. Some jails have glass rooms near the command center to maintain close observation over possible suicidal detainees.

It is common knowledge among jail personnel (or at least it should be) that the most likely suicide candidate is a young man with no arrest record who is depressed and has been drinking or taking drugs. That is part of jailer training and something to which they should pay attention during the initial classification process and thereafter. And the worst thing to do is provide the means or situation whereby detainees can end their lives. They are silently crying for help.

Federal courts have loosened jail oversight in recent years—not that it was ever very comprehensive—making it more difficult to hold jailers liable for malfeasance. Those lawsuits traditionally had been litigated under standard civil rights statutes for denial of due process.

However, the ADA helped fill the court-created vacuum. The ADA requires that government programs and facilities accommodate people with mental and physical disabilities. The US Supreme Court has made it clear that this includes jails. The three Tom Green County lawsuits illustrate how the ADA came to be a powerful legal tool.

Tom Green County has a serious suicide problem, with a rate surpassing both state and national averages. One would think that reality would call for additional caution in attending to jail detainees.

The first case, in 1985, was under traditional civil rights law for denial of due process, that is, for not protecting the young man's life. The lawsuit successfully settled. He was a young Hispanic man, fitting the profile described above, placed in a cell that had a solid steel door with a small rectangular window, maybe the size of a dollar bill, which allowed only minimal direct observation.

The jailers provided little supervision and issued him a bedsheet. It is beyond imagination how the jailers could have done anything worse to set up a suicide scenario. Either sheer senselessness or callous indifference was at play. That the young man was Mexican American probably figured into the equation.

He hanged himself from the showerhead with the sheet. He left behind a wife, two children, and an extended family. He was in his early twenties. It was very tragic. The law was clear at that point in those circumstances. The jailers had liability, and the county settled with the family for monetary compensation. But the county could not give back the man's life to his family.

By the time the second lawsuit happened a couple years later under remarkably similar tragic circumstances, the law had become more problematic and less favorable to the family, but to its credit the county still settled. This was a young Anglo man under age eighteen who was still living at home, had been drinking, was severely depressed, and was acting out. His parents did not know what to do. They called the police and lived to regret it. Guilt and sadness filled their hearts.

The third Tom Green County case occurred about the time the ADA became law in 1990, again involving a Hispanic man in his early twenties; he was depressed and had been drinking. By then the courts had so undermined earlier law that it was doubtful it would apply in jail suicide cases.

However, the ADA provided a lifeline by showing that the jail's intake process was deficient in detecting mental illness symptoms and depression and for not protecting potential suicide victims from harming themselves. The county settled with the family. Yet another needless death.

ADA liability is strict in jail confinement situations. The sheriff or operator for each jail facility in Texas must implement a suicide prevention and mental disabilities plan, which includes staff training in recognizing and handling prisoners who may be suicidal or depressed or express mental health concerns. The ADA has saved the day in many instances—and many lives.

The fourth case also would anger anyone. It involved another young guy with kids, in his early thirties, who was depressed that his marriage was breaking up. He had been drinking and was driving from New Mexico to see his family in Austin. A deputy arrested and jailed him for DWI in Andrews County in West Texas. They put him in a cell with a blanket, which he used to take his life. Utterly irresponsible!

The jail did not even put him through the classification interview process. I asked the sheriff, one of those old, gruff, stereotypical West Texas sheriffs, "Why not?" in a deposition. His inane answer: "I looked him in the eye and could tell he was not suicidal." This was the first and only time the sheriff had met the victim. The county had no choice but to settle, and we set up a small trust to benefit the man's two children.

I wonder if guilt ever weighs down officials like the sheriff when someone unnecessarily dies because of their utter idiocy or callous attitude. Suicide cases of young men pained me. There was no reason the suicides should have happened. The victims were deeply troubled when they took their lives and left behind immense pain for the survivors who loved them. Their deaths could have been avoided. Kids lost their fathers. I grieved for the families, especially when interacting with them during the litigation. Their sorrow was profound.

Another significant suit that TCRP tackled to help improve the justice system addressed recidivism of parolees with disabilities. An important TCRP ADA lawsuit with significant statewide ramifications came out of federal court in Laredo. It was to help make the parole system less problematic for parolees with mental disabilities. The percentage of such individuals is large. The Meadows Foundation published a 2016 report finding that 34 percent of Texas inmates have mental health disorders.

Often, and for various reasons (such as not taking prescribed medication), parolees with mental disabilities will act out in ways that could lead to revocation of parole granted by the court for relatively minor infractions. Or they might not report to parole officers when required. The recidivism rate for parolees with mental disabilities when we filed suit was about twice as high compared to parolee recidivism generally, which was about 20 percent. (Recidivism here refers to a person's relapse into criminal behavior that causes reincarceration for violation of the terms of parole. It also includes reincarceration for myriad noncriminal violations of parole terms, such as not reporting to one's parole officer regularly, failing to get a job, leaving the jurisdiction, etc.)

Parole is a "program" as defined by the ADA and must accommodate people with disabilities. Its objective is reintegration back into general society. As a result of our lawsuit, which the state settled, parole officers for individuals with mental disabilities took on fewer cases and acted more like mental health social workers.

These officers were trained to spend more time interacting with parolees with mental disabilities so that those under supervision could find jobs, learn how to use public transportation, and so on. These specialized case officers gained a better understanding of coping with minor infractions (like "acting out") so that they would not quickly revoke a person's parole.

The Texas Correctional Office on Offenders with Medical or Mental Impairments already existed under the Department of Criminal Justice, and the lawsuit did much to help revamp its policies and practices. Texas became one of the few states to adopt this type of specialized case manager. For once, Texas was ahead of the curve. Too bad not more often.

The other important facet of the settlement was convincing the agency to help inmates obtain federal disability benefits, typically through the Social Security Administration, from the moment they walked out of prison on parole. Otherwise parolees were stuck with $100 that the state puts in their pocket when they pass through the front gate of the prison (thus the slang term "gate money" for this munificent sum). Disability benefits under Social Security provide income, which helps stabilize a parolee's life. It is federal money with no cost to Texas and aids the state and people in so many ways.

Within a few years of implementing the settlement, recidivism for parolees with mental disabilities dropped to the same general rate for all parolees, if not a bit lower, and has continued to decrease.

One might wonder why it took litigation to kick-start an obvious goal, but this is Texas, and logic does not necessarily carry the day with lawmakers and officials. Sometimes federal litigation provides a crack of the whip before the legislature lurches into action. And sometimes legislators and officials know better but wait for the political cover of litigation before doing what they know to be the right thing.

To underscore again how important the ADA is as a civil rights law: this kind of case would not have been possible under standard civil rights laws.

Given this promising model of training parole officers to be more like social workers with fewer people in their charge, one might wonder why Texas shouldn't experiment with applying this to the parole system generally. The rub is the short-term expense; but if rehabilitation and reintegration are the goals, then investment might be worth it in the long run.

THE FIFTH CIRCUIT'S (NON)ENFORCEMENT OF THE ADA

Some contrary examples notwithstanding (such as Franklin Johnson and Romney's battle with the brewery in Shiner), the Fifth Circuit is no friend to people with disabilities. The judges serving in this conservative appellate court seem to go out of their way with tortuous reasoning to rule against the disability community, even when people win in the trial court. Not infrequently, outright disingenuousness seems to be afoot back in chambers.

The Fifth Circuit is now one of the most conservative appellate courts in the country. It oversees trial court decisions brought from Texas, Louisiana, and Mississippi. At one time, it covered the entire South. Ironically, Fifth Circuit was in the past a champion of civil rights and effectively desegregated the South during the 1950s and 1960s, even though most of the judges were Republican appointees. No one imagined that the court would become so reactionary, that it would become a wrecking ball for civil rights lawsuits, issuing plainly awful edicts.

Our lawsuits suffered from this precarious turn of historical events. TCRP still managed to eke out victories, albeit sometimes partial, or at least make it clear that victory was coming with the next lawsuit. The circuit judges failed to completely halt the march of progress but sure made the road rockier and the detours hazardous.

The Michael Hainze shooting case demonstrates how bad the Fifth Circuit can be. Sometimes the results of an appeal are just plain awful—there's no way around it. No lawyer likes to confess making bad law, but I must.

This case from 2000 revolved around a late-night suicide call to the Williamson County sheriff by Michael Hainze's aunt. Michael, a veteran, was experiencing suicidal ideation. She requested that deputies take him to a hospital for emergency mental health treatment.

Michael had a history of depression and was under the influence of alcohol and antidepressants. He was barefoot on a cold night, carrying a knife, and threatening to commit "suicide by cop," which is to provoke an officer to kill him. Suicide by cop is not an uncommon phenomenon with some folks who are mentally ill. When police get a suicide call, particularly a suicide-by-cop call, their job is to approach the scene accordingly, deescalate the situation, and prevent a suicide from happening.

Sheriff deputies went to the convenience store where Michael was. When they arrived Michael was standing by the passenger door of a pickup in the parking lot, talking with the two men inside it.

One deputy immediately pulled out his gun and ordered Michael away from the truck. Michael responded with profanities and began walking toward the officer with a small knife in hand. The deputy ordered Michael to stop, but Michael ignored him. When Michael approached within four to six feet, the deputy fired two shots into Michael's chest. Michael miraculously survived. The bullets went through his chest without significant damage.

We filed suit on Michael's behalf, alleging the deputies violated the ADA in the way they managed the suicide call. We argued the deputies should have stepped away, protecting themselves by standing on the other side of a patrol car. They should have engaged Michael in a prolonged conversation until convincing him to go to the hospital. The deputies had no training about handling suicide calls, even though since 1990 the ADA required such policies and training. The American Psychological Association pegs at 20 percent the number of police calls related to mental illness.

Confrontation—which typifies most police encounters—is counterproductive in mental health calls and often leads to increased risk of violence. The standard operating procedure is for police to talk calmly and back away when encountering someone experiencing a mental health emergency. The process takes longer than a quick arrest but has better outcomes for all involved.

The district judge dismissed our lawsuit, and the case made its way to the Fifth Circuit. In a stunning ruling, the appeals judges decided that the ADA did not apply in this situation because the law comes into play only *after* a person is arrested and secured. The judges simply conjured up this exception out of whole cloth. Nothing in the ADA expresses such a "prearrest exemption" from the law's application.

This decision was ridiculous, contrary to the purpose and language of the ADA, and dangerous for people having mental health crises. Moreover, the import of this ruling is that family and friends will hesitate to call police for assistance with a loved one, fearing what the officers might do. In Michael's case, the deputies did everything wrong and escalated the precarious situation. They almost obliged Michael's suicidal ideation by shooting him rather than transporting him to the hospital.

I went to the hospital late that night to see Michael and his family. I was so outraged at what happened and how close the police had come to ending his life—all because his family had called for help.

Other federal courts around the country have reacted adversely to the Fifth Circuit's decision in Michael Hainze's case and fortunately have ruled just the opposite: police must manage mental health calls differently and carefully.

Shortly after the Fifth Circuit's *Hainze* decision, we had a case that showed its dreadful ramification, that of Sophia King, whom the police shot and killed at the Rosewood Courts housing project in Austin in June 2002.

TCRP lost the case on behalf of her children. Their twenty-three-year-old mother had a history of severe mental illness. Sophia had long bouts with schizophrenia and had been a patient at Austin State Hospital various times. Sophia, already known to the police as an emotionally disturbed person, was acting out—throwing around dishes, pots, and pans outside her apartment. She was in an ongoing heated dispute with the housing project's manager, who called the police.

This was not Austin PD's first call about Sophia in a mental health crisis or for acting out. There were many. She needed emergency treatment. Nevertheless, a single officer arrived and created an immediate direct confrontation, which is the last thing to do during a mental health call.

The result was predictable: Sophia blew up in anger and paranoia, grabbed a kitchen knife, ran out a rear door, saw the manager, and began chasing her in the complex's grassy area. Another officer arriving on the scene shot and killed Sophia on the spot.

Sophia King's death created an enormous uproar in the African American community, in which the housing project was located. Both officers were white. She was African American.

Austin PD issued a report eighteen months after the killing and called for the department to improve its mental health response procedures. The department didn't really need to wait a year and a half to underline that self-evident truth. The report was underwhelming, if not vacuous. What the report didn't say, and what added to the pathos of the killing, was that months earlier then–Chief of Police Stan Knee had ended Austin PD's contract with the Travis County sheriff's mental health unit to respond to such calls.

The Travis County unit was one of the best in the country. The officers went to mental health calls in plainclothes—no uniform and no weapon. Their approach was deescalation, which meant talking and talking and more talking. They did their job well and were a model for other law enforcement agencies.

Knee told us (yours truly and Nelson Linder from the Austin NAACP) in a meeting eight months before Sophia King's killing, when we complained about his breaking the contract, not to worry: Austin PD would do better than Travis County. But the department hadn't done anything, as the report reflected, two years and two months after our meeting with Knee. Was his conscience disturbed by this?

Sophia King's death was not Austin PD's first fatal police shooting of a citizen with mental illness, nor was it the last. But the ramifications of the *Hainze* case relieved them from concern or liability about prearrest situations.

It would not be a reach, in my view, to argue that Knee's failure to do what he said he would do led to Sophia's death. The pathos of Sophia King's life and death is also an indictment of the lack of community mental health services.

A BIRTHDAY TRIP TO JAIL

While the Hainze and King cases agonizingly show how much further we need to travel toward justice, it's important to appreciate how much progress has occurred in people's day-to-day lives.

This concluding case is about how a restaurant and a clueless cop ruined an elderly couple's birthday breakfast but still turned it into a celebration, albeit a little delayed. Richard Bell was deaf and blind, and Joan, his wife, was also blind. They communicated through a kind of sign language in the palms of their hands, which was fascinating to watch and quite amazing in how well it functioned between them. Richard walked with a cane because of physical issues.

The Bells often visited the old Catfish Parlour restaurant in North Austin because of its breakfast buffet. One day they went to celebrate Richard's sixty-ninth birthday. Unfortunately, they arrived right after the buffet had ended at 11 a.m.

Since there was no buffet, Joan asked for a Braille menu, which the ADA requires, or a reasonable alternative. However, there wasn't any, and the discussion with the waitress was fraught because of communication issues and her lack of knowledge about accommodating patrons with disabilities.

The manager intervened and made the bad situation worse. She grabbed Richard's cane from him for some inexplicable reason and summoned the police. When an officer arrived, the manager told him that the couple was unruly and would not maintain peace. The officer could not communicate with either Joan or Richard and thus had no idea of the situation from their side.

Doing the most unhelpful thing he could, the officer arrested both, even forcibly pulling Richard from the restaurant booth without his cane, and took them to the county jail. The jail staff correctly sized up the situation and refused to accept the couple for booking. Facing that situation, the police released them from custody.

It was harrowing for Joan and Richard that their disabilities caused their arrest and doubly distressing because the officer did not follow Austin policy, which required an interpreter to be on hand before deciding to arrest an individual with visual or hearing disabilities to help clarify the situation for the police.

Even though Austin PD had this policy, the officer did not know about it, which speaks to lack of police training. Had the officer abided by the policy, he could have avoided the whole farce and saved the couple from the trauma he needlessly inflicted upon them.

The restaurant promptly settled the federal lawsuit that we brought and had Braille menus printed. Austin PD stalled in settling their part of the lawsuit and was preparing to go to trial until the federal judge met with us in his chambers and said to the city attorney: "Do you really want to have a trial on this?" The city's lawyer got the message and settled. The city paid damages and doubled police academy training from two to four hours for handling disability issues and implemented an in-service training program.

Joan and Richard received appropriate compensation for the humiliation they suffered at the restaurant. The city also provided them compensation and affirmed their inspiring commitment to live as independently as possible as members of society.

Richard expressed it well through Joan: "We were very scared to begin this lawsuit because we had never done anything like it, but we decided to stick with it and try to change things not only for us, but also for all of the members of the disabled community so we could all be treated with dignity and respect." He could not have said it better. We were so proud to represent them.

FINAL WORDS: FRANK LOZANO

Being involved in so many disability lawsuits gives me deep pride and joy. It was a privilege to work so closely with so many individuals in the disability community. I respected them all enormously for their undaunted struggle seeking dignity and human rights. Many were characters in the best sense, especially the ADAPT folks. We made personal friendships in addition to professional relationships.

They helped me grow in understanding the disability community and appreciating and respecting their gritty tenacity for justice, equity, and equality. They inspired me to dig deeper into my own life and work. They honored me with their confidence and companionship. They brought me into their community and made me part of it.

As with many oppressed people with whom we worked, they formed their own internal community. They weren't just defined as a community by the larger society but were their own mutually supportive community to each other. "Community," as I came to understand, had two different meanings in this sense: from the outside and from the inside.

It's important to wrap up this chapter with a tribute to Frank Lozano, a blind disability advocate from El Paso and a leader of Desert ADAPT. He passed away in 2020 at age seventy. We were friends and loved to joke with each other. The community called him a "spiritual warrior," a title that fit him perfectly. He was a fellow badass and one of my favorite plaintiffs. He had a calm dignity and happiness about him, which he shared with everyone.

One particularly emblematic memory of Frank was how he would help others despite his own disability. I often saw Frank pushing one of his colleagues in a wheelchair to court hearings or to press conferences. He and his friends represented the disability movement: helping each other and pushing for greater inclusion in the larger society. We could always count on Frank.

I know from our conversations that Frank staunchly believed in nonviolent direct action. He practiced it with creativity and courage, even when facing arrest and police mistreatment. He relished the struggle and unselfishly shared his life with others. His commitment to equality and social justice summoned us to action when things were tough and the odds appeared insurmountable. Frank was a hero and a moral companion to all.

What this says of Frank could describe scores of people with whom TCRP worked across the years. Frank, I know, would be pleased with the comparison. Human rights is a way of life.

TAKEAWAYS: DISABILITY RIGHTS ARE HUMAN RIGHTS

Sometimes it is incumbent upon us all to raise a powerful voice for justice as Frank did. At times, we label this as a "prophetic voice" but rarely associate it with ourselves. The phrase, whenever I hear it, reminds me of an occurrence I was part of one night at about 1 a.m. where I saw a prophetic voice in action. I was returning home from toiling over a legal brief at the office. I stopped to buy milk for the kids' breakfast at Fiesta Mart, an Austin store catering to the Hispanic community.

I was third in the checkout line. The first was a poor, middle-aged Mexican American woman, short and bowed with the years. She was trying to pay for her groceries with food stamps, which, back in those days, was like Monopoly money only very complicated.

Second in line was a well-dressed Anglo woman, also about the same age as the woman in front of her. I was musing about how well she was attired for that hour compared to my dingy shorts, sandals, and crumpled t-shirt.

The cashier was giving the first woman an extremely difficult time, even though she, like the woman, was Latina. It was excruciatingly embarrassing, watching the cashier demean the older woman, probably twice her age and completely confused with sorting out the food stamps.

When it was the Anglo woman's turn with the cashier, it was night and day. You hear stories like this but rarely see them unfold before you. The cashier was ultra-attentive to the woman and very polite. As they finished their business, the Anglo woman said to the cashier: "Thank you so much for the respectful way you've treated me. I'm grateful for your kindness and patience. I only wish you had treated the woman in front of me the same way."

Her words thundered through my soul and sent chills across my shoulders. Hers was the prophetic voice for justice in action. Over the years since, I have wondered how many times and how many people (me included) have had the opportunity to lift their voice against injustice, as did the Anglo woman, but demurred. And how it might have changed society, if only one step at a time.

I have not used this powerful phrase—"prophetic voice"—enough in this memoir in reference to some of the people with whom we worked, even though I've told their stories. They, Frank, and the Anglo woman are models for all of us.

9

THE PEOPLE PUSH BACK

Free Speech and Assembly

Free speech and assembly lawsuits on behalf of community groups popped up frequently throughout my half-century as a lawyer. They received high priority at TCRP because they backed people's organizing efforts and were about reining in arbitrary government power that sought to quash democratic impulses from any corner. Litigation also signaled a warning shot to others who might harbor similar repressive propensities.

Most free speech cases that came across our legal docket were for community groups, but some were for individuals whose lawsuits affected a larger audience than just a private dispute.

Free speech cases happen suddenly. There is no advance planning. It all depends on when some government entity decides to choke off opposition. The haphazardness of this reality shows up in this chapter. There is no good way to organize all the lawsuits. They came at different times and from different areas of Texas. The facts of the cases are interesting, usually entertaining, and best appreciated in the context of people vehemently protesting about something in which they zealously believe. These are emotional events.

REPRESENTING THE DEMOCRACY COALITION AGAINST TRAMPLING HORSES

Shortly after becoming president, George W. Bush returned to Austin in April 2001 to dedicate the new Bob Bullock Texas State History Museum. Protesters, still smarting from the US Supreme Court handing him the election over Vice President Al Gore, banded together for their version of a Texas welcome. The capital city and its police department would have none of it and did their best to thwart any protest within earshot or eyesight of Bush.

After the dedication, from which the police kept them a block away and mostly out of view, the demonstrators began marching to the Governor's Mansion, where Bush was to lunch with Rick Perry, his successor as governor.

Their goal: conduct a respectably large and noisy protest on the sidewalk across Lavaca Street from the mansion's westside vehicle entrance. The Lavaca Street site had long been a traditional remonstrance gathering point, especially when capital punishment was to occur. It was the only location where protests could take place that state officials and the governor had to witness during comings and goings at the mansion.

As protesters marched peacefully along the sidewalk north of the mansion, coming from the direction of the Capitol, Austin police moved in with horses to block them from getting to the coveted protest site where they could draw Bush's attention as his motorcade exited.

The police intended for Bush to leave without having to hear or see any adverse political discourse. They did allow reporters and a handful of sign-waving Bush backers at the Lavaca Street site, belying any security argument they might have made.

Democracy Coalition, an ad hoc community group, and thirteen of its members, with TCRP's assistance, sued the city of Austin and two officers on horses, alleging free speech and assembly violations under the federal and state constitutions.

We drew an overtly hostile judge for trial, Margaret Cooper, who outright dismissed the case against the city without letting the jury hear it. She summarily rejected the idea that there was a special free speech and assembly site across from the mansion because, she said, every public place was a special free speech and assembly location. A novel comment and legally off the wall.

That left only the two mounted officers for trial. The jurors cleared them, finding they had not injured any demonstrators or personally prevented marchers from moving forward. Intimidating protesters with horses apparently wasn't serious enough in this scenario. Or maybe they picked up on the judge's antagonism to the case and her dismissal of the city as a defendant.

Democracy Coalition appealed the judge's dismissal of the case against the city and won. The Court of Appeals in Austin sent the lawsuit back for trial as to whether city policies violated the protesters' free speech rights under the Texas Constitution.

Judge Cooper threw out the case once again, saying, quite contrary to logic and settled law, that, if the two officers weren't individually culpable, then the city itself couldn't be culpable. A second appeal ensued, and Democracy Coalition notched another victory.

The lawsuit came back again, this time to Judge Gisela Triana (Cooper having retired). She moved the trial forward.

Democracy Coalition won, buttressed by the testimony of the veteran Austin officer who had overseen protests for years. His responsibility was to supervise police interactions with demonstrators and keep it all running smoothly while respecting people's free speech and assembly rights.

The captain testified that, contrary to Austin police protocols, he was not in charge that day, opining that the Secret Service may have called the plays, although higher-ups kept mum on that point.

He was forthright that the police had managed the protest wrongly and that he would have allowed the demonstrators to proceed to the Lavaca site, which he acknowledged was a traditional protest assembly point. He

LAW STUDENT SCHOOLS ASSISTANT AUSTIN CITY ATTORNEY

TCRP's customary practice with law student interns was to involve them as much as possible in the mechanics of legal practice and not just sequester them away to write legal memoranda (a fate that befell their peers at big law firms).

In the Democracy Coalition case, one of our summer interns argued against the city's pretrial motion to dismiss the lawsuit. She won, and the city's lawyer literally had a hissy fit in the courtroom, slamming a book on the counsel table. How dare a second-year law student prevail against a seasoned and opinionated city attorney! That, of course, made the intern's victory even sweeter; she relished the win.

The student was later chosen to introduce Barack Obama at a huge outdoor Austin rally on a campaign swing during his first run for the presidency.

summarily deep-sixed the city's defense in a matter of minutes on the witness stand, and the judge lauded his honesty.

Judge Triana awarded judgment and attorney fees against the city. The city wisely opted not to appeal.

THE CRAWFORD 5 AND VISITING THE BUSH RANCH

We had a second Bush case two years later. Before becoming president, then-Governor Bush had bought the Prairie Chapel Ranch seven miles outside Crawford in 1999 to pump up his newly found man-of-the-people ranch cred as he moved toward seeking the White House.

Crawford, a half-hour drive southwest of Waco, had seven hundred inhabitants at the time. Bush stationed the "Western White House" there and often retreated to the ranch for long weekends and noticeably extended vacations.

Right after Bush was elected president, the town, whose residents were fans, enacted an ordinance making it a misdemeanor crime to hold a procession, parade, or demonstration in any public space in Crawford without giving fifteen days' notice, paying a $25 fee, and obtaining the sheriff's permission. The law also confined demonstrators to the local high-school football field and did not define how many people constituted a procession, parade, or demonstration.

With the March 2003 Iraq invasion, the Western White House became a focus of antiwar demonstrations when Bush was there. Peace organizers managed to locate a house in the middle of Crawford as their base for demonstrations at the ranch, typically on weekends. They dubbed it the "Peace House."

The townsfolk were chagrined at being catapulted into national politics, or so they claimed, while certainly enjoying the economic boost that the protesters and attendant radio and television reporters brought.

The advance protest notice requirement, which the city later reduced to seven days, was an impossible requisite, since, for security reasons, no one knew that far in advance when Bush would arrive. And being confined to the high-school football stadium nullified the goal of demonstrating directly against Bush.

The ordinance effectively outlawed any protest caravan leaving or moving through town on the way to the Bush ranch. It was the closest to a total First Amendment ban I ever encountered, and local constabulary was dead set on enforcing it.

Inevitably, the ordinance snared a group of five folks in early May 2003. A police blockade stopped them on their way to the ranch when the Australian prime minister was visiting, which, for the activists, was a national media opportunity. Police arrested them and threw them in jail for the night. They became known celebrity-wise as the "Crawford 5." Not surprisingly, the police did nothing about the counterprotesters flying Confederate flags at the blockade site.

On the appointed trial date, the Crawford 5 "miscreants" and fifty or so friends gathered at the Peace House and, chanting, marched through the neighborhood with antiwar placards to the Tonkawa Falls Event Center a mile away. The trial was to take place there because the regular municipal courtroom was too small. The morning was cool and sunny, perfect for a march.

At the event center, basically a dance hall, the part-time municipal judge sat at an old wooden table on the band stage. Even though elevated above us, he was clearly in over his head. It might have been his first jury trial as a judge—or so it seemed. The city attorney spent much of the trial up on the large dais next to the judge, directing him.

The trial came as close to a kangaroo court as one could imagine. An array of townspeople filled the front seats as prospective jurors. Selecting six fair jurors was an impossible challenge. As many as half the assembled individuals, including an Episcopal clergyman, flatly said up front they could not be fair and impartial. At least they were honest, more so than those eventually seated as the jury.

Crawford Police Chief Donnie Tidmore, one of those older, small-town career chiefs, offered some remarkable trial testimony that, under the ordinance, he could arrest someone for simply wearing a "Peace" button while walking on a sidewalk (he said it was a procession) or for distributing leaflets anywhere in the city, even to friends or others who might want to read them.

The chief floundered around, with a deer-in-the-headlights look, when trying to explain why the ordinance did not apply to the game-night caravans that raucously paraded throughout town on Fridays. He eventually just shrugged his shoulders. Nor, according to Tidmore, could a caravan simply leave town on the way to the Bush ranch without running afoul of the ordinance. He could not articulate any reason for blockading the exit from the town toward the ranch. Not that making any sense was paramount in his mind. He just knew they wanted to suppress out-of-town protesters.

It was a classic political trial, the Crawford 5 testifying about why they were protesting the Iraq invasion. The activists admitted they never obtained a permit but pointed out they were not engaged in a demonstration when the police arrested them as they left town.

When the case finally went to the six jurors for judgment, to our wonderment, they stayed out for a few hours. Then we realized it was so they could have a free dinner, courtesy of the town, a benefit of jury duty.

To no one's surprise the jurors returned guilty verdicts. They convicted four of the protesters but acquitted one, a softspoken matronly church worker from Dallas. The jury fined our folks between $200 and $500 each, the only discernible difference being how much jurors disliked a particular activist.

We promptly appealed to the McLennan County Court at Law in Waco. The judge there was attuned to the ordinance's severe First Amendment flaws and promptly overturned the convictions. The judge relished his position against the ordinance, which was so poorly crafted that it was a gift to any jurist looking to do the right thing.

The Crawford 5 then filed a civil rights lawsuit in federal district court in Waco, which the city quickly settled for $43,000; it also repealed the ordinance. Crawford paid a hefty price for not tolerating relatively mild dissent in Bush's backyard and gratuitously jailing people overnight.

POLICE RUN AMOK IN SOCORRO SCHOOL DISTRICT: THE MONTWOOD HIGH SCHOOL WALKOUT

Representing students was a TCRP priority. Society typically overlooks them and easily disregards their rights. Student groups also have a hard time finding attorneys to help them vindicate their rights.

One important case happened in El Paso. TCRP became involved in the aftermath of a 2003 walkout and protest by a thousand Montwood High School students in the Socorro School District, adjacent to El Paso. The school administrators called in the El Paso police to make sure everything stayed peaceful. Instead, they brought chaos and violence into a nonviolent protest.

The school's sudden, radical reordering of the curriculum structure—going from the usual hourly classes to a solid block schedule—provoked the demonstration, which the school permitted the students to hold.

About a hundred officers showed up and, unbidden, decided to intervene. They rampaged throughout the campus, clubbing students, a teacher, and a pregnant young woman. The police tried to physically force students back into the school. The building had only four doors that they could use for reentry, which compounded the chaos. Police arrested five students for rioting but prosecuted none. Twenty people ended up in the hospital. Not a single officer faced discipline for excessive force.

We partnered with Texas RioGrande Legal Aid and two local attorneys in a federal lawsuit on behalf of the arrested students and the teacher beaten by an officer. The police knocked one plaintiff, a junior, to the ground with a baton, then handcuffed and pepper-sprayed him. One officer held a knee to his head. The young man ended up needing professional counseling because of the trauma. The injured teacher had been outside checking on the students' well-being. An officer assaulted him from behind while he was ushering kids back into the building. His offense? Asking for the officer's badge number.

During the lawsuit, we learned people had lodged more than 4,300 excessive force complaints against El Paso police in the prior eight years, which averages out to more than one per day. That is an astronomical number given the general reluctance of aggrieved individuals to file complaints against officers. The numbers betrayed a toxic culture of brutality. I had never seen a police department with anywhere near that number of excessive force complaints. It was mind-blowing and made me wonder what was going on with El Paso PD.

Within a few months the attorneys defending the school and the police realized that litigation would be prolonged, expensive, and likely result in an unfavorable outcome. Facing the music, they agreed to a daylong Saturday mediation and settled the case in the late evening with monetary compensation for the students and the teacher ($195,000, including attorney fees), as well as the creation of a police deescalation program. Jack Ryan, a respected law enforcement expert, retrained the entire police force on how to appropriately oversee protests, and at schools specifically, according to constitutional norms.

That more students and faculty did not join the suit was disappointing. Those who did sign on as plaintiffs took pride in the result they obtained

THE ORIGIN OF TCRP'S EL PASO OFFICE

Because of TCRP's involvement in earlier civil rights cases in El Paso and the Montwood school case, El Paso community members asked us to open an office there, which we did: the El Paso del Norte Civil Rights Project.

The invitation to establish a presence in El Paso and get proximate to that community, which had its own civil rights struggles, was an honor. El Paso was always a hotbed of "good trouble." The El Paso office also oversaw a West Texas Violence Against Women Act program and eventually opened a satellite office in Odessa that became a free-standing TCRP center.

It was quite painful that TCRP shuttered the office sometime after I retired.

for themselves and their community thanks to their perseverance. They had a keen sense of outrage that was good to help channel.

KKK RALLIES IN AUSTIN'S FREE SPEECH PLAZA

On the sunny Saturday morning before the November 2005 state constitutional referendum that banned gay marriage and comparable arrangements, a dozen American White Knights of the Ku Klux Klan, with advance publicity, roared in from San Angelo riding motorcycles to demonstrate at Austin's City Hall Free Speech Plaza. A few (a very few) individuals of similar ilk joined them in favor of the referendum and the "white Christian values" embraced therein and "supported by God."

Not surprisingly, Austinites organized a march and counterdemonstration, outnumbering the Klan squad by the thousands (three thousand to be accurate). However, two hundred Austin police officers set up a blockade around a two-block perimeter of the rally, prohibiting counterprotesters from getting anywhere close to the KKK. Even more bizarre (and intimidating) were officers, visibly armed with rifles stationed atop building roofs, lining the counterprotesters' four-block parade route. Police helicopters whirled overhead. The police suppressed the anti-Klan protesters.

What the police chief called a "safety zone" was in fact a police-engineered deconstitutionalized zone that effectively silenced the anti-Klan demonstrators. They were neither within earshot nor within view of the White Knights. Police have a duty to maintain order, but people also have a right to make their voices heard.

The Wednesday before the KKK event, the city suddenly notified media representatives that they needed special credentials to attend. They either had to be full-time news staffers or submit a "reference letter" from two news agencies that had recently hired them as freelance staff. The new policy blocked alternative, non–mainstream press representatives and documentarians. The credential requirement was such that neither Ben Franklin nor Tom Paine would have qualified as a press representative.

On the Monday after the Klan rally and thwarted counterrally, TCRP filed a federal suit on behalf of eight plaintiffs. Five were individual citizens blocked by the police buffer zone. The other three were independent media producers challenging the city's process for censoring which media had access to the plaza.

Our lawsuit sought to invalidate the city's bogus credentialing process as unconstitutional and to ban its use in the future. The plaintiff activists also requested a court order requiring the city and its police to better plan and organize for demonstrations yet to come so they didn't interfere with, or impede, the First Amendment rights of protesters, counterprotesters, and media.

Thanks to the help of one of our star volunteer cooperating attorneys, the city settled the case and put in place new measures that allowed counterprotesters to get near to protesters, like the procedures the Texas Department of Public Safety uses at state Capitol protests and counterprotests. The city also set up a neutral credentialing system for the future.

THE ROUND ROCK 99: STUDENT IMMIGRATION PROTESTS

In March 2006, teenagers across the nation cut school for a day and joined protests against proposed federal legislation to increase penalties for illegal immigration and to classify as felons undocumented people and anyone who helped them enter or remain in the United States. If passed, the law would ensnare benevolent charities and church groups that provided food, water, and temporary shelter. For churches, such assistance was part of their religious missions. The students' activism was inspiring, and the country took note.

The protests not only rejected the proposed law but also demanded comprehensive reform of the country's immigration laws, including a path to citizenship for undocumented immigrants. Millions of protesters marched and rallied across the United States. Some viewed the mobilizations as a turning point in Latino politics, especially as to Latino civic participation and political influence. Sponsors of the prospective legislation gave up the ghost and did not proceed.

The responses to the walkouts were as varied as the locations. In some areas, the community supported them and school officials tolerated them. In other places, students faced consequences ranging from stern lectures to suspensions to having their right to attend school prom revoked.

Several Texas schools joined the day of action, and administrators mostly practiced tolerance or issued mild rebukes. Round Rock Independent School District was an outlier. The district went into full-throttle overreaction and enlisted the local constabulary's help, which issued 209 criminal misdemeanor citations to protesting students, accusing them of violating the city's youth daytime curfew or disrupting class. Punishment for these infractions was a fine up to $500.

The collaborative heavy-handedness of school administrators and police drew public outrage and rebuke locally and around the nation. A group of upset parents came to TCRP, mostly proud of their students' budding political consciousness and arguing their kids had First Amendment protest rights. Ensnaring their children in the criminal justice system for legal activity was downright reprehensible.

TCRP organized a cadre of sympathetic pro bono (meaning there is no charge for legal services) criminal defense attorneys, including former Attorney General Jim Mattox, to represent eighty-two arrested students. The city prosecutor was adamant about convicting these up-and-coming leaders of the community, even if it meant tying up municipal courts in jury trials for the next year or two.

The city was hard-pressed to defend itself, since the ordinance that required students to be in school provided an exception for exercising free speech rights. But prosecutors wanted to evaluate each case individually because they contended some students had skipped school merely for the fun of it. This meant many students and their families would be on edge for months, if not a year or more, awaiting criminal trial outcomes.

After several jury trials with varying results (mostly good) and some case dismissals by judges, it became obvious that a strategy of waiting until all trials had concluded before filing a civil rights case against the school district and police was unsupportable.

Several students' trials would go past the statute of limitations, which in this case required any lawsuit to be brought within two years of the event complained about. Not filing a case within two years forfeits the right to sue.

Besides this concern, such an extensive number of criminal cases was a burden on the pro bono defense lawyers. Moreover, some cases would come to trial after a student had graduated and left for college. They would have to return for trial at the family's expense.

We decided to go ahead with a First Amendment federal lawsuit, arguing that the students had the right to protest without repercussions under the criminal law. We had ninety-nine plaintiffs, which included seventeen who had not been arrested but were facing school discipline. These were the famous "Round Rock 99."

We faced head-on a problematic issue with this approach, imposed by the US Supreme Court in *Younger v. Harris* (1971), which decided that, in most lawsuits, a federal judge should not move forward in a civil rights case until underlying state criminal cases were resolved one way or the other. *Younger* is nearly an impossible wall to hurdle, with very few exceptions; it's a very narrow doorway indeed. The delay would have been onerous to our clients.

We drew US District Judge Lee Yeakel for the Round Rock 99 case. He held a preliminary hearing on a Monday in early January, in the middle of a snowstorm. We proceeded by phone. Opposing counsel confidently argued that *Younger* applied and that the judge should not proceed with our case.

However, the judge responded, "Well, what if I find that the *Younger* criteria have been met and they are entitled to proceed with the federal case?" There was audible stunned silence on the line from opposing counsel, almost a gasp.

That telephone chat with the judge moved the police and school district immediately into mediation and settlement talks. Two pro bono attorneys from respected Austin law firms jumped in to help champion our cause.

As a result of settlement, the city dropped all criminal charges against all of the students who had participated in the immigration protests and were part of the lawsuit. The city also set up a fund to pay $400 to each

TEACHING THE *YOUNGER* DOCTRINE

By the time of this meeting with Judge Yeakel, I had taught every kind of case in my UT constitutional law seminar from my own experience, except one. I had never litigated a case that involved the *Younger* doctrine. The Round Rock 99 case completed my journey of living through all the cases and legal theories covered by the textbook, sometimes happily, sometimes sadly, depending on their outcome. But it was quite something to realize that I had finally litigated every type of case included in the casebook.

student for legal fees if they wanted to expunge their arrest records, giving them a clean slate.

In exchange, the students took a three-hour, Saturday morning civics class on constitutional rights and duties, with instructors agreed upon by the students' lawyers and sometimes including those same lawyers. That gave us a prime opportunity to empower the students with helpful knowledge about protests and the First Amendment.

From the time of the demonstration through settlement, more than eighty students who were not part of the suit opted to plead guilty or no-contest to their citations, agreeing to pay fines or perform community service. They wanted an easy way out and declined to stand up.

It was a good lesson for the Round Rock 99 who stood their ground: they could organize and prevail against the police and school district in the face of injustice. It was also a good lesson for the other students, the police, and the school district.

Jim Mattox summed up the irony and pathos of the situation: "We criticize our young people for not being interested in civic affairs. We send them to school to have them study government and political science and then, when they decide they're going to exercise their rights, we're trying to slap them down. It's un-American."

The police captain, who vigorously led the issuing of citations to the students, frankly admitted that most of them were passionate about their cause, but we "don't turn our heads when a crime is committed, no matter if it's just a little bitty one, because it's important to hold people accountable."

The brazen nonsense of such a comment didn't seem to dawn on him. How much better off the Round Rock community would have been had the authorities helped guide the students' legitimate voices of dissent rather than slamming down an iron fist? In the end, the students helped the captain and his cohorts learn accountability under democratic norms.

The Round Rock settlement set aside $45,000 to cover the cost of expunging students' arrest records. Only $41,000 was necessary, leaving a $4,000 balance. Under the settlement TCRP could use that balance to award a college scholarship to a Round Rock protestor. We did so based on the "Shout Out for Your Rights" writing contest.

The scholarship went to a graduating senior so she could begin community college that summer. Her essay described how she was pulling her life together after having a baby, who had a disability, at age fifteen. Her parents had divorced, and she was caring for her very ill father. Her life was rough. Being part of the protest was a step in her developing maturity and social responsibility, which she articulated poignantly in her essay.

This story closes with a comment by student Kim Arteaga: "I think it was on my mind, and so I spoke it. I knew that they [immigrants] were afraid to go out there because they thought, 'Well, I could get sent back to Mexico,' and so I wanted to do it for them." Kim, a junior at the time, is only one of the amazing and inspiring people whom we were honored to represent throughout the years. She made her parents proud.

Often, potential clients like the Round Rock kids and parents would assemble in our offices and make clear that their fight and potential lawsuit were not just for themselves but for others in the community lest they suffer similar affronts to personal dignity and basic human rights. That commitment and sincerity always strengthened the litigation and frequently impressed judges, juries, and even opposing parties.

It is good to see that students at Round Rock High School have continued their walkout tradition on issues like gun violence, reproductive rights, and inadequate COVID-19 protocols. Hopefully, TCRP's legal assistance had something to do with that. That was our aim.

OCCUPY WALL STREET BUT NOT AUSTIN'S FREE SPEECH PLAZA

TCRP had to bring the city of Austin to federal court again, this time in 2011, representing two demonstrators who challenged "banning" prohibitions imposed by the city on protesters during the nationwide Occupy Wall Street movement.

Ironically, the city was objecting to the Occupy Austin protesters' use of its spacious, vaunted public Free Speech Plaza in front of City Hall, staying all day and into the night, even though the protest was peaceful.

The city, invoking a hastily issued change of use policy, arrested people who stayed past a 10 p.m. curfew and then took the startling prior restraint step of banning ninety-five protesters from all city property. The bans ranged from weeks to months, even years, and applied to all municipal property of whatever kind—even the city's public service and utility offices. Nor could they even get into City Hall to see their council representative.

The new rule empowered city administrators with the discretion to ban any person from a public city space whom they deemed unreasonably disruptive, regardless of their free speech and assembly rights and whatever "unreasonably disruptive" meant to the official.

The capricious and arbitrary bans clamped down on the Occupy Austin protesters, about eighty to a hundred individuals during the day and twenty or fewer into the evening. Prior restraints on speech and assembly are anathema to the First Amendment, something to which the city seemed oblivious. They are doubly abhorrent when imposed arbitrarily.

Of the two plaintiffs whom TCRP assisted, one was charged with criminal trespassing after taking pictures of police officers. He showed up in court, impeccably dressed in suit and tie, and testified that his Christian beliefs moved him to protest Wall Street's aggrandizement of wealth to the detriment of poor people. The police arrested the other banned man at the Occupy Austin site on an outstanding warrant for running a stop sign on his bike. He appeared in court in what I would describe as a standard "Keep Austin Weird" outfit.

The case concluded in the protesters' favor. US District Judge Lee Yeakel excoriated the city in a written decision peppered with sharp language about flaunting First Amendment law.

RETALIATION BY POLITICIANS AGAINST CITIZENS

Another genre of First Amendment issues that came TCRP's way dealt with retaliation against people who offended political leaders by word or deed. Nonurban politicians are major offenders. Two TCRP cases stand out in this area of litigation.

The first case addressed whether there is meaningful protection under the First Amendment in some areas of rural Texas. TCRP litigated a federal case on behalf of two West Texas juvenile probation officers, Paula Savage and John Denton, who were fired by the joint juvenile probation board, which was composed of four judges from three local counties. They were terminated in late 1981 and early 1982, respectively, after angering the judges by advocating for an African American boy with an intellectual disability who was having trouble with the legal system.

It began when Denton and Savage upset Clifton Independent School District administrators by insisting that they place the young boy in a school with remedial teaching to accommodate his mental disability. When the district refused, they complained to the Texas Education Agency (TEA), asserting the district acted adversely to the young student because of his race.

School districts in rural areas are often the largest employer in a county and wield considerable political clout. The superintendent was upset at the TEA complaint and got word to the judges, who then fired the two probation officers.

Denton and Savage together sued the judges for unlawfully terminating them in retaliation for the exercise of their First Amendment rights. John had served eight years as a probation officer. One of the defendant judges even testified at trial that John was one of the best probation officers in the state.

Through the skillful work of staff attorney Peter Hofer, John and Paula won their jury trial in 1996. The judges appealed, but the US Fifth Circuit Court of Appeals affirmed the $228,506 judgment against them. The judges also had to pay TCRP's attorney fees, making the victory even sweeter.

The judges' obstinacy cost the three counties dearly; but politicians rarely care about wasting taxpayer money to defend their own egos. There was no question that the judges cavalierly spurned John's and Paula's First Amendment rights. To their credit, John and Paula did their part to make that area of Texas a more just place. It took courage and involved risk.

It was heartening that a West Texas jury stood behind them. For TCRP, it was crucial to bring this message to rural areas, where political leaders often act like the constitution doesn't apply to them.

Three unrelated but successful lawsuits help illustrate how elected politicians easily slip into abusing power and reveal their tissue-thin skins when community activists call them out. This trio of cases helped ordinary citizens push back against city mayors who were intent on abusing their official powers.

In 2007, the *LareDOS* newspaper sharply criticized the mayor's development plans for Laredo. He took umbrage and ordered all copies of the newspaper seized ($400 worth) from its racks at City Hall and the airport visitor center. An absurdly amusing video showed the mayor running around the airport purloining the papers. The mayor apologized, and city taxpayers had to lay out $15,000 for his foolish First Amendment violations.

A former mayor named Pat Townsend and the then-current mayor of Mission, Norberto Salinas, together sued the activist Ester Salinas (no relation) for slander in 2005 because of her extremely strong complaints at city commission meetings and on Spanish television, ripping the officials for not addressing the problem of heavy pesticide drift into poor residential areas from a nearby chemical factory.

The mayors called her a "troublemaker," a title she wore even more proudly in 2012 after winning an impressive free speech victory against them in the Supreme Court of Texas thanks to the outstanding effort of our South Texas director, Corinna Spencer-Scheurich.

The third mayor case involved Othal Brand, featured in earlier chapters. This happened when I was still in the Valley. Residents of Colonia Balboa south of McAllen were at a city commission meeting, complaining again about the abysmal lack of public services in their impoverished community. Brand lost his temper and rammed through a new city ordinance on the spot prohibiting people from Colonia Balboa from ever again speaking at city commission meetings. We were in court the next day, and Brand was put in his place. This is another of those cases you can't make up.

Litigation tamed the mayors. While these cases were slam dunks, we had to step in because our clients could not afford to hire lawyers. The cases reflect a trend of small local jurisdictions (and sometimes larger ones) retaliating against individuals for exercising their First Amendment rights.

How often do politicians get away with this stuff because no one is around like TCRP to beat them back for low-income community folks?

FREE SPEECH AND ASSEMBLY RIGHTS ON PRIVATE PROPERTY UNDER THE TEXAS CONSTITUTION

In June 1983, promptly after arriving at the Texas Civil Liberties Union, I partnered with another attorney to use the Texas Bill of Rights to extend state constitutional free speech and assembly rights for a local peace group in Austin's expansive Barton Creek Square Mall, even though the group had no federal First Amendment protection.

The First Amendment applies only to public property and public actors, not to the private sector. Our federalist system allows states to provide greater protection than federal law, but never less. A few states had moved in the direction of deciding that shopping malls—given their extensive physical layout, marketing, and commercial practices—functioned in modern times like the old public square. Therefore, state constitutional protections safeguarded the exercise of free speech and assembly rights within a quasi-public mall.

A small team of Nuclear Freeze campaign representatives were collecting signatures from passersby on a petition to the local Congress member. They limited their efforts to a single stationary booth.

Our gambit succeeded, and we won a trial court order in 1983 against the mall on behalf of the campaign. The district judge applied the logic of the public square and protected the activists' exercise of free speech. The mall did not appeal, and the court order became permanent.

An interesting twist was that years later, in 1999, TCRP was conducting an anti–race discrimination Equality Under the Law campaign against local businesses. We were holding a press conference inside Barton Creek Square Mall with three Mexican American plaintiffs in front of Johnny Rockets, an offending restaurant.

The mall called the police, who arrested me for trespass, no matter how much I insisted on the earlier court order. We filed suit against the mall, arguing that the 1983 court order meant that the mall was a public space for Texas constitutional purposes. The mall dropped the trespass charges.

Unfortunately, appellate judges decided that the earlier court order

ANOTHER VISIT TO JAIL BY YOURS TRULY

A funny sidebar to my Barton Creek arrest is that the TCRP staff all went to lunch when I was jailed. Nobody was there to answer the phone to give me a ride back to the office after posting personal bond. Fortunately, the walk from the county jail to the office was only a couple of miles.

Sometimes the thought has crept through my mind that maybe the staff was there and chose not to answer the phone and rescue me. This was the last of my three or four arrests for pushing the civil rights envelope (and one narrow escape from contempt of court).

This arrest drew a biting, tongue-in-cheek article about the mall from the *Texas Observer* headlined "Johnny Racist."

protected only the Nuclear Freeze campaign and no one else. The judges were clear about where they were going on this issue. The courts had become markedly more conservative. That put a damper on pursuing free speech and assembly breakthroughs under the Texas Constitution.

We had similar mixed luck with an earlier civil suit against Albertsons. Four United Farm Workers members were doing consumer leafleting at the grocery store on a Saturday, asking shoppers not to buy non–UFW produced grapes. Albertsons had them arrested for criminal trespass.

The boycotters then sued the store for transgressing their free speech rights under the Texas Constitution. The Austin jury awarded $750 to each picketer. This was a breakthrough case in that there could be a monetary award for violation of Texas constitutional free speech rights on private premises. Up to that point, our success had been limited to securing a court order to allow access to private property.

The victory was short-lived, however. Albertsons appealed, and the appellate judges decided in 1993 that, even if the state constitution protected free speech access to private property, it did not mean there would be monetary recompense. The most would be a court order allowing entry to private premises. Not a bad result, but it was not what we had hoped. Prospective money damages and paying attorney fees are always a good deterrent against unconstitutional actions.

We had a free speech clash with Whole Foods Market five years earlier, before it became a conglomerate, when the store had four people arrested (the "Whole Foods 4") and sued to halt a grape boycott picket. The store settled after a UFW volunteer acquired damaging information about health department inspections and the store's deceptive repackaging of baked goods. It had rewrapped Sara Lee products as its own specialty item. The truth became known when a customer, who had unwittingly bought the Sara Lee item, went into sugar shock after eating the pastry.

TWO EARLY VICTORIES: STUDENTS' FREEDOM OF THE PRESS

In fall 1987, we helped on a case where students drew cartoon depictions of the school principal as part of a contest. Four rebellious Bryan High School students published a satiric underground newsletter, "Twisted Times," critiquing the school, as one might expect (and hope). They distributed their limited edition publication from the sidewalk across the street from the school.

The editor had a creative slant on criticizing Principal Jerry Kirby, whom many students thought didn't have much of a visible presence on campus. The middle of the front page featured a large blank square, advertised as a "Draw Principal Kirby" contest, complete with prizes of a sardonic nature.

The principal took umbrage and suspended the novice journalist and squelched the newsletter. We wrangled a quick Friday afternoon court hearing; the judge restored the budding publisher to school, and the newsletter went forward.

We later settled the case by clearing the student's record and winning compensation because the suspension affected his college and scholarship applications. We also negotiated a student publication policy to protect students going forward.

Such a shame to punish ingenuity rather than celebrate it. The newsletter had a prominent spot in my desk drawer for years, always good for a smile. Unfortunately, Principal Kirby would probably win these days, at least from a First Amendment perspective, given the US Supreme Court's continuing erosion of high school students' rights.

There's something profoundly disturbing about teaching students that they are to be productive citizens and leaders in a democratic society when they turn eighteen but denying them basic rights until they reach a magic birthday or graduate from high school, whichever occurs later. They can vote at eighteen if they are in school. That's pretty much it.

Principal Kirby predates the modern "Mr. Kirby" meme. How that meme would have played into the students' newsletter is fascinating speculation.

Another case centered on the suppression of a college newspaper and how events led to awarding scholarships. Writing about the Bryan High School case in the previous section caused me to reflect on my first student free press case in 1977 while with the South Texas Project. The president of Pan American University (now University of Texas Rio Grande Valley) prohibited further publication of the *El Sol* student newspaper and seized all copies on campus. *El Sol* had reported on possible financial irregularities involving university funds. Another certain reason, unspoken, was its activist Chicano bent. There was no love lost between the students and the president, who represented the Anglo old guard.

We filed a lawsuit and held a hearing in federal court. When it became clear we were going to win, even with a conservative judge, the university caved. Part of the settlement, besides reinstating the newspaper, was a $3,500 fund, from which *El Sol* awarded two $250 scholarships per semester until exhausting the fund. The scholarship value in today's dollars would be $1,250 each.

TAKEAWAYS: STUDENT ACTIVISM IS CRUCIAL

It was fun working with students. Our society gives them so little legal support, and often penalizes them, while we tell them to get ready to be future leaders. "Back-ass-ward," as Texans would say. I found students to be creative and refreshing and regretted that our culture was corrupting their innocence.

Our free speech lawsuits are among many examples of providing free legal assistance to people and community organizations that could not otherwise afford legal help. Were it not for TCRP, the authorities would have gotten away with trampling on the people's rights and undermining their organizing. Sometimes, governmental entities did succeed in undercutting the organizing but eventually paid a price. Our hope was that the penalty would keep them from repeating their nefarious deeds, although that may be hoping for too much.

Free speech and assembly lawsuits were always a pleasure to manage because the groups and individuals whom we represented were intense and passionate about their causes. They were fervently committed to protecting the rights of the entire community and knew the impact lawsuits would have in furthering laudable goals.

Such lawsuits gave people the space and protection they needed to organize, and they punished officials who trespassed on that hallowed democratic space sheltered by the federal and Texas Constitutions. The litigation fit perfectly into TCRP's vision of offering legal defense to those striving to vindicate social justice and human rights.

10

POLICE BRUTALITY, ACT II

The More Cops Change . . .

When I arrived in South Texas to work in 1973, I never dreamed that my career from that moment until retirement would involve suing law enforcement officials of all stripes; I filed more than seventy such lawsuits, some with significant impacts. The circle of attorneys who have overseen so many police lawsuits is small indeed.

At the South Texas Project and later at TCRP, we felt compelled to tackle police litigation because few other lawyers would risk it (for a variety of reasons) and because poor people and minority communities suffered the brunt of police brutality and misconduct. Abusive police power angered me. It was such a barefaced manifestation of oppressive physical force that unjustly altered people's lives that it had to be resisted. Compassion for the victims drove us forward in many instances.

Some of the most grievous cases that follow are divided by regions of the state, which makes it easier to track. A chronological sequence would be impossible, since over the years the litigation actions we undertook overlapped and intersected with each other and with our civil rights cases.

CORPUS CHRISTI: LOSING A THIRTEEN-WEEK TRIAL

After the McAllen C-Shift litigation wound down, staff attorney Richard Flores and I litigated a thirteen-week trial in 1983 in Corpus Christi over five police misconduct lawsuits, ranging from excessive force to false arrest, much like the McAllen cases. These cases, except for one, were consolidated into a single trial. The lawsuit overlapped with my joining the Texas Civil Liberties Union in 1983.

Because of the lawsuit's politically charged nature, the assigned judge brought in a former judge, Stanley Kirk, to oversee the litigation. In Texas, a former or retired state judge can be brought in as a visiting judge when local judges need assistance or have a politically contentious case.

No one disclosed that Kirk, originally from Wichita County, was a former judge because he had been criminally indicted (or was about to be) for attempting to surreptitiously alter a court reporter's trial transcript at night. He did not want the official transcript to reflect how he had berated jurors in a felony trial for ruling contrary to how he wanted them to rule. Jurors had complained to the State Commission on Judicial Conduct about his abusive behavior.

Kirk entered a plea deal. The criminal charge was dismissed (or not filed) in exchange for his resignation as a judge. Under Texas law at that time, he could still serve as a visiting judge, which he did. We would have fiercely objected to him as a judge had we known about his criminal history and lack of integrity. Because of the Commission on Judicial Conduct's secretive procedures, none of this information was publicly available.

We learned later that, during our trial, Kirk went sailing with the police chief, who himself had an unsavory reputation. By chance we ran into the chief chatting amicably with the judge in his office one morning before trial resumed. All this was inappropriate and unethical on Kirk's part given that the chief was also a defendant.

Kirk's conduct on the bench was so erratic at times that we took to calling him "Judge Quirk" behind his back. He obviously favored the police. After we lost the jury verdict, the police took pictures with him in the courtroom, all laughing.

When I vigorously called out Kirk's background in the media after finding out about it, long after we had lost the trial, one of the city's lawyers filed a grievance against me with the State Bar for impugning the judge. The First Amendment saved the day. Short shrift was made of the grievance, although that would have been a fun case to take to a jury and cross-examine a judge like Kirk on the witness stand.

Our next move was convincing the legislature to close the loophole and amend the law so that any judge who resigned or retired under a legal cloud could not later serve as a visiting judge. Kirk lost his gig and future boondoggles. It was small payback.

In retrospect, the situation was a setup. The city hired three high-powered attorneys to assist in the case. The establishment came together and plotted. They surely knew about Kirk's lack of integrity. They wanted him because they could keep him on a string. He was dependent on their largesse, not only for his time in Corpus Christi but also for prospective appointments.

Kirk played along and was compensated handsomely with taxpayers' money, but their conduct was outrageous and corrupted the legal system—and showed how easy it was to do.

Perhaps our mistake was filing in state court rather than federal court.

REVENGE AND SILENCING THROUGH STATE BAR GRIEVANCES

The Kirk-related grievance was the second time a judge's surrogate attempted to silence and punish me for speaking out against a judge. Both times, I prevailed.

Usually, the State Bar tries to resolve such matters quietly by asking the attorney to accept a private reprimand, that is, with no publicity about the disciplinary action. Of course, a second such complaint can escalate to more serious punishment.

I decided early on that judges were open to criticism. Most colleagues avoided doing that for the realistic fear it would adversely affect their cases. I would never accept a private reprimand because the First Amendment protected speech that was important to the public. Nor would I be cowed by an attempt to silence me.

In another instance, the *Wall Street Journal* quoted me in a front-page article taking to task US District Judge James Nowlin of Austin and other conservative judges for their ideological bent in rolling back civil rights protections. They were part of the initiative begun under President Ronald Reagan to add a political litmus test for selecting federal judges, an effort that has intensified in subsequent Republican administrations.

As fate would have it, I had to be in his courtroom the same day the article came out. He got in his dig from the bench in his typical understated, sarcastic fashion.

Being a badass can be risky, but not calling out those with power prolongs the community's oppression. It was my job to be vocal.

We had sought to avoid the federal court because the judge in that district was very conservative. He was going on senior status (semiretirement) but could have ended up overseeing the litigation had he wanted to. His incoming successor was equally conservative, a scion of one of the city's eminent powerbrokers.

Maybe another mistake was trying the individual cases together. The better approach might have been to litigate one case at a time, as we did with the McAllen police. Given the setup that played out, it might not have mattered. Our clients got railroaded. The case that was kept separate from the consolidated litigation went to trial with a different judge and was successful. In that case, the police wrongly arrested, searched, charged, and harassed a woman and her ten-year-old son.

It took a good while to recover from this loss. Remorse kicked in about failing our plaintiffs—working-class folks—who not only had to endure the adverse verdict but also walk away doubly abused by the police and the system. I admired their self-respect and dignity and felt deeply pained that we could not help deliver justice on their behalf.

Looking back on this, I am chagrined and regretful about how naïve we were as to what was going on around us and not putting two and two together. It left a painful scar on my soul that will never fully heal. How did I fail them? What could I have done differently? How much more humiliation did they end up enduring because they trusted in me? Even when you know the odds are heavily against you, being a civil rights attorney can be especially tough at times.

SAN ANTONIO AND THE SLOW DEATH KNELL OF NO-KNOCK WARRANTS

In recent years, no-knock warrants have found increasing disfavor with the courts, Congress, and local authorities—and rightly so. A no-knock warrant does not require police officers to announce themselves or knock on the door of an alleged suspect before bursting into a residence or any other location with guns drawn. The US Supreme Court allows such warrants only in very narrow circumstances. Whether no-knock warrants are prudent is another matter. Police love them in suspected drug cases, but they present great jeopardy to all involved.

The danger is obvious to both the officers and the people whose premises they are searching, particularly when the police execute a no-knock warrant in the middle of the night, as cops often prefer. These warrants are particularly dicey these days when weapons are abundantly available to people in a hyped-up gun culture of fear. Added to the high-risk level is that officers often do not wear uniforms. An officer could suddenly be facing a resident's weapon. One or the other or both might well end up dead, but usually it is the citizen.

TCRP had a signature no-knock warrant case that created major systemic change in 2009. It involved a San Antonio police officer who secured a no-knock warrant based on a confidential informant's tip. The warrant was to search the house of two women, a lesbian couple, on the informant's claim they ran a drug operation there.

Eight police officers (only one in uniform), using a battering ram, busted into the women's house in 2009 in the middle of the night and completely terrified them. It was a miracle that an officer didn't get shot. One of the women was grabbing for a pistol on the nightstand, but an officer entered the bedroom and intervened.

The police stayed in the house for two hours and humiliated the women, although both were cooperative. The police forced one of them to lie on the floor while handcuffed. Eventually, the police realized they had no justification for being there and unapologetically departed, leaving behind a smashed front door.

We suspected that the warrant was bogus because the officer lived near the women and may have had it in for them because of their sexuality. The federal district judge blocked us from finding out who the anonymous tipster was or any related information so we could discover whether there was justification for the warrant. The judge summarily threw out the case, leaving the two women with no remedy and allowing the police to operate with impunity by hiding behind an alleged informant.

We did not let the case die. A cooperating attorney from a respected New York law firm picked up the appeal for us and won a major victory in the US Fifth Circuit Court of Appeals in July 2018. San Antonio did not appeal. An appeal from a circuit court decision goes to the US Supreme Court for discretionary review at the court's option. There are twelve regional circuits in the United States.

Thanks to our cooperating counsel, the court lowered the boom on the San Antonio police in 2012, allowing the officers no good-faith excuse for how they executed the warrant. They violated the search and seizure guarantees of the Fourth Amendment and were liable in damages to the women. The court pretty much banned no-knock warrants in drug cases.

The general constitutional rule for executing a warrant is that the officers knock and identify themselves as the police, then serve the warrant on the person. If a person with an outstanding warrant doesn't respond but is on the premises, the officer is entitled to enter.

The US Supreme Court made some exceptions. One is that there is no need to knock and identify if a person's life is in grave danger (such as a hostage situation). The police may go ahead and burst into the premises.

That exception was extended to drug cases in which police allege that the person with the drugs would destroy them (flush them down the toilet, for example) before opening the door to receive the warrant. It got to the point that police were abusing this loophole so much that, even as law enforcement tried to enlarge the loophole, the courts began to narrow it significantly.

No-knock warrants are extremely dangerous both to the people inside the premises and to the officers, as history has repeatedly shown. They are even more dangerous when police execute them at night and in plainclothes, as they tend to do. They can, and commonly do, end in the death or injury of the inhabitants and, sometimes, of the police.

The trend now is to severely limit no-knock warrants and ban them altogether in drug cases. The city of Houston finally narrowed its no-knock policy in 2019 after the shooting death of a couple during a botched nighttime raid, precipitated by a fraudulent police affidavit on which the no-knock warrant was based. The man shot four officers during the raid, leaving one paralyzed, before the police killed him and his wife. An unnecessary tragedy all around. Houston ignored the Fifth Circuit San Antonio decision, and two innocent people paid for it with their lives.

After the Fifth Circuit victory, TCRP surveyed 161 of Texas's largest sheriff and municipal police departments regarding their no-knock warrant policies. At the time, only fifty-three agencies had a written policy about when no-knock entry was permitted.

TCRP's contribution to changing the no-knock law was enormous and undoubtedly protected the lives of many individuals in the future.

San Antonio banned no-knock warrants altogether in 2020.

CAPITAL AREA NARCOTICS TASK FORCE RUNS AMOK

TCRP's second warrant-related lawsuit (actually no warrant was issued) came about because of the ludicrous search in 2001 of a woman's rural property near Spicewood Springs. It was cowboy-like in its execution. The handful of residents there appeared to be of retired hippie vintage and referred to the fifty-six-year-old owner Sandra Smith as "Mother Sunshine." It is hard to imagine a debacle more comical and yet dangerous.

The pilot of a Department of Public Safety airplane searching overhead had the visual acuity to identify a small plot of marijuana in the yard. Alerted by the pilot, an ad hoc Capital Area Narcotics Task Force SWAT team helicoptered to the parking lot of a nearby convenience store, changed into their regalia, and rushed up the road helter-skelter onto the property, terrifying the occupants. They had no warrant and made no effort to obtain one from a judge.

After they realized that a thicket of common ragweed, not marijuana, had gotten the better of them, they left the premises ransacked without any apology, gratuitously kicking the dog on their way out.

Not only was the raid downright asinine and bungled, it placed Mother Sunshine into the Texas drug suspect database, for which she would be flagged in any police encounter, even a traffic ticket. It didn't take long for the county to settle.

The *Austin Chronicle* summarized it well: "No Weed, Just Dopes."

Police behavior of this type is perilous. This raid and two others, also in 2001, in which people were mistakenly killed (including a deputy) prompted the Travis County Sheriff's Office to pull out of the task force.

AUSTIN POLICE, PART 1: THE NAACP'S JUNETEENTH PETITION TO BLOCK FEDERAL FUNDING

The Austin NAACP, under Nelson Linder's steadfast leadership, and TCRP joined forces on a variety of important issues, most often about the Austin police. We shared a bully pulpit calling out police misconduct. Linder, a longtime advocate, characterized by his pencil mustache (now gray) and intensity of purpose, has acute political insight. We labored together for many years and were sharp thorns in Austin PD's side—and deservedly so. Linder, now in his midsixties, over the years single-handedly brought significant changes to bad police practices.

Austinites quietly accepted the differential between police conduct west of Interstate 35, which cuts through Austin, versus the eastside, where the minority communities reside. Police conduct on the westside was deferential. Mistreatment of the eastside communities was unshackled, sometimes with excessive brutality and a questionable police-caused death about once every year. Austin PD lacked moral or constitutional restraints.

It would not be unusual for an officer to tell an African American driver to exit the car and sit on the curb while the police searched the vehicle pursuant to the driver's manufactured "consent." Such searches were problematic constitutionally but a fact of life in East Austin. Despite styling itself as a progressive enclave in Texas, Austin was not much different from other big cities when it came to how the police treated the African American and Mexican American communities.

This misconduct continued to be so egregious that the Austin NAACP with TCRP's legal help petitioned the US Department of Justice to defund the police department of $3.2 million in federal grants until such time as it formally agreed to remedial steps. We filed this complaint, appropriately enough, on Juneteenth in 2004, announcing it with an outdoor press conference the morning of the annual march. We chose that date as symbolic. Ending slavery did not in itself end oppression and police violence.

The Juneteenth petition drew considerable publicity. Its sixteen pages detailed Austin PD's unabated unconstitutional conduct and discrimination over the years. Worse, though, was the number of individuals killed by the police. Between 1999 and 2003 alone, eleven people died from problematic police encounters. Only one who died was Caucasian; the rest were either Hispanic or African American.

To our surprise, given the few times that the Justice Department intervenes, it accepted our complaint and began an intensive review of Austin PD in 2007. Four years later, the police formally agreed to 160 detailed reform measures put forward by DOJ.

The retirement of the police chief and the hiring of a new one during this period facilitated the agreement. The new chief, who did not have an Austin PD background, used the DOJ report for reform measures without having to worry about being caught up in Austin PD's historical culture.

The 160 reforms looked good on parchment. However, as usually happens with police bureaucracies, implementation was another story. A year later, we had to hold another press conference to announce a new petition for DOJ to return to Austin and make good on the reforms. Nothing seemed to have changed, and there had been another dubious death at police hands. DOJ did not return but made the necessary inquiry. Austin PD clearly got the message.

AUSTIN POLICE, PART 2: MISCREANT COPS, LIES, AND VIDEOTAPES

Sometimes TCRP could find willing lawyers in Austin and other urban areas to oversee lawsuits against the local constabulary so we could dedicate our resources to other worthy endeavors. Some cases entailed egregious police misconduct and brutality that merited TCRP and media attention, as the following story illuminates.

Little did Austin police officer Michael Olsen know that a random outdoor surveillance camera on the nearby Texas Lottery building would be his undoing. The camera recorded, blow for blow, the beating he gratuitously inflicted on Jeffrey Thornton.

Jeffrey and a friend had been on Austin's iconic Sixth Street, celebrating Juneteenth 2002, when they witnessed Olsen roughing up another young African American man, seemingly for no reason. Jeffrey commented to his friend about it, mentioning the racial dynamic at play. Olsen overheard him, arrested him, and then beat him unconscious against the patrol car to the point that an ambulance had to come and transport Jeffrey to the hospital.

Olsen, a white officer, filed a resisting arrest charge against Jeffrey. Fortunately for Jeffrey, his uncle was an Austin police officer. He prompted an internal affairs investigation during which the video eventually came to light. Olsen's patrol car video camera was not operating during the brutal beating (by "happenstance," he said, as officers in similar beating situations often claim). But unlike Olsen, the nearby camera told no lies.

The video showed Olsen slugging Jeffrey with such force that Olsen raised him upward above the patrol car's roof and then showed Jeffrey falling to the ground. Jeffrey was of medium stature and build. Olsen, who was taller and looked like a gym regular, outweighed him by at least fifty pounds.

TCRP filed a civil rights case for the vicious thrashing. I still vividly remember taking Olsen's deposition on a cold, cloudy afternoon around Thanksgiving. We were in a small room together. He was a big guy and made no effort to be polite, as do most people during depositions. He was overtly hostile, spared no words, and left no doubt what an encounter on the street with him would be like. It was an unpleasant experience.

Austin PD Internal Affairs compared the video against Olsen's written report and determined he fabricated details of the beating. The police withdrew the criminal charges against Jeffrey. A grand jury indicted Olsen for filing a false government report.

The city settled the case, including a damage award for Jeffrey.

One wonders how many other victims Olsen had beaten, lied about, and convicted because no cameras recorded his brutality and rebutted his perjured testimony. Nor had an advocate inside the department.

Austin PD did not dismiss Olsen. He was terminated in 2007, five years later, for the unjustified killing of a twenty-five-year-old African American man. Olsen shot him in the back twice. Kevin Brown might still be alive had the department appropriately responded in the aftermath of Jeffrey's beating. The city settled the wrongful death suit for $1 million. The question in the minds of many: How could the police department leave a cop patrolling the streets after the Jeffrey Thornton incident and not risk exposing other African Americans to danger?

HOUSTON: A DEADLY POLICE BARRICADE PERMANENTLY INJURES TWO YOUNG MEN

The most emotionally wrenching lawsuits involve death or permanent disability. TCRP helped file a tragic permanent injury lawsuit with cooperating attorneys in Houston in August 2010.

A Harris County constable responded to a stalled vehicle call. An altercation took place with the driver. She knocked him down and took off in his patrol car. This began a high-speed freeway chase exceeding eighty miles per hour in which the Houston police became involved.

Houston officers decided to set up a roadblock on the freeway. They created a barrier for two of the three lanes by stopping other drivers so that their cars would be a barricade to her. They left one lane open and spiked it to flatten her tires if she sped through that lane, as they assumed she would for some foolish reason.

Instead, as anyone might foresee, she barreled into a car the police had stopped as part of their barrier. Two young men, ages nineteen and twenty, randomly detained as a part of the barricade, sitting in the car, suffered severe injuries and brain damage when the woman rammed into them.

What the police did—using the men as involuntary human shields—was incomprehensibly inane. How they could not have anticipated what might happen is beyond belief, yet the city of Houston fought the case. It landed in front of a federal judge who had formerly served as a Houston police officer. They may have thought he would give them a break, but the opposite happened. He wrote an opinion that their "conduct shocked the conscience."

The city eventually settled for $5 million, but no settlement could restore full body and brain capacity to the two men, who had young children. Both would require extensive in-home assistance or in-patient facility care for the rest of their lives and cannot provide for their kids. A very distressing case, one that still makes me angry.

WEST TEXAS: THE EL PASO SHERIFF AND IMMIGRATION HARASSMENT

There is another case worth mentioning because it underscores the importance of TCRP's reach into rural Texas.

At some juncture, El Paso County Sheriff Leo Samaniego, allegedly seeking higher employment in the US immigration apparatus, took it upon himself to enforce immigration law and deployed deputies in San Elizario, a small, poor Hispanic town twenty-two miles east of El Paso on the Rio Grande.

POLITICIANS' USE OF PUBLIC MONEY TO DEFEND THEMSELVES

José Rodríguez, the El Paso County Attorney and a longtime colleague, once advised me that, any time we were going to sue Sheriff Samaniego, we should file only against the county and not name the sheriff individually.

Whenever the sheriff was personally summoned to court, rather than relying on the county attorney, he would hire his own lawyer, who was much less amenable to working out cases. He preferred to fight regardless of merit.

José was an anomaly for county attorneys. He was interested in looking at an issue raised in litigation and seeing if there was a way to resolve it in the interest of justice without having to go to the mat. That was his approach to the cases we pursued there. It was easy to see why he was so well-respected, reelected, and then tapped to serve in the state senate.

The deputies' job was to stop regional buses and search for people who did not have legal documentation to be in the country, a barefaced unconstitutional operation. Police cannot randomly stop people and ask for proof of citizenship or question their status in the country.

The owner of Pepe's General Store near the roadblock disapproved of the operation and, after a deputy came in to his store to harass a customer (claiming the customer was evading the immigration checkpoint), displayed a protest sign in the window. The deputies arrested him for "unauthorized display of sign, signal, or marking." The district attorney dismissed the absurd charge.

TCRP's El Paso office sued the sheriff and deputies. The federal judge summarily rejected the lawsuit. We appealed and won in the Fifth Circuit, after which the county settled the lawsuit and ended the roadblock nonsense.

Sometimes I wonder what would have happened to the people in this unlawful scenario if TCRP had not staffed an El Paso office. Or if reaching into poorer rural areas of the state had not been a priority of ours.

THE HEARTBREAKING UNSUCCESSFUL CASES

Even though the number of TCRP's successful lawsuits is impressive by any measure, some heartrending lawsuits were lost. I have noted two of the most agonizing here. Another, Sophia King, appears in chapter 8 in the context of protecting disability rights.

In some cases, especially those that significantly alter people's lives without helping to lift them at least a little from their pain, one wants to cry. Doubts and remorse plague me about whether I could have done a better job with a better result. Did my ego get in the way during the trial and affect the outcome?

One of the toughest parts about being a civil rights attorney is losing a case for the people you are representing and then having to be back at the job early the next day. Sometimes I almost felt as if I had to place a stone coating around my heart and keep going, knowing in my mind that the legal system cannot always be on our side but still feeling sorrowful in spirit because of the loss.

A Death at the Border

One incredibly sad lawsuit involved the death of a nine-months' pregnant mother in 1977. She had gone to Las Flores, a dusty village on the Mexico side of the border south of Progreso, Texas. It was common for families to have relatives on both sides of the Rio Grande. The mother was bringing back a relative or family friend to help take care of her eleven children while she had the new baby.

Immigration officials detained her when she crossed back into Texas and viciously interrogated her, accusing her of illegally smuggling the young babysitter-to-be. During overbearing interrogation, witnessed by her children, she had a sudden seizure and died, along with her baby.

It did not take long for the UFW to assemble a picket at the bridge. We spent the night there, occupying the immigration offices, until the United States Attorney promised an investigation, which he followed through on. Nothing came of it.

We litigated the case before a federal jury in Brownsville. The jury did not find in favor of the family based on the doctrine of qualified immunity that lets law enforcement off the hook if they thought they were acting in good faith. I don't see much good faith here.

In addition, the judge ruled that, even if the officers had negligently mistreated the mother, her death was unforeseeable. The agents had no liability once her seizure happened because the ambulance could not have come from Weslaco, thirty minutes away, and carried her back to the hospital in time to render live-saving medical assistance for her and the baby.

The judge's argument was circular at best. This is one of those cases where a judge's discretion made all the difference. Here he could have helped, and maybe saved, the family. They were extremely poor, and the children appeared thin from malnourishment. I have always feared that the family fell apart because the mother was holding everyone together. The father was problematic, to put it charitably.

I can still see the girls in my mind, all of them together, the oldest being a young teenager, holding each other and supporting each other, unsure. I felt so bad, so very sad. The case still rends my heart.

Austin Police, Part 3: Sixteen-Year-Old Boy Shot in the Back

Another very painful loss involved a sixteen-year-old high-school student in 1985. He was out target shooting at a small campfire one summer with teenage friends, all Mexican American, at about 10 p.m. They were in a large and deep drainage ditch in South Austin. Neighbors called the police.

The officers arrived and decided to scare the kids. They snuck up on the teens in the dark and charged down the side of the ditch, terrifying the four boys, who panicked and scattered. A younger officer, confused by the chaos they caused, shot the boy in the back and killed him as he ran away. The case went to a jury, which ruled against the family. We were stunned.

Afterward, I asked the presiding juror, an Anglo, why the jury could possibly have ruled against the family. Her answer was emotionless and matter-of-fact: the boy should not have been out after curfew. Her statement was dumbfounding. Death should not be a consequence of violating curfew, an ordinance that the city rarely and spottily enforced. The city repealed the curfew ordinance (11 p.m. to 6 a.m.) in 2013.

When you lose a case, you have to turn and face your clients sitting next to you. That is difficult enough, but it was devasting in this case. The boy's parents took the verdict very hard and cried. I was despondent. I remember aimlessly walking around in a Sears the next day, Saturday morning, blaming myself, not sure why I was even at the store. I just had to get away. I returned home and went jogging for four miles.

This case exemplified the double standard of social and economic class unconsciously at play in police lawsuits, coupled with race and age (younger men of color have more difficult times with juries). Predominantly Anglo juries will tolerate excessive force and police misconduct in minority communities on the other side of the tracks (or the interstate, in Austin's case). But God help the police if they cross that line and bring their abuse into the white community.

Recent studies like that by Stephanie Romeo are exploring this double standard more, although I have seen it at play in my litigation. I first observed it in the McAllen police cases. It's a mutual experience with my colleagues. It underscores the critical importance of having juries that truly represent a cross-section of the community, as chapter 4 on grand jury reform discusses. I share the view that jury selection is the most important part of a trial, and that depends on having a cross-representative pool of prospective jurors from which to choose.

To experience this latent disparate bias in the context of a young boy unnecessarily killed and suddenly ripped from his family is excruciatingly sorrowful.

POLICE LITIGATION: ANY HOPE FOR CHANGE?

Police misconduct and brutality never seem to abate. The media's glaring spotlight may shine on grave misdeeds, but history teaches (and my experience affirms) this is only a momentary hiatus. We have been witnesses to this so repeatedly that it tends to numb our sensitivities, and we wonder if there is any solution.

It is a mystery why taxpayers do not revolt at the sky-high cost of litigation settlements and court judgments, which fortunately for victims have increased significantly over the years. Those settlements and judgments mean that something is badly amiss with the police. Why should taxpayers pay hefty sums for systemic incompetency or negligence that ends in injury and death? Until taxpayers rise up and without internal reformation, verdicts against the police will be seen as the cost of doing business.

Following are brief insights from my career on what works, what does not work, and what might work to curtail police misconduct.

The Police Subculture

Plenty of police officers are good folks who do not lie or engage in misconduct. We all have met many such officers and respect them, but they are up against a system that corrupts and co-opts those who want to do good and shores up those who do bad.

As the McAllen C-Shift thugs demonstrated, and as Captain Alex Longoria testified in that case, police live in a mutually reinforcing subculture, which, when corrupted, can suck good cops into that muddy quagmire. In this subculture, police view the world as "us" versus "them." They are the ones holding society together against anarchy. They are the warriors defending the gates. They feel the rest of us do not understand that or appreciate the difficulty of their job.

In this existential dilemma, police justify lying and abuse. They (the "us" in this scenario) know who the criminal is and who needs to be locked up (the "them"). They dislike legal technicalities, which they see as tying their hands as they try to protect society. Experience and history show how deeply flawed this thinking is, but it is engrained in police subculture. Good cops must resist this enticement.

Police live within the Blue Wall of Silence (also called the "Blue Code" or "Blue Shield"), an informal code of silence not to report on a colleague's errors, misconduct, or crimes, especially brutality. It can be personally dangerous to break this code.

Review Boards and Monitor Offices

Nearly a half-century of suing law enforcement agencies and officers taught me that police review boards offer no panacea, contrary to the public's hope, and typically do not operate well for various reasons. The one in McAllen failed, no matter how carefully we structured it, and that is a medium-size city. Larger cities are more difficult.

These boards come into being in the wake of egregious police misconduct but become defanged quickly, if they ever had bite to start with.

Monitoring systems do not have any real power at the end of the day. Police unions oppose them. They are bereft of the ability to create systemic change. Their best tool is the bully pulpit if they happen to have that kind of leadership. Typically, the establishment quickly co-opts them. Who gets appointed to serve on the review board or employed to a monitor's position seals the deal.

No Passing the Buck: Holding Supervisors Accountable

As I see it, probably the most effective option for changing police culture is holding supervisors accountable for misconduct or brutality that happens on their shift by an officer they are overseeing. Because of bad court decisions, federal law does not provide a mechanism for suing supervisors in this context. One can sue a supervisor only if he or she is actively complicit in the brutality.

Under a private-sector corporate model, supervisors pay the price if someone for whom they are responsible is seriously delinquent on the job. That should be the paradigm for police departments as well.

In my later years with TCRP, I had this discussion with Art Acevedo when he was Austin's chief of police and William McManus, the chief in San Antonio. Both agreed on the necessity of punishing supervisors. But when push came to shove it was a different story. Only McManus, to my knowledge, publicly disciplined a supervisor for a subordinate officer's misconduct.

Corrective Police Training and Procedures: Only Minor Benefit?

Every time we settled a case we insisted, apart from monetary compensation for the victim, on what we thought would be two corrective outcomes: new or extra training, and (sometimes) updated written procedures.

Training is important and, if taken seriously, can be a pivotal step toward change. We tried all kinds of training: formal classes, integration into the academy curriculum, annual training, and short trainings at the beginning of a shift change. We consulted with experts on training and procedures. Sometimes they helped implement a settlement agreement.

In my experience and that of special trainers brought in from the community, police do not take civil rights training seriously and resent it when it is imposed by litigation. Sonia Pruitt, a police expert and former Montgomery County (Maryland) captain, says that "the police eat training for breakfast." Amen to that!

TAKEAWAYS: BRUTALITY CAN'T BECOME ROUTINE

Nothing in my commentary is new or startling. Learned studies abound, and even popular culture has picked up the themes from time to time. But nothing changes.

To buttress this point, McAllen's C-Shift Animals appeared again, so to speak, in the self-styled "Goon Squad," a group of officers in Rankin

County, Mississippi, known for using excessive force and not reporting it. Three of them pleaded guilty, along with three other cops, in August 2023 to federal civil rights crimes of heinous brutality and torture.

This raises the question of the adequacy of preemployment and post-employment psychological screening and whether it is sufficiently tailored to account for police subculture pressures.

Only litigation will bring about change. Only litigation will compel internal change in a department. Experience over five decades has brought me to this conclusion.

TCRP handled police litigation because few other attorneys would. Our hope, besides bringing justice, was to show other attorneys that police litigation was feasible for them. We helped their efforts. It is fair to say that TCRP went a long way toward achieving that goal over time. Likewise, the steep rise in jury verdicts against miscreant cops, made viable by smart-phone videos taken by witnesses, has helped encourage more lawsuits by more attorneys.

11
VIOLENCE AGAINST WOMEN AND SEXUAL BULLYING

While our other work was ongoing, TCRP in 1999 initiated the first of its two salient community assistance programs. One was pursued on behalf of immigrant women suffering violence from husbands or partners. The other, begun a few years later, was on behalf of students, usually young women, enduring sex discrimination and bullying in Texas schools. These were stand-alone programs in the sense they had their own staffs and funding, were shored up by local volunteers, and were part of the TCRP family.

THE VIOLENCE AGAINST WOMEN ACT

Domestic violence and abuse have long seared the country's family fabric. Only slowly has our society begun to confront it and care for its victims. Spousal beatings and psychological abuse unfortunately are more frequent for undocumented immigrant women, as much as three times the national rate, especially for those whom US citizen or resident spouses bring into the country.

Multiple barriers worsen the plight of abused immigrant women: culture, religion, being strangers in a strange country, language isolation, constant threat of deportation, lack of financial resources, and fear of law enforcement based on experience in homelands.

TCRP made a program decision to help undocumented immigrant women to liberate themselves and their children from a life of violence and to remove themselves from abusive relationships. It was a program about which I always talked in speeches because it helped rescue hundreds of immigrant women and their kids from the dark shadows of fear and violence and brought them into the light of hope.

The 1994 Violence Against Women Act (VAWA), a federal law, protects women against domestic violence; it includes in its protections undocumented women whom men with US status (legal residents or citizens) bring into the country as spouses or partners and then subject them to abusive living conditions.

If the relationship becomes physically or psychologically violent or abusive, VAWA allows the woman, along with her children, to separate from the abuser and seek protection in the United States. The first step after obtaining protection against deportation is to acquire a work permit and then begin the regular route toward residency.

Typically, the partner/husband frightens the woman with deportation if she reports him to the police by threatening to keep the children after her deportation. Sometimes the abuser wreaks violence on the children as well. One TCRP case involved a father holding a knife to a young son's throat while making violent threats against the wife.

Abusive men wield the power imbalance like cudgels over the heads of wives and partners while they beat them with real ones. Given the record of police maltreatment in their home countries, women tremble at calling law enforcement, that is, if they can even figure out how. Cultural restraints come into play, too. Marriage is final; that's it. Pray, if you must, but endure it.

VAWA applies only if the abusive spouse or partner has legal status in the United States. However, a crime victim's U visa, which functions like VAWA and which TCRP also managed, is potentially available when undocumented abusers are involved. The U visa is for victims of crimes (assault, for example) who have suffered mental or physical abuse and are helpful to law enforcement officials in prosecuting the crime.

Privacy reasons narrow the discussion of TCRP's individual cases, but I can discuss two that were typical.

A serendipitous event occurred while I was penning this memoir. I was returning from a writing week in Mexico, secluded in a quaint old *posada* (inn) not far from the beach. A middle-aged Hispanic woman walked up to me at the crowded Austin boarding gate in the Houston airport and asked, in Spanish, if I was who I am. I replied I was. María then began to talk excitedly about how she had been a client in 2009, eventually getting her U visa, and how it had saved her life. She expressed thanks over and over, almost crying. I felt a little embarrassed but was happy for her. The surprise encounter was a wonderful gift.

She was now a school-bus driver. Her younger daughter was studying forensics at Texas State University, and her older daughter was a physician in Guatemala, preparing immigration papers to come to the United States to practice.

María followed up on her work visa and attained US residency, and then citizenship three years later, having handled her own application. She was so proud that she was able to vote for the first time. María was returning from visiting her mother in Guatemala, whom she had not been able to see in twenty years. Because of her prior undocumented status, she feared leaving the country and not being able to get back in. She proudly showed me her US passport.

A week later, I visited María at her neatly kept modular trailer home in East Austin. She gave me permission to tell her story. María's history is reflective in so many ways of the brave and courageous immigrant women whom TCRP assisted over seventeen years.

María and her siblings all came to this country separately but for the same reason. The family, living in a small agrarian town outside Guatemala City, did not have enough food to survive. Her mother struggled every day just to put tortillas on the table, nothing else.

In 1996, María made the hellish, weekslong journey across Mexico, then through the inferno of Arizona's Sonoran Desert to Los Angeles. She eventually came to Austin for employment opportunities. Because of her undocumented status, she took jobs typical for immigrant women (small restaurants, house cleaning) at pittance wages, often $6/hour.

In 2000, she partnered with a man whom she called her husband. She endured eight years of escalating physical and psychological abuse from an increasingly drunken partner. She often showed up to her job in the morning with black and blue bruises on her body from the night before. Her culture told her this was to be her life.

She prayed on her knees at the foot of the bed while her husband slept in an alcoholic stupor. She prayed for salvation or death. She cried to me as she described her "terrible depression." She even considered buying a gun and killing herself, she said, as she pointed to her right temple.

One day at 4 a.m., her husband's rage was such that he chased her into their young daughter's bedroom at the front of their trailer home, threw her on the bed, and began choking her, her head hanging over the side of the bed.

She managed to get free and ran to their bedroom in back. She reached 911 services on the line—she doesn't remember how—before her husband shoved her down on their bed and again began choking her. Remarkably, the police showed up immediately and probably saved her life. This all happened in front of their nine-year-old daughter, as had his earlier beatings.

Gaining freedom from her husband was traumatic. She felt guilty she had sent him to jail. His relatives harassed her at work. She felt safe only after the authorities deported him to Mexico.

She volunteered at hospitals and church until the government approved her work visa. Her own and her daughter's lives were very tough before the visa came through. Subsistence was difficult.

After a year, the psychological tide turned and happiness set in (*Ahora,*

A LETTER FROM THE SON OF A VAWA MOM

Thank you for all you have done. You have helped my mother, but you have also given my family hope. Hope for the future, that we may one day be a prosperous family. I do not mean prosperous, as in economically successful. I mean prosperous in the form that my family will one day live a comfortable and peaceful life in this world. A world that has not always been merciful to us. One that allowed us to suffer hunger, and to be abused by its inhabitants. A world that could cause so much harm to a person because they lack paperwork.

This idea seems silly to me now, but as a child it frightened me. Watching my mother be mistreated and threatened, all because she didn't have a green card. Living with the fear that she could be taken away from me at any time. It was our own personal hell.

You may or may not know this feeling of despair. But if you do, you must know why you must continue. Many of these people are helpless, and you, like any doctor or fireman, are their heroes. You save them from terrible life situations, and you give them hope for a better life. And for this I admire your organization.

SINCERELY, ALEJANDRO HERNÁNDEZ [PSEUDONYM]

siento feliz, which translates as "I now feel happy"). She learned how to forgive her former husband and came to the aid of other abused women in our *promotora* program, described a bit later.

The eloquent letter in the preceding sidebar is from the son of another VAWA client, printed with permission.

Our VAWA program began in South Texas in 1999 under the able guidance of Jaime Ortiz, our paralegal there. Not too long after that, a funding prospect suddenly opened to expand the VAWA program statewide. As often happens when opportunities unexpectedly arise, one must quickly seize them. We needed to find an attorney, a prerequisite of the grant, as soon as possible.

My son Isaac was a recently minted attorney. Given the short time frame we had to submit a proposal, I recruited him for the VAWA program. It was with some reservations as to how the dynamic between father and son, supervisor and supervisee, would play out. It went well, and he did excellent, meticulous work.

Even though the Austin office housed the expanded VAWA program, its mandate was to reach into rural areas around Central Texas and East Texas, where VAWA resources were scarce. Other organizations were providing VAWA assistance in Austin. Our peripatetic staff dubbed themselves the "Circuit Riders." The El Paso branch of our VAWA program, expertly headed up by Paulina Baca, also had a Circuit Rider component that reached into West Texas as far as Alpine and Presidio; they established a satellite in Odessa. Yessica Gonzales, a former VAWA client, eventually joined the South Texas staff. She went on to be the star witness in our case against the Supreme Court of Texas to expand legal services for the poor, discussed in chapter 13.

As María's account reflects, acquiring status in the United States was only the beginning of the clients' journeys. For example, they had to go through the divorce and child custody process, maybe obtain a protective order against the abuser, and find financial assistance, since they could not officially work without a visa.

After our VAWA program had been underway for some time, a prospective funder showed up one day at the office unannounced, asking for what he might offer a grant. A sudden golden opportunity. An obvious need existed to follow up and help VAWA clients live on their own in a new way of life and to provide psychological help to try to heal the trauma they and their children had internalized and endured.

We outlined a *promotora* program so we could support recent VAWA clients by organizing clients who were further along on their VAWA paths. The veterans would meet with the newer folks regularly to offer encouragement and suggestions as they went forward.

Promotores de salud ("health promoters") is a model originally developed in Latin American countries of lay health workers who visited and organized poor communities, offering advice to watch over their health. The *promotores* come from the same social and cultural backgrounds as the people they served. They knew how to relate to the people on the ground.

We were fortunate to employ Laura Gómez-Horton, a skilled and respected social worker supervisor, to help organize our *promotora* effort, a component of which included Laura enlisting university social work student interns to design the *promotora* program and provide individual guidance. All three TCRP offices that served VAWA clients created *promotora* programs. The *promotoras* were all volunteers, dedicated to helping other women on the journeys they were just beginning. María was one of the first *promotoras*.

I was struck by how the program formed a community of VAWA women. It wasn't just them helping one another; they fostered a supportive and nurturing group. The logistics were tough, since getting together involved traveling and often child care. We helped offset costs because the mutual bonding was so helpful and important to them. This was heartwarming to watch happen.

The VAWA experience helped me understand that human rights was not only about righting injustices but also about people freeing themselves, and becoming free, to live as their sense of dignity and individuality would have it, drawing them into a fuller community.

Thanks to the staff's remarkable professional performance, our VAWA program had a well-earned reputation as one of the best in the state. The estimate from surveying former staff is that TCRP served about three thousand women and their children over the seventeen years the program was in place. Not everyone qualified as a VAWA recipient, of course. Many women came only for advice and orientation. Many, sadly, just could not take the final step of separating from their abusers.

The VAWA program had an immediate impact on the lives of women and children. Their courage, single-minded sense of purpose, resilience, and care for their kids inspired us all. The pain of their brutal abuse—psychological and usually physical—at times would move our staff to tears.

There were tears of happiness, too. Many clients would bring gifts of food and flowers to our offices, especially at Christmastime. It was so heartwarming to hear how their lives had changed for the better and how they were on the path to full residency and then citizenship. A few had even set up their own small businesses. They all were so glad for their kids' sake. We were honored to have played a helpful and healing part in their life journeys.

TITLE IX, PEER/STUDENT HARASSMENT, AND THE TEXAS ERA

Thanks to special attorney fellowships, TCRP was able to take on several lawsuits protecting young women in school from sexual harassment. We earned different fellowships at different times, which brought us attorneys to help and gave our effort continuity.

We filed the lawsuits under Title IX, the federal law that requires equal treatment of girls and boys in educational and school-sponsored settings. Equal sports opportunities have drawn the most public attention, but there are other facets as well.

Bryan Independent School District

We became particularly involved on behalf of Debbie Rowinsky with Bryan Independent School District over peer sexual harassment. Her two daughters in eighth grade endured vile, degrading, ongoing physical and verbal sexual harassment from boys on the school bus during the 1992–1993 school year. The driver made no effort to halt the abuse, despite Debbie's repeated demands.

We filed a complaint with the US Department of Education's Office of Civil Rights in Dallas, which enforces Title IX in Texas schools. The Office of Civil Rights eventually reported 254 student-to-student "sexual incidents" in Bryan ISD during 1992–1993. Female students were victims four times more often than males. Those numbers are startling and shameful. According to the Office of Civil Rights, Bryan ISD had a "sexually hostile environment" that violated Title IX. In other words, Bryan was an out-of-control nightmare for female students.

We went the federal litigation route in 1993 to obtain relief for the Rowinsky sisters while the Office of Civil Rights investigation was underway. It did not take long for Bryan ISD to quickly enact a peer sexual harassment

GRADUATION DIPLOMAS AS A GIFT

During our annual Texas Bill of Rights dinner in the fall of 1997, Debbie and her two daughters unexpectedly walked up to the podium and presented the young women's high-school diplomas to TCRP as a gift, saying that, were it not for TCRP, the sisters would not have graduated. Their presentation was emotionally moving for everyone at the dinner. Not many people give away their diplomas. It was and continues to remain a deeply felt honor. The diplomas hang on my wall at home.

policy. It had none before the suit. At least on paper, this improved the situation.

The district judge ruled that the school or its agents had not caused the abuse; the students did. Therefore, the ISD could not be liable. Quite a sleight-of-hand. Two years later, in 1996, the federal Fifth Circuit Court of Appeals agreed with the district judge, burying our case under a mound of contorted logic. The absurd result: the school district could sit back, allow sexual harassment to run rampant through campus, and wash its hands.

We refused to give up and went to state court, invoking the Texas Equal Rights Amendment, which prohibits sex discrimination and guarantees equal rights, as a way of holding Bryan ISD liable for not reining in the abusive students. But we had no success here because the girls had graduated and were no longer in school. Besides, said the court, because Bryan ISD adopted new policies, the situation was different.

SHIPS

Even though Debbie Rowinsky's litigation hit the end of the road, she was undaunted and became involved with TCRP staff in fashioning the "Stop Harassment in Public Schools" (SHIPS) initiative to address the increasing number of sexual harassment complaints in middle and high schools and bring attention to school administrators' refusal to correct them.

Debbie did a considerable amount of speaking and met with many parents in Central Texas. She was a formidable and articulate proponent of protecting girls in school. No surprise given the pain she and her daughters suffered.

In two-years' time, SHIPS, by its count, educated 5,000 students in classrooms across Texas about sexual harassment; it also trained five hundred education professionals and two hundred parents and Girl Scout leaders. Debbie helped staff produce a documentary segment that Channel 1, the internal broadcast network for schools, aired in fall 1997 to 12,000 schools across the nation.

SHIPS morphed into TCRP's SAFE Schools antibullying initiative, training high-school students how to conduct peer workshops at their schools. The volunteers partnered with the Anti-Defamation League, which had a very active program, to create the culture change necessary to prevent and eliminate harassment and bullying.

Even though TCRP didn't hesitate to bring lawsuits against districts for not protecting students from harassment, we much preferred the peer-to-peer training model. Schools are often too overwhelmed to deal internally with bullying, and lawsuits only hit a gnat's worth of the problem.

Any effective antibullying effort must move beyond punitive measures and deal with bullying behavior as a social issue. Peer programs help teach bullies that what they do is wrong. They also help educate victims and other students on how to deal with bullying. If not corrected, bullies will carry their behaviors forward into workplaces, relationships, and family situations, affecting their own kids.

These programs resulted in significant impacts because of the volunteers who were inspired to help students minimize sexual harassment and bullying. Those behaviors themselves have all kinds of serious consequences on young people, one of the most dangerous being depression, which can lead to self-harm and suicide.

The coda to this section is our 2009 federal lawsuit against Georgetown Independent School District for the peer sexual bullying of a young African American student that continued from fourth through ninth grades, both in person and on social media. The boy had been the victim of sexual physical assaults in school, including being spit on, tripped, having his head slammed into a metal window frame, and being beaten unconscious. Fellow students derided him as gay and phoned his home, threatening to castrate him. He eventually took on suicidal thoughts.

This case caught the attention of the *New York Times* in 2011. We eventually settled the lawsuit for new policies, training, and monetary compensation. His mother, Kime Mitchell, became an impassioned speaker and activist with TCRP to push back against school bullying.

Luling Independent School District

Our Title IX endeavors included Luling Independent School District, which was a not-so-proud recipient of two TCRP lawsuits. In 2002, Luling ISD settled the first lawsuit on behalf of two pregnant high-school students whom it had expelled, thereby depriving them of the equal opportunity to attend school and receive other educational services while pregnant. Denying pregnant students educational opportunities increases the possibility that girls will drop out of school.

The settlement required Luling ISD to provide facilities where girls could leave their babies and attend to them as needed during the school day. The case had another component: equalizing sports opportunities for girls. This was also important for pregnant girls. Sports are important for teenagers because they help with physical development and teach teamwork, goal-setting, leadership, and competition.

This was a solid victory against school pregnancy discrimination, which was common in rural areas with conservative, often reactionary, mores. This case drew considerable public attention.

In the second lawsuit, a Luling High School assistant principal brought three boys whom he surmised were gay to his office and brandished a butterfly knife to "convince" them to "like girls." The district settled our lawsuit for $300,000 and terminated the assistant principal after his criminal conviction for possession of a prohibited weapon. Two of the boys were so traumatized that they transferred out of the district.

HUMAN TRAFFICKING AND FORCED LABOR

Another important case related to the abusive treatment of women involved human trafficking, which is a severe, under-the-radar problem in Texas. Human trafficking exploits persons for coerced sexual services or forced labor. At any given time, the 2016 Statewide Human Trafficking Mapping Project of Texas estimated more than 313,000 victims were in Texas, two-thirds being victims of labor trafficking and 79,000 being youth and minor victims of sex trafficking.

Criminal prosecutions are few for various reasons. One is that it's not a law enforcement priority. Another is the grave physical danger to someone attempting to break out of a smuggling ring of ruthless captors. And there are other factors, like language and victims' lack of familiarity with the United States, a foreign country to many, and how it operates.

The South Texas office handled a trafficking and forced labor case in 2005 for two Guatemalan women caught up in a couple's scheme in Mission. It was a representative case in many respects, but it was not typical of the larger cartel-like operations seen in Houston, for example.

The couple had lured and transported them to Texas by promising jobs. They then used physical force and threats of deportation to compel the women to work long days without pay over the course of two months (we calculated at least 1,300 hours). They worked at the couple's adult daycare center and had to perform domestic labor in several homes.

At the daycare center, said one of the women, "they wanted us to dance and flirt and even kiss old men, make them fall in love." She also reported how "they would take us to the flea markets to flirt with older men to recruit them to visit the daycare center." This invited sexual harassment.

Besides not paying the captives (that's what they were, in effect) for their work, the couple denied them adequate food and water and kept them from contacting family or friends. The man forced himself on one of the women and tried to drug her for sex.

They finally escaped the house through a window and made their way to our Valley office, desperate for help. Thanks to our staff, the police arrested the couple for trafficking and obtained a conviction. The judge ordered restitution and back pay for the women. One of the victims was able to obtain a U visa and, through our VAWA staff's creative footwork, bring her daughter to the United States. Today mother and daughter are citizens living in California. While I was writing this memoir, the mom wrote to Jaime Ortiz, who had helped her, to report her joy at now having a grandchild. Years had passed, and she was so happy.

TAKEAWAYS: TOUGH WORK, UNFINISHED

The efforts described in this chapter were pain-racking for everyone—victims, families, advocates, and legal workers. It goes to the heart of community living in a democratic society and dealing with the institutional imbalances afoot. TCRP tried to do its part toward making life fairer and more just, albeit addressing only a fraction of what remains to be done. The heartwarming part is how parents and other community members became part of the organizing to lessen bullying and to help other kids. This is tough work, and it remains unfinished business.

12
PRIVACY
AIDS, Lie Detectors, and the Case of the Purloined Baby Blood

Another prominent series of issues into which TCRP dived concerned privacy, the results of which benefited millions of Texans. Many lawsuits of similar genres ran through various stages of my career journey from the Rio Grande Valley to TCRP. The privacy cases, though, had their beginning at the Texas Civil Liberties Union and continued into TCRP. The Houston polygraph lawsuit, for example, which TCLU had filed in 1982, a year before I arrived, did not wrap up until 1996, six years into the Texas Civil Rights Project.

Privacy is one of the most important issues facing modern society. Neither government nor the private sector has respect for our privacy and retreat from abridging it only when we push back. That unfortunately assumes that we know when a privacy invasion is afoot, especially with ever more sophisticated technology. We often aren't aware of any issue so insidious, myriad, and masterful as the ways of privacy intrusion. Artificial Intelligence (AI) will be a formidable foe.

TWO SIDES TO PRIVACY

Privacy has two components—two sides of the same coin, if you will. The facet of privacy that usually pops first into our head is protecting deeply personal information from disclosure without consent. Medical privacy is a prime example.

The other side of privacy is self-autonomy: the right to live and define our individuality as we see fit so long as we don't tread on another's rights. Autonomy privacy often interlocks with other rights, such as freedom of religion, association, and assembly. Gay marriage is an autonomy right. The right to be left alone is another autonomy privacy. Measuring autonomy rights against society's predilections is a fraught enterprise.

In some instances, both aspects of privacy are in play. The right against unlawful search and seizure invokes the dual protections of nondisclosure and of autonomy. The idea of privacy has evolved and continues to do so. Not until 1890 was privacy itself named as a right in American law, although many rights have privacy implications.

Society must sort out when it has an overarching right, which the law calls a "compelling state interest," to infringe upon an individual's privacy. The Bill of Rights is an attempt to balance state and individual rights and interests. This is no easy task. The abortion debate is about the intersection of self-autonomy and societal rights.

These two sides of privacy, in differing degrees, show up in the lawsuits we handled.

AIDS

Some of our earlier AIDS-related work bears mention, given the public uproar and consternation at the time.

To Quarantine or Not to Quarantine

My first brush with the intersection of AIDS and privacy came in 1985 when Texas Commissioner of Health Robert Bernstein proposed quarantining people with AIDS. That was back in the day when AIDS-related deaths were beginning to skyrocket and appropriate medical care was not yet available. AIDS was a death sentence, often within eleven months of diagnosis. Panic in the gay community is not an understatement. The general community distanced itself from gay people just in case AIDS was contagious.

The quarantine idea did not fly. The backlash was swift and fierce from all sides, including medical professionals and civil libertarians. Outrage poured in from the gay community, and privacy became a critical legal issue. Besides the sheer infeasibility of quarantining everyone with AIDS, it had no medical value and was akin to consigning someone to a cold state facility until death.

We were able to beat back the quarantine idea through public pressure.

The commissioner, after having to backtrack, assembled an advisory group to study the issue, headed by in-house counsel Susan Steeg. He named me to the committee, and I chaired its Law and Ethics Panel. Steeg adeptly helped deep-six any notion of quarantining people with AIDS. The quarantine idea was farfetched and bizarre, but it reflected the hysteria of that time in our history.

Discrimination and Gossip by Medical Professionals

AIDS carried a stigma, a scarlet letter with social ostracization and discrimination in the tailwinds.

Among a trio of issue-related lawsuits, our first dealt with the landlord of an Austin facility housing Roy Lozano's Ballet Folklórico de Texas. He evicted the ballet in 1992 when he found out that Roy had AIDS. TCRP succeeded in stopping the eviction. It was a pleasure to run into his mother a few hours later and tell her the good news. She was a dignified elderly woman, always quick with a kind smile. She loved Roy and worried about his health.

Roy's soul was in the ballet. In the beginning, he supported himself as a waiter and financed the ballet's wardrobes from tips and savings. Roy founded the ballet school to open up cultural heritage possibilities for youth. Roy died in 1994 at age forty. His ballet lives on and thrives.

Even as medical treatment for HIV and AIDS steadily improved, social stigma and fear toward those with the disease did not quickly abate. It was in this context that we brought two privacy lawsuits against medical personnel who should have known better but disclosed a patient's HIV status in public.

In one case, a West Texas nurse revealed a patient's AIDS status to shoppers in a convenience store. Word of the disclosure circled back to the patient. The other case involved an HIV/AIDS clinic in Austin. Two staff publicly discussed the status of one of their patients during happy hour at a popular outdoor venue near the clinic. One of the young man's friends sitting nearby overheard their discussion. He did not know his friend was HIV-positive. Both lawsuits settled quickly in favor of the two men who suffered the privacy violations, but they could never recover the privacy that was stripped from them. It had been set loose to the fickle winds.

POLYGRAPHS AND PUBLIC EMPLOYEES: "YOU'RE LYING BECAUSE I SAID SO"

Another large-scale privacy intrusion that appeared on the scene about the time of the AIDS epidemic involved a state agency's use of random polygraphs on its employees.

State Agencies Know Best

One case, filed in 1984, was monumental in its outcome.

We represented the Texas State Employees Union (TSEU) and brought a halt to a practice by the Texas Department of Mental Health and Mental Retardation (as it was known then). It began randomly polygraphing its staff and terminating employment if they refused the polygraph.

Polygraphs have two major flaws. One is that they are about as accurate as flipping a coin, which is disturbing if your job depends on how a nickel lands. The second is that the claim of accuracy rests on the whacky idea of asking a series of control questions at the beginning that are intrusive, invasive, and personal, such as questions about a person's sex life, drug use, marriage fidelity, if they stole anything as a child, and so on.

Control questions range wildly over the person's private life and understandably make the examinee nervous. The presumption is that people will not answer candidly or will lie and dissemble. The polygrapher then forms a purely personal, subjective baseline for measuring whether the examinees' subsequent answers to "pertinent questions" are true, grounded on the degree of the examinee's observable nervousness, according to the polygrapher's intuited opinion, upon which your future pathway may be doomed.

The phrase "control questions" does not imply any orderly plan or prescribed script. The examiner is free to range at will without restriction for as long as desired and ask questions that intrude into a person's solitude, seclusion, private affairs, and concerns. The examiner's tone of voice can be as accusatory or sarcastic as desired—whatever inquisitorial style the examiner sees fit to adopt. The style and range of inquiry are designed to be highly offensive and nerve-wracking to a reasonable person. The process is invasive and sometimes abusive. It is an unwanted interrogation.

The machine, connecting the examinee to a box with a few wires, cannot itself detect honesty or lies. It is the examiner's interpretation of the machine's zigzag scratches and the examiner's idiosyncratic perception of the examinee that fuels the "truthfulness" interpretation.

During the 1973 Watergate hearings, Senator Sam Irvin, who was leading the inquiry into the infamous political scandal, labeled polygraphs "twentieth-century witchcraft." He was responding to a culprit's assertion that he had passed the polygraph. That may have been so, Irvin said, but he was still a liar. Irvin was right.

Random polygraphs are inaccurate and invasive. The only time in which a polygraph may be useful is in a focused investigation on a particular person and event and if that inquiry takes place without use of control questions. Just the intensive questioning itself may provoke a confession. That renders the touted magic of polygraphing meaningless.

Our lawsuit was on behalf of the caregiver staff in state mental health facilities. TSEU, the employee union, was confident that the real reason for the agency's compulsory polygraphing was to target union organizing among the employees. The union was seeking higher wages and better job security. The agency vehemently opposed the union movement and was resolute on undercutting TSEU, even if that meant trampling on the staff's privacy rights.

TSEU held this suspicion because employee polygraphing began at a facility that was known as an organizing hotspot, and some of the organizers were among those called first for testing. Polygraphing was mandatory. An employee who refused would be shown the door, soon to be looking for another job. The agency could require any staff member to submit to polygraphing at any time.

Given how arbitrarily polygraphs operated, the union feared the agency would use the polygraphs to provide pretextual reasons for terminating union advocates. Officials claimed they were administering the intrusive polygraphs for patient safety, although they had no specifics linking any employee to malfeasance.

Taking the same approach as with the Texas ERA farmworker and free speech cases discussed in earlier chapters, we wanted to use this case to expand privacy protections under the Texas State Constitution beyond those accorded by the United States Constitution.

Privacy is not a right specifically expressed in the federal Constitution. Our goal was to create a strong privacy right under the Texas Constitution. Our federalist system allows states to provide greater-than-federal protection but never less.

In this case, some of the privacy-intrusive questions were: "Do members of your family smoke dope?"; "Have you stolen anything in your life or in the past 10 years?"; "Have you used alcohol, prescription drugs, or marijuana?"; "Have you beaten your kids?" These were the questions listed in the court's written decision, but there was a whole range of offensive and embarrassing questions about a person's sexual life and marital fidelity that the court chose not to describe in writing. The agency's position was that such control questions were necessary for a proper polygraph examination, even if it meant trespassing on the examinee's privacy.

We filed our lawsuit before the agency could implement the new policy and terminate any staff members. We won an injunction in the trial court banning the agency's use of polygraphs. We lost on the first appeal, then won a terrific victory in the Supreme Court of Texas in 1987. The nine jurists, in a written opinion by the chief justice, unanimously ruled that privacy was an implicit fundamental right under the Texas Bill of Rights, even though it was not specifically written there.

The court declared that the Texas Constitution recognizes a right to privacy and, without distinguishing confidentiality and autonomy cases, adopted a "strict scrutiny" test in privacy cases: the state must show a compelling interest for intruding upon a person's privacy. That test kicked the use of control questions out the window. Just generally claiming patient safety was insufficient. Our lawsuit rang the death knell for random polygraphs in Texas. The court's decision was clear, direct, and forceful.

This case at the time was momentous, and it remains so today, because there is no specific privacy right under the federal Constitution. In other words, Texans have a stronger privacy right under the state constitution than under the federal document. That has profound ramifications. It was the Texas right of privacy, not federal law, that interred random polygraphing by government employers.

I count this case as one of the best legal victories any civil rights lawyer could wish for, as it created new constitutional protections. It also exemplified how a union protects its members and the public at the same time. The beneficiaries of TSEU's suit are roughly 1.6 million government workers in Texas, of whom the state itself employs 330,000.

It was personally disgusting to me that the agency was treating dedicated employees with such indignity. Working in mental health facilities is difficult and sometimes dangerous. The pay is low. Texas should honor the people in this occupation, not disrespect them.

This case was followed by a similar ruling in a Houston lawsuit that incorporated the precedential impact of the TSEU ruling, as explained in the next section. That case also illustrates the coarseness and intrusiveness of the city of Houston's polygraphing regime, which was not atypical at the time.

The City of Houston: Sacked by Its Own Polygraphy Expert

The TSEU success did not mean that all government agencies would suddenly toe the line and stop random polygraphing. The next case up addressed polygraphing as a preemployment requisite. This kind of random polygraphing is even more adrift and unanchored in a sea of "voodoo thinking," as our expert put it.

Houston had already arisen (or stooped) to the occasion and was a defendant in a 1982 TCLU federal class action on behalf of three rejected applicants for positions of firefighter, airport security staff, and police officer. Each man had impressive credentials, experience, and background but was denied employment based on how the city's polygrapher interpreted their prehire polygraph exams.

We could never get a good figure for how many applicants Houston had rejected because of polygraphing. However, the total workforce involved was ten thousand employees. Given how the polygraphing program played out in our case, it would not surprise me if the polygrapher's whim had rejected thousands of otherwise competent individuals for city employment.

I had taken over the Houston case in 1983 but, truth be told, did not push it forward because federal law was not helpful. The odds of winning were stacked against us. That dynamic changed with the Supreme Court of Texas's TSEU decision, which greatly strengthened our hand. I added the Texas constitutional privacy law to the federal case and moved forward.

Houston did not back down. The city asked questions of applicants, which, in the words of US District Judge Lynn Hughes, who was overseeing the lawsuit, were

> insulting, intrusive, argumentative, embarrassing, and wholly unrelated to any legitimate interest. There were questions about consensual sex, marital harmony, sex with animals, lifetime recreational drug use, non-violent criminal acts as minors, misdemeanors as

> adults, religious preferences, political associations, and other subjects wholly unrelated to the applicants' ability to perform the job.

This was only the judge's summary of the detailed and extensive polygraph questions, which would make many a person cringe. The judge suggested that the city's polygraphers showed more of a "morbid and prurient interest" than a search for loyal, efficient officers. This aptly describes the caliber of control questions that the judge chose not to repeat in his decision.

The judge's written opinion came after a three-day jury trial. Testimony by the city's chief polygrapher at trial underscored the arbitrariness and craziness of a procedure that could deny someone a worthwhile livelihood without rationality. He could offer no good reason that the city had, or even had the right, to ask questions about consensual sex, marital harmony, teenage recreational drug use, religious preferences, and political associations. Religious and political association questions are absolutely taboo, but he didn't seem to get that. Nor could he concoct a reason why they might be useful. His floundering search for answers on the witness stand buried any notion of credibility he might have struggled to present.

None of the questions had anything to do with job performance, and many were about activity protected by the state and federal constitutions. The city had no legal authority to ask them, let alone base a hiring decision thereon. His hemming and hawing during testimony was pathetic; the jurors visibly picked up on that if one was to believe their body language.

The head city polygrapher's most bizarre defense was trying the explain why polygraphers asked prospective employees questions about sex with animals. His answer was that some police had taken dogs to motel rooms for sex. You could feel and see the jurors' visceral reaction. Particularly noticeable was the NASA scientist on the jury, who was elected foreperson. He was almost audible in his disgust.

The city's polygrapher did much to bolster our case. He was so repulsive on the stand that he was our best witness. The city could produce no witnesses to credibly underpin its case. The one witness that it did produce dug a six-foot grave. He was pathetically mismatched against our expert, who had also testified in the TSEU trial and was one of the country's preeminent experts opposing use of polygraphy in these circumstances.

The jury ruled in our favor, and the judge ordered a halt to the polygraphing. Houston appealed. The US Fifth Circuit vacated the judgment in 1991 due to technical errors at the trial level. The appeals court returned the case to Judge Hughes to modify his judgment.

Hughes hammered Houston again in 1996, this time also applying the TSEU case, and kept his ban on polygraphs firmly in place. The city finally waved the white flag and ended its preemployment polygraphing regimen and allowed the plaintiffs to reapply if they chose to do so. The plaintiffs received lost pay, ranging from $69,000 to $184,000, plus interest, which was considerable after fourteen years of litigation. We received a respectable amount in attorney fees.

By then all three applicants had found other jobs. John Woodland, the lead plaintiff, became a substantial TCRP donor for a few years thereafter to show his appreciation at finding a lawyer who would handle his case.

Two Follow-ups

The polygraph lawsuits involved government agencies. Constitutional protections apply only to government actions. As for the private sector, Texas recognizes a strong common law right of privacy, which the Supreme Court of Texas indicated in the TSEU case may even prohibit private employers from asking control questions. Employers seem unwilling to take any chance. The phrase "common law" refers to traditional legal principles engrained in society that the courts apply when making decisions. They are not explicitly memorialized in writing and are applied on a case-by-case basis.

We also attempted to limit in the private and public sectors testing for

TEXAS'S DARTH VADER

During our efforts to limit preemployment drug testing, the Texas Association of Business (akin to the Chamber of Commerce) invited me to its state convention to offer my views (to which employer members rolled their eyes). The emcee introduced me as the "Darth Vader of Texas," which was quite funny. I appreciated that as an indicator of doing my job well. At family dinner that night, as I was humorously telling the story, my younger son became upset. He was too young to get the irony, but not too young for family loyalty.

drug use, but the effort was short-lived. The courts were not receptive. Our argument was that drug testing revealed an examinee's private medical information that a potential employer had no right to know and might later use as a reason not to hire someone (for example, a person with a heart ailment).

We did block drug testing of students at Amarillo's Tulia High School in federal court in 2000. A set of parents objected that their two girls, who wanted to play in the band, had to submit to drug tests. The US Fifth Circuit made short shrift of that on appeal and reversed the district court judge.

ANOTHER BIG PRIVACY WIN: SELLING BABY BLOOD TO BIG PHARMA AND GIVING IT TO THE US ARMY

The astounding "baby blood" scheme is another case carrying great consequences for privacy and the enormous number of people benefiting from it.

Texas has close to 400,000 births every year. One reporter, who had been in Minnesota, learned how that state had a baby blood spot collecting operation, which gathered and stored the spots indefinitely. When she returned to Texas, she found out that the Lone Star State was doing the same. She called me out of the blue for a comment about Texas's program and families' privacy rights. She got quite a comment—and Texas got a lawsuit.

For years, the law throughout the United States has been that, when a new baby is born, the medical team takes blood spots (samples) from the newborn, usually by pricking the bottom of the foot. They then screen the blood for disabilities or disease propensities as a way of informing the parents about how they might consider raising their child. The current list enumerates fifty-five disorders and diseases. Standard medical protocols called for destroying the samples after two years.

Texas, however, had another idea. Since 2002, for six years, and completely unknown to parents, Texas had been collecting baby blood spots and surreptitiously storing them indefinitely without parental consent in a Quonset hut at Texas A&M University in College Station.

The state health department, we learned, sold about 8,000 samples to pharmaceutical companies or used them to barter for lab supplies, HIV test kits, and maintenance contracts. Even more alarming, the health department was sending blood spots to the US Armed Forces Institute of Pathology, which conducted research on a half-cocked idea that DNA might show criminal propensity. A theory floated around that, if there was a criminal in the family tree, the miscreant's DNA might predict a predisposition for malfeasance in other family members.

The objection was not to the state collecting and storing the blood for appropriate scientific purposes; it was that it did so behind everyone's back without consent. Not telling parents what it was doing with their children's blood was unconscionable and raised the specter of misuse by Big Brother for financial gain, even for horrifying eugenicist research, as indeed was the case.

My grandson was born in late 2008. His mother, a University of Texas School of Law graduate, was beside herself with the idea that the state would secretly store and use his blood however it saw fit. She and four other families became plaintiffs in our federal litigation in San Antonio in 2009 against the state health department and Texas A&M.

The suit alleged that the agencies' activities constituted unlawful search and seizure and violated fundamental privacy rights. Law requires newborn screening, but there is no legal authority that allows the state to then "seize" the blood, keep it on ice indefinitely, and use or sell it without consent. Moreover, the agencies violated standard informed consent protocols for medical research.

The state agencies asked the judge to dismiss our case. Instead, US District Judge Fred Biery ruled that we had presented a formidable case. Bowing to the inevitable, the state destroyed the 5.1 million baby blood samples it had collected over many years. The health department preferred that option to seeking retroactive permission from parents. Their secret hairbrained stratagem cost the taxpayers a good deal of money.

The Texas state legislature then inserted itself into the process. This created a strange set of bedfellows: conservatives and progressives banding together, unnerved by the Orwellian potential of the baby-blood scheme.

The result was a 2012 law requiring destruction of blood spots after two years unless parents give written consent otherwise for research purposes. In the case of research, the state must abide by a set of protocols that mirror the US Department of Health and Human Services regulations for medical research involving minor children. The agencies had not followed a single one of the protocols before that.

BRILLIANT FUTURE LEGAL CAREER

My grandson was part of the baby-blood lawsuit press conference at the tender age of eleven months, winning this—his first case—thereafter. At the time, a funny picture was circulating from a press conference of two balding characters. One is the young plaintiff, laughing, with outsized sunglasses and facing the Capitol Building; the other, his grandfather, is carrying him down the Capitol steps.

This case helped inspire similar litigation and legislation in Michigan and New Jersey. The struggle continues.

COACHES OUT A STUDENT

A final case illuminating TCRP's privacy work involved two high-school softball coaches at Kilgore Independent School District in rural East Texas who outed a lesbian student to her mother. They confronted and bullied sixteen-year-old Skye Wyatt in a locker room about her sexual orientation and then summoned her mom to the school so they could out her daughter. They also kicked Skye off the softball team, for which she was a star player. Such heartlessness was stunning.

The girl's mother responded impressively. Her comfort and compassion were important to Skye, who was severely traumatized and had cut herself more than once and was thinking of suicide. The cowardly district simply hunkered down and supported the coaches' utterly shameful conduct.

The federal lawsuit, filed in 2010 by TCRP legal director Wayne Krause Yang, lasted four years and involved one interim appeal by the district that TCRP won. Kilgore ISD finally settled the case two weeks before trial with $77,500 paid to the young woman. The district also agreed to an annual training program for all its staff and faculty so this painful situation would never befall other students. A statewide LGBTQ+ organization conducted the first training, which was received positively.

I admired Skye's public visibility and personal witness. She undoubtedly was a help and inspiration to other students, a true example of standing up for justice. Skye and her mother Barbara showed courage, demonstrated through their mutual care for one another and other students, and vindicated their personal dignity. It was an honor to accompany them on this difficult journey.

TAKEAWAYS: INTO THE FUTURE

The privacy litigation I describe was important because it curtailed government power, at all levels, to intrude on individuals' privacy. It was a matter of respect and dignity. The TSEU case was more than just a great victory. It may become key precedent in litigation yet to come as abridgments of personal privacy continue to be experienced by countless people in the private and public sectors.

The baby-blood case raised even greater alarms about the state acting secretly to collect personal health information. It was necessary to beat back Big Brother's avaricious appetite, which, although benignly couched, had serious consequences for our democratic society.

This was important work. I was proud to be part of it.

13

DARING TO SUE THE SUPREME COURT OF TEXAS ON BEHALF OF LOW-INCOME TEXANS

One of TCRP's most important cases (among the top three for its significance benefiting working people), suing the Texas state supreme court, had immense impact on ratcheting up legal services for poor and low-income Texans. This audacious, if not quixotic, venture originated as an effort to require attorneys to provide a certain amount of pro bono help each year to the low-income community, as much as a week altogether. This would be a condition of keeping one's law license active.

POOR PEOPLE IN TEXAS AND NONEXISTENT LEGAL ASSISTANCE

Television programs sometimes portray Texans as richer than we are. A good deal of wealth indeed is packed into the tip of the economic pyramid, but poverty sharply expands as one scales down the pyramid. The Texas triangle is squat and broad-based; there is nothing elegant about it.

About 14 percent of Texans live in poverty. Texas is the thirteenth poorest state in the nation and the poorest of the six most populous states. Hispanic and Black Texans represent 54 percent of the state and are disproportionately within the poverty group. Their hands hold little of Texas's wealth—not surprising given Texas history.

With poverty goes the need for legal aid, which is gravely deficient for poor people.

The numbers are staggering. About 5.2 million Texans qualify for legal aid. The majority of those in need do not receive it, even though legal aid organizations help more than 140,000 families each year. Texas places forty-sixth among the states in legal aid access. Only about one legal aid lawyer is available for every 7,000 Texans who qualify. Fewer than 10 percent of low-income and poor Texans have their legal needs attended to.

These statistics, as bad as they are, are devoid of the flesh-and-blood suffering of persons represented by a number. They do not show the agony of a young construction worker wrongly terminated because he had to take his baby daughter to the emergency room, or of a single mom whose family has lost their apartment because the janitor service that employed her didn't pay her all month.

I have overseen enough employment issues and wage claims during my lifetime to know how easily a lawyer's call resolves them. Employers will not risk litigation knowing they are wrong. Not having an attorney on your side can mean personal or family devastation. The stories of people whose lives have been wrecked or made more unbearable for lack of a lawyer can fill volumes, volumes we don't want to read because they point the finger back at our democracy.

Legal problems that poor people face run the gamut: domestic violence, claiming veterans' benefits, disability access, housing conditions, health care, consumer and finance issues, rental problems and evictions, divorce and child custody, and school. Often these problems cascade. Eviction sets in motion a chain of dreadful events, even the possibility of becoming homeless. Loss of employment can lead to a repossessed car and a need for food assistance. And so on. The possible scenarios are endless and not experienced with the same frequency or ferocity in middle- and upper-class households.

On the criminal justice side of the system, not being able to afford bond for a minor traffic offense, a routine public intoxication arrest, or a DWI charge keeps a person in jail and sends the dominoes cascading (loss of job, or maybe short-term loans at exorbitant interest to buy food and pay utilities—one unfortunate result after another).

There is no question about the drastic need to increase legal aid. The assistance provided by the federal government is nowhere near what poor Texans need.

Those acquainted with this distressing situation, mostly attorneys and judges, profess solemn concern but proffer only lip service of the highest degree and action of the lowest. The Supreme Court of Texas instituted a voluntary program in 1984 to collect funds from the interest generated by attorneys' client trust accounts and convert those funds to supplement legal aid programs. Even that relatively small fund was shrinking at the time we filed the lawsuit. Attorneys would not part with the interest their accounts garnered from holding other people's money in trust, even if the money wasn't coming out of their pockets.

SUING THE STATE BAR TO GET PRO BONO HELP

Poor people were not gaining access to the labyrinthine legal system because they lacked an attorney to protect their interests. Lawyers, however, were getting fatter and living well financially thanks to an exclusive license provided by the state to practice law.

Troubled by this dismal situation, Austin attorney Chuck Herring helped spur our litigation in 1991. Our offices were close to each other when TCRP was housed in the Peace Building on Congress Avenue. Chuck and I would sometimes meet at the famed Las Manitas restaurant to plot legal strategies. Las Manitas saw any number of progressive stratagems hatched there. It is now gone, gobbled up by a hotel chain.

Chuck laid out the legal strategy to engineer more legal help for poor people by requiring attorneys to do pro bono assistance, all 60,000 of them at the time, or lose their license. That would be an enormous influx of legal help for low-income folks. The idea seemed eminently reasonable, morally required, politically problematic, and certain to stir lawyers' ire. The case needed to be done. It was time to be a badass. My kind of lawsuit. Chuck drafted the lawsuit and later the appellate briefs and guided us along before the courts.

The defendant was the State Bar of Texas, to which all lawyers must belong, grudgingly. It functions as the administrative arm of the state's judicial branch charged with supervising attorneys. Our three clients spearheading the lawsuit were poor people from the Valley, who had various cases; Texas Rural Legal Aid would typically assist but couldn't because its staffing was incommensurate with need. A budgetary deficit.

María Gómez, the lead plaintiff, was a luminary in her own right. She said what needed to be said when it needed to be said. Her political instincts were superb. Serving as her attorney was a pleasure.

María was in her midforties at the time, with four children. She had been a farm laborer all her life, harvesting melons, cauliflower, and all kinds of crops. She became a fearless organizer, especially against the excessive spraying of pesticides on crops that would drift into her *colonia* from the fields nearby. When that happened, people and their kids had to go inside and shut the windows despite the heat. It was not a healthy or happy experience. She developed a respiratory ailment from the pesticides that caused her to wheeze.

María also single-handedly made a local hospital change its security personnel uniforms because they mimicked Border Patrol outfits. That deterred people from going to the hospital. Even if they were citizens or had legal status in the country, people feared the government could take it away or they could be deported if they didn't have proof of status on their person. Given the Valley's history, such fear was not unfounded.

A dedicated, compassionate person, María fit the "servant–leader" ideal to a T.

María and her two colleagues, all United Farm Workers members, laid out the stark, in-your-face facts that approximately 90 percent of the serious legal needs of indigent Texans went unmet and about 80 percent of Texas's 60,000 lawyers did not help one bit in delivering free legal services to them. Our folks represented a class of poor and low-income Texans who were entitled to legal services but had been denied them for budgetary reasons.

The lawsuit, using the State Bar's own data about the desperate need, contended that the Bar has an affirmative legal duty to require lawyers to provide the needed legal services Texans for professional and ethical reasons. Our legal arguments were varied and complex.

It has always seemed to me that the strongest legal argument was in the Texas Bill of Rights: "All courts shall be open, and every person for an injury done him, in his lands, goods, person or reputation, shall have remedy by due course of law." The courts in all practicality are not open for relief unless an individual has a lawyer. The legal system is almost impossible to navigate without using an attorney as a compass. Too many eddies in a fast-moving river.

A Travis County district judge heard us out but dismissed the lawsuit, deciding he lacked authority over the State Bar because it was an entity ultimately responsible to the Supreme Court of Texas; only that court had the power to order the State Bar to require attorney pro bono assistance, according to this judge.

Our luck fared better in Austin's Court of Appeals, which reversed the district judge, deciding that he should indeed proceed to hear the lawsuit and decide what to do about our request. The appellate court opinion was sympathetic to our plaintiffs.

LAWYERS SENDING HATE MAIL

TCRP received its fair share of hate mail. One epistle-length screed was addressed to the "Texas Civil *Tights* Project." We enjoyed the misspelling. The biggest batch, volume-wise, came from lawyers in response to the litigation to require them to provide pro bono legal assistance. One lawyer issued a condemnation for acting contrary to the Thirteenth Amendment, which had abolished slavery in the 1860s. Another sent a newspaper photo of the mobster John Gotti on the way to jail with my face superimposed on his.

The most striking aspect of the hostile attorney letters was how poorly written they were—rife with misspellings, lousy punctuation, and frequent incoherence of thought. I must confess they gave me second thoughts about the proposition of requiring lawyers like them to help others.

The State Bar then appealed to the Supreme Court of Texas, which in 1994 ruled the trial judge was correct in ruling that no lower court had authority to regulate lawyers; only the state supreme court did. Not to worry, however, said the justices, they would put this matter on their administrative docket and figure out at a later date how to handle it. In the meantime, people could send suggestions and legal briefs.

John Cornyn, who was on the court then and earlier had wanted to defund TCRP, wrote the majority opinion that showed scant concern for his less-well-off fellow Texans. Justice Raúl González dissented, lambasting his colleagues for dodging the crisis, which he noted had been overstudied for years. In his opinion, only funding by the state legislature would nudge everything in the right direction.

At the end of the day, this political potato was too hot to juggle. No way on earth would the court impose a mandatory pro bono requirement on attorneys and law firms that lavish campaign funds on judges of all stripes and hobnob with them. Providing a week of pro bono help each year was too much of a revenue loss for the silk stockings.

Nor was it surprising that the court issued its decision on Thursday, December 22, just before the Christmas holiday, not an uncommon maneuver by politicians who like to bury bad news during the weekend and holiday deficit of media coverage.

Nobody had a clue what it meant to be on the court's administrative docket. Nothing happened. For four years, I wrote to the supreme court, asking what was going on with our case. For four years, no response. Finally, in the fifth year, I called. After a while on hold, the clerk informed me there was no such thing as an administrative docket with our case on it.

That was startling given the supreme court opinion saying there was. Our clients felt stiffed by the judges, rightly so, and wanted to press ahead, even suing the court for sandbagging us.

TAKING THE BULL BY THE HORNS

The same three individuals then filed a lawsuit in federal court in Brownsville, naming the Supreme Court of Texas justices as individual defendants. That alone was eyebrow-raising, but asking for what the plaintiffs wanted was somewhere over the moon in the eyes of the press and dogged court watchers.

That case, in December 1999, represented the last TCRP case of the millennium. Our legal argument was that the Supreme Court of Texas was denying the plaintiffs and low-income Texans due process by promising a hearing and then never holding one.

The lawsuit drew considerable publicity. The idea that an attorney would sue the Supreme Court for pro bono assistance seemed like a reckless act of professional suicide, although I had crossed that bridge long before and was still charging at windmills.

It didn't take long for the federal judge in Brownsville (who no doubt did not want this on her plate) to transfer the case to federal court in Austin, where the Supreme Court of Texas was located. US District Judge Sam Sparks, whose court received the lawsuit from Brownsville, did one of those "I happened to be walking through the clerk's office and look what I found" orders and forthwith dismissed the case without a hearing. Obviously, judges protecting judges.

The chances of winning the case were slim, if not nonexistent, but something had to be done, even if on the edge of career self-jeopardy. The lawsuit did what we designed it to do. Our action wrangled the supreme court's attention, and the public's, and it deservedly embarrassed the judges.

To their credit, the judges did not react defensively and lash out. Rather, they took the opportunity to conduct the promised hearing on what to do about the dearth of legal services for the poor, although it took them a few years to crank up the car.

The hearing finally took place in December 2008 at the Supreme Court of Texas, with furniture rearranged so the judges did not sit up on the dais behind their marble bench. People crammed into the large, majestic courtroom. Its walnut wood walls held large oil portraits of earlier jurists, all white men, who undoubtedly would have disdained the goings-on under their gilt-framed likenesses.

The directors of all kinds of legal aid programs in the state showed up to testify passionately as to the need for greater financial help. We wanted to try a different approach by adding flesh and soul to the statistics and calling persons directly affected by legal services programs to testify—our clients. Let the judges hear personally from the affected people, we decided, not just the clamoring lawyers (yours truly included).

Yessica Gonzales from our South Texas office stepped up to testify. She was a perfect spokesperson. She was young, attractive, a bit shy, and personally engaging with a friendly smile. She had been a client of our South Texas Violence Against Women Act program. She eventually became a VAWA paralegal for our office, assisting Jaime Ortiz, the program director, to help rescue other immigrant women and their children from spousal abuse and violence. Yessica could speak personally from her soul and professionally from her work.

It was Yessica's first time flying, and she was petrified. To compound her anxiety, bad weather postponed her flight for a day. She had to disembark from the plane. The experience wracked her nerves, but she arrived on the second day, just in time to bear eloquent witness. She was nervous, but within minutes she had put that aside.

Yessica was the hearing's leading light by all accounts. Perhaps "hero" fits just as well. Her testimony was gripping. Not a sound in the courtroom was heard as she emotionally laid out her own story of peril from her abusive spouse, and she included the stories of others with the same need for legal rescue from awful physical and psychological abuses. They needed an attorney with a lifeline to help save them. "There was the risk of life and death from the abuser in many situations," Yessica said quietly, "and only someone with legal experience can guide the victims through the danger and their trauma."

Yessica describing her own need for legal assistance in such intimate terms resonated a hundred times more eloquently than all the program directors' pleas. Her riveting testimony was so powerful and poignant that it moved the judges and all present. Yessica, one person empowered with courage and purpose, helped nudge Texas forward that day. An ordinary person doing an extraordinary thing.

María Gómez also testified and did so very well, explaining her family's unmet legal needs and those that she knew about from relatives and friends.

That hearing moved the Supreme Court of Texas to commit itself to expanding legal aid resources. It is a very conservative court, but it is also deeply dedicated to the principle that all people, regardless of economic status, should have access to justice. The court created the Texas Access to Justice Commission in 2010 to implement initiatives for legal aid. Forming the commission was an ingenious move; it let the judges invite powerful and prominent attorneys and law firms to serve as members and help raise funds.

The court also convinced the legislature to begin appropriating additional legal aid funding and now wraps legal services financial backing into the court's budget, a masterful stroke. The Texas Access to Justice Foundation, which predated the 2010 commission, continues its work as the partner allocating legal services monies to nonprofit organizations.

TCRP, a recipient of Texas Access to Justice Foundation funds, drew on these augmented resources to extend our services and create special programs, including for prisoner rights and veteran rights. We also enlarged our VAWA program and geared assistance more toward rural areas.

Supreme Court of Texas Chief Justice Nathan Hecht (and Justice Deborah Hankinson before him) helped shepherd all this along. They became leaders for other state supreme courts. Hecht developed a rock star's reputation among his colleagues around the country and helped them expand legal aid programs in their home states.

Hecht appeared at TCRP's twenty-fifth anniversary Bill of Rights Dinner and brought with him an award honoring TCRP's efforts to expand legal services to poor Texans, the Harold F. Kleinman Award from the Texas Access to Justice Commission. Kleinman was the founding chair of the commission and one of those respected Texas legal giants. The heavy, solid glass award sits on a small antique wood table by my front window. The morning sun shines into it and reflects rainbow colors on the blueish-purple wall and white ceiling as the sun moves across the sky—symbolic, it seems to me.

TAKEAWAYS: CHALLENGING THE BIGGEST POWERS IN TEXAS LAW

The lawsuit's outcome was very good but not a panacea. Too many lawyers still avoid pro bono assistance and don't contribute financially to the Texas Access to Justice Commission. The Supreme Court has let them off the professional-ethics hook, so to speak. And the legislature, never a friend to the poor, still has a large say over funding levels. But this case was a giant step. It created and legitimized a financial support mechanism that had never before existed.

I've always been grateful to Chuck Herring for his shove in this direction. It was because of another Las Manitas lunch with him that we got to discussing ADA compliance as a TCRP priority. Chuck was good at rattling the cage and then stepping back after I was on board. I am appreciative that the opportunity came my way.

This chapter is short, but its saga is long and deep. No fancy trial happened, just a bit of legal creativity. Ultimately, it is about all kinds of good people wanting to do the right thing. Sometimes all that is needed is a l'il ol' badass lawsuit to help move things along.

This is a wonderful legacy for TCRP. The poor people of Texas benefited greatly, but this was only the start of expanding legal assistance for them. *¡Adelante!*

14

CONTINUING THE GOOD FIGHT

Other Fronts

TCRP helped bring forward other major lawsuits with successful outcomes, not linked to themes in the previous chapters but nonetheless significantly impacting people's lives and meriting honorable mention because of their results. These cases also defined TCRP's role in taking on tough cases at the spur of the moment on behalf of the community. They are an important part of TCRP's legacy.

CRIMINAL LAW AND GARY GRAHAM: WRONGFUL EXECUTION?

TCRP rarely engaged in criminal cases unless they might create systemic change. One such lawsuit early on was for Gary Graham, who was on death row for a Houston murder. Texas law at the time did not allow him a due process hearing before the Texas Board of Pardons and Paroles for a reprieve, commutation, or pardon as a last chance before execution.

Graham had received a divided 10–7 vote against clemency from the board. The board had voted remotely "on the paper," meaning only his file. He took the position that due process entitled him to a full, in-person hearing before the board prior to any execution. He argued that his court-appointed attorney, Ron Mock, was incompetent at trial and did not call witnesses who would have testified that Graham was not the murderer. The lawyer was equally inept on the appeal.

The State Bar had disciplined Mock various times, once suspending him. Harris County judges liked appointing him because his trials were short, which saved the county money. Hardly commendable goals when a person's life is at stake. Capital punishment trials are typically long and expensive to make sure no mistakes happen and that the jury is as fair as possible.

Mock was widely viewed as a cog in the local aggressive death penalty machinery, doing little to vigorously fight executions in a county where the district attorney consistently sought them. Of the nineteen capital murder cases that Mock handled between 1986 and 2001, sixteen of his clients landed on death row.

The crime alleged against Graham took place at a store entrance. Graham was convicted on the testimony of a single witness, who testified saw the murder as she sat in her car in the parking lot. No forensic evidence connected Graham to the crime, and two witnesses inside the store could not identify Graham as the murderer. Graham's case took on national attention over his likely innocence. The trial lasted little more than a day. Alibi witnesses came forward after his conviction.

We sued in July 1993, a month before Graham's scheduled execution, and succeeded in halting it. We were able to establish a mechanism for the state parole board to more than perfunctorily review claims of innocence for persons sentenced to death. The Texas Court of Criminal Appeals upheld the ruling in favor of Graham.

Other attorneys, experts in death penalty litigation, then picked up his case and represented him throughout the ensuing process. The Board of Pardons and Paroles did adopt new due process rules, but it didn't matter. Graham was executed in 2000.

Graham made a desperate call to TCRP the day before the state put him to death, but we could do nothing given all the court hearings that had transpired. It was tough that he telephoned. We were as helpless as he was desperate. Not a good feeling, and it hung over me for more than a few days.

This experience again churned up sentiments inside me about capital punishment in general and questions about how often we have executed innocent people. Since 1993, 196 former death row prisoners have been exonerated nationwide (twenty-nine people thanks to DNA testing). That is an unconscionably high number of individuals wrongly sentenced to die and a harsh commentary on our criminal justice system. How many people are wrongly executed, especially when no DNA evidence was available that might have exculpated them, as was the situation with Gary Graham?

Since 1989, 466 Texans have been exonerated of crimes for which they had been convicted, according to the National Registry of Exonerations. That's an unconscionably hefty number. About a third of those convictions were overturned due to perjury or false accusations. Nearly one in five was due to inadequate legal defense counsel. That 466 total represents 2,503 lost years in prison for people wrongly convicted (or 5.37 years average). These figures should nag on anyone's conscience and doubly so when executions are involved.

THE SEPTEMBER 11 TERRORIST ATTACKS AND ANTI-MUSLIM DISCRIMINATION

After the 2001 terrorist attacks, the country witnessed a sharp rise of bigotry against Muslims, Central Asians, and Arabs. TCRP represented Mohammed Ali Ahmed, who sued American Airlines for arresting and removing him from a plane headed from Austin to Chicago two weeks after the attacks. The airplane captain refused to fly any passenger of Middle Eastern descent or who was Muslim. The airlines called the FBI, who interrogated Ali for an hour and released him.

Ali, a pleasant, respectful gentleman with three small kids, an American citizen originally from Pakistan, belonged to the American Airlines frequent flyer program because of employment-related travel. He and his family were on the way to the funeral of his father-in-law, who had died the day before. Islamic religious practice calls for burial soon after death. His arrest prevented the family from attending the funeral. He also felt humiliated. Ali's case was one of six similar suits filed across the United States on June 4, 2002, against four major airlines.

American Airlines eventually settled with compensation for Ali and a commitment to retrain its employees about not discriminating because of national origin, religion, or any impermissible reason. Serendipitously, at the time of settlement, the US Department of Transportation granted the airlines $3 million for training along these lines, which facilitated the settlement's implementation.

SEXUAL VIOLENCE

Two cases the TCRP became involved in highlight a common occurrence in the corrections and law enforcement systems: sexual violence against vulnerable individuals.

A Judge Uses Discretion for Justice

My most striking experience of how a judge can use discretion to do justice when the law was unfavorable came from US District Judge Royal Furgeson. It happened in El Paso during a pretrial hearing in federal court in 2004 regarding a young Mexican American man in his early twenties, who had been raped in the jail after being incarcerated on a minor credit card fraud charge. He was short and of slight stature and had a drinking problem. The jailers placed him in a cell with much bigger rogue guys with criminal records. That he was gay put him at outsized risk. The thugs were ruthless.

The sheriff had done away with special celling for inmates vulnerable to predatory sexual assault. At least seven other inmates had suffered sexual assault in the jail since the sheriff—contrary to commonly accepted penological practices—abolished the protective cell areas. National averages at the time showed that about 20 percent of jail inmates were susceptible to brutalization by violent inmates.

What made this case worse was that the young man's mother, who was in the courtroom, testified she had rushed over to the jail booking desk when she found out about her son's arrest. She asked that he be protected because he had been in jail before and was sexually abused then. The jail officers ignored her.

The chance was slim that we could prevail under federal law because the appeals courts had tightly narrowed prisoners' rights in this context. We would have to prove that the jailers deliberately intended that he be assaulted or knew he would be. Of course, no officer is going to get on the witness stand and testify to that effect. More likely than not, this had to do with their callousness overall and probable homophobia.

This was one of those lawsuits we had to take on, even if the chance of success was low. It was the only way of calling out the El Paso sheriff and jail personnel for allowing this vile conduct on their watch. Jail rape cases are revulsive, vicious, and degrading. They deeply wound the victim's psyche.

After mentioning our case's legal weakness, the judge engaged the sheriff in a remarkable fifteen-minute conversation from the bench in a soothing, smooth cajoling, filled with praise. The dialogue (actually, more monologue) was something close to: "I know, Sheriff Samaniego, you are a good man, dedicated, and genuinely want to do the right thing and that we really don't need to have this trial because this young man was hurt badly. And you really would want to make this situation right. Isn't that a good plan, sheriff?"

What could the sheriff do after that "dialogue" but settle the case, although we all knew it viscerally pained him to do so. It is not good to be on the wrong side of a federal judge given the number of lawsuits involving sheriff's departments that end up on the court docket.

That exchange was so transfixing that it is visually embedded in my mind after all these years. I can still see each character and our positions in the courtroom as this scene unfolded. It was astonishing to witness the judge exercise his discretion so effectively in such good-old-boy fashion to do justice in a way that the law might not accommodate. It was quite a dance.

We settled for monetary damages and getting the young man transferred to a less restrictive correction facility, much like a halfway house. He did well there, according to the staff. It was good to be able to help him out with what he had gone through without having to relive his awful experience at trial. To me, he was a nice kid with a drinking problem, and the new place was helping him deal with it. Rehabilitation should be the goal of the corrections system in many, if not most, situations.

Mother and Daughter Sexually Abused by Border Patrol

Some cases are so despicable that they fill you with stomach-churning disgust. One such instance involved a Border Patrol agent who detained and sexually molested a mother and her thirteen-year-old daughter in the barren desert east of El Paso after they had crossed the Rio Grande into the United States. He then deported them.

The mother, to her credit and bravery, went to the Mexican consulate in El Paso to complain. The consul, quite angry over this disgusting incident, called our office.

After filing a federal lawsuit in 2006, we went into mediation with the US government about the assaults. The result was a respectable sum with which the woman and her daughter could purchase a very modest home in

Ciudad Juárez, across from El Paso. That obviated their need to migrate to the United States.

The Border Patrol terminated the agent, Pablo Rosario. He was criminally convicted in another case in 2007. Given how brazen Rosario's conduct was, one might wonder how many other women he had molested but were not courageous enough to report him. How many times did the Border Patrol ignore his reported sexual assaults?

Before this awful event, the consul had appointed me Abogado Consultor del Gobierno de México (Lawyer Consultant for the Government of Mexico). The title reflected our close working relationship. Sometimes the Mexican government would grant limited funds to our El Paso office's VAWA program.

There was a formal swearing-in ceremony as Abogado Consultor at the consulate. The El Paso consul had a history of working closely with *mexicanos* on the American side of the border. Our relationship, which he wanted to formalize, was passing on to us information that he felt needed TCRP's attention so we could partner informally. This was a personal honor and gave me great pride in that he respected our work so much. It certainly worked to the benefit of the mother and daughter sexual abuse victims we were able to assist.

A BISHOP TAKES AWAY WORKER PENSIONS

We had to bring a lawsuit in 2003 against the Catholic bishop of Brownsville, Raymundo Peña, for abolishing the diocesan pension plan for nonclergy workers. He retained the pension plan for clergy. The plan was overfunded. By abolishing it, he could recoup the funds.

Because this reduced their retirement incomes 30–50 percent, especially among senior colleagues, thirty staff workers in four parishes formed a union in 2002 and associated with the United Farm Workers, the most viable union option in the Rio Grande Valley. The pastors signed contracts with the workers, paying into the UFW pension fund. The bishop intervened and reassigned pastors, one of whom then terminated four staff who were union members.

Our suit, brought under the state right-to-work law with two local volunteer attorneys, was legally problematic because churches generally have immunity from labor organizing laws. We made a sufficiently strong enough argument, however, that the judge refused to dismiss the case and let us proceed. He reinstated the four workers.

The funny thing was that, every time we scheduled the bishop for deposition, he objected to the judge but made more concessions to the workers. After doing this two or three times, we finally coaxed the bishop into mediation (though he did not personally attend) and reached an agreement to reinstate the pension plan for the workers until it vested for them.

The bishop also agreed to meet with workers to develop employee hiring and termination policies. However, he would not get together with the workers until the judge, quite exasperated, told the bishop's lawyer he was in contempt and could face incarceration. That got the ball rolling.

It was good we could help the workers. Their wages were low as it was, and they were such dedicated folks. They deserved better treatment. This is another one of those cases no one else would have handled had we not been there to help.

WELCOMING THE KKK TO THE CONVENTION CENTER

In June 2005, the city of Tomball leased its convention center to the local White Camelia Knights of the KKK, whose policy was to exclude African American and Jewish people from their events. Protests rankled the town. Wayne Krause Yang, TCRP's longtime legal director, represented United Concerned Neighbors, a grassroots organization, as well as two individual African Americans and a Jewish woman.

Tomball settled the federal litigation, agreeing to a policy not to rent to anybody that excluded attendees for impermissible discriminatory reasons. To the end, city officials had a tough time understanding what they had done wrong, but they learned the lesson not to do it again.

PRISONER RIGHTS: A SPECIAL PROGRAM WITH SINGULAR RESULTS

TCRP was offered funds to create a program to protect prisoners' rights, which Scott Medlock superbly headed up. He became one of the nation's leading voices and litigators on behalf of prisoners. TCRP ran the only prisoner rights program in the state.

Scott also did an equally admirable job as TCRP's pro bono coordinator, engaging attorneys at major law firms in and outside Texas to furnish thousands of hours in assisting TCRP's ability to provide free legal services. He also brought in cooperating lawyers to help with the prisoner program.

Prisoner litigation is problematic because the legal standards regarding imprisonment are different and less protective than in the outside world. Prison cases most often involve mistreatment or brutality by guards. Besides the myriad legal obstacles, prison lawsuits are difficult practically speaking because prisons are typically in rural areas, the same areas from which the juries would be drawn. Prisons are large local employers, which means everyone has relatives or friends working in them, if not they themselves. The local culture is very pro–law enforcement.

Nevertheless, TCRP had some success in those lawsuits. Scott was adept in getting into mediation and settling rather than trying the cases in court. This is another area of the law where the US Fifth Circuit Court of Appeals is downright dreadful. "Better to mediate than litigate" was the motto.

Texas Youth Commission: The Pyote Scandal

The Texas Youth Commission (TYC), which is responsible for juvenile corrections and operates the incarceration facilities, is a notoriously inept agency. It is often under investigation because of the horrible treatment of minors in its facilities. The guards do not control the violence perpetrated by inmate thugs. And guards themselves will inflict their own brutality upon the boys.

In 2007, TCRP filed federal litigation against the TYC juvenile detention center in Pyote in West Texas, which was even more notorious than others for rampant cruelty and sexual abuse. We represented four teenage victims. Their cases were horrendous and indescribable here. The state settled for $625,000 and pledged a series of significant changes. TYC admitted that Pyote staff sexually molested at least ten teenage boys.

The settlement was good for that time, but I could not help cringing at imagining the unbridled violence and sexual abuse and the devasting impacts on the boys, experiences that would deeply scar them for their entire lives. Hardly rehabilitation. TYC finally shut down the Pyote facility in 2010.

Opposing Prison Censorship

TCRP successfully represented *Prison Legal News* when the state tried to ban it from prisons. The respected national newsletter, published by a former inmate, advises prisoners of their rights, which of course the Texas Department of Corrections found offensive. Scott Medlock was similarly successful with counties trying to ban the publication from their local jails.

The corrections agency's propensity for banning the written word extended to an enormous exclusion of books that included literature and specific topics. One cannot fathom why they would distress the censors. They included books by William Shakespeare, Jenna Bush, Sister Helen Prejean, Sojourner Truth, Juan Williams, John Grisham, Noam Chomsky, Stephen King, John Updike, Kurt Vonnegut, Jack Kerouac, George Carlin, Gore Vidal, George Orwell, Gustave Flaubert, and Jon Stewart. That became the basis of TCRP's eighty-one-page Human Rights Report in 2011 titled "Banned Books in the Texas Prison System: How the Texas Department of Criminal Justice Censors Books Sent to Prisoners."

Air-conditioning for Medically Fragile and Elderly Prisoners

TCRP also did modestly well in litigation to expand air-conditioning for medically fragile and elderly inmates. Prison units in South Texas and East Texas typically have triple-digit inside temperatures during summer, day and night, even reaching a staggering 120 degrees Fahrenheit, making the prisons unsafe and inhumane. Under Texas law, county jails must maintain temperature levels between 65 and 85 degrees, but the law did not apply to state prisons.

Two federal lawsuits helped spur the Department of Corrections to increase the number of air-conditioned units from one-fifth to one-third of total units as of 2022. The federal Fifth Circuit Court of Appeals, increasingly hostile to prisoner rights, hemmed us in so that we could not go as far as we wanted on the lack of air-conditioning. Lieutenant Governor Dan Patrick blocked an appropriation in 2023 by the Texas House of Representatives to retrofit all prisons immediately. So the slow pace continues, as will litigation.

WILLIAMSON COUNTY CONSTABLES

Texans tend to have a difficult time understanding the idea of keeping religion and state separate. It was inevitable that TCRP would have to slap a federal lawsuit on someone sooner or later. The Williamson County Commissioners volunteered for this in 2013 when the county instituted religion-based hiring tests when replacing a constable who had resigned.

The commissioners refused to employ any of the three most qualified law enforcement applicants because of how they had answered questions about abortion, gay marriage, their religion, where they went to church, which political party they had supported, and how they had voted. The questions had nothing to do with a constable's duties to serve warrants and lawsuits on people and keep the peace.

The Bill of Rights in the state constitution states: "No religious test shall ever be required as a qualification to any office, or public trust, in this State; nor shall any one be excluded from holding office on account of his religious sentiments." The federal First Amendment is similarly prohibitive.

It was impressive that these three middle-age veteran officers from a county known for its solid conservative bent stood together against the commissioners. The county paid out more than $600,000 to a well-appointed Houston law firm to lose a case it had no chance of winning. Another reprehensible example of officials misspending taxpayer money. The rejected applicants received $50,000 each from the county, courtesy of the commissioners' inanity.

ANTI-IMMIGRANT BIRTH CERTIFICATE RETALIATION

One important class-action lawsuit came my way in 2015 as retirement loomed on the horizon. The Texas Health Department issued a new rule to make it more difficult, if not impossible, for immigrant parents without documentation to obtain birth certificates of their children born in Texas.

The department narrowed the kinds of identification it would accept from a parent who wanted a child's birth certificate. Few undocumented parents possessed or could obtain the specified documents. The agency admitted there wasn't any problem before the change that needed correcting. The goal was overtly political, to make life more difficult for families with undocumented parents.

Birth certificates are important for parents. They need them to enroll their kids in school, baptize them, qualify them for government programs, and so on. Birth certificates also allow parents to obtain a passport for their children with which they can visit family in other countries. Without a birth certificate and thus no proof of citizenship, the child is in limbo and in danger of adverse immigration consequences, even deportation.

TCRP had to do the litigation thing and collaborated closely with the Mexican Consul in Austin to apply appropriate political pressure. We became close allies. Texas backed down. It not only returned to status quo but even somewhat loosened the previous rules. What started as an anti-immigrant tactic backfired. Immigrants were a bit better off, but not much.

We shared mutual disgust that the state would so crassly use young children as pawns for its political agenda.

TAKEAWAYS: SOMETIMES IT'S THE PEOPLE VERSUS THE STATE

Only three of the cases mentioned here involved community organizing, one of our litigation goals, but they were all important in helping make structural change in their communities or in the state at large. No one else had stepped forward, so TCRP did what was needed—and with good results.

It was disconcerting to see how often government entities and officials fought us because of personal feelings rather than trying to work out litigation for the public interest. They unwisely squander taxpayer money at a rapid clip, sometimes simply for ego's sake. Private businesses were more responsive to early settlement discussions. They didn't allow egos to affect their pocketbooks. It should be a lesson learned, but alas such lessons don't always uptake with bureaucrats.

15

INTERNATIONAL HUMAN RIGHTS

Solidarity

Doing high-profile civil rights work inevitably led to invitations to be part of international human rights trips and conferences. I jumped at such opportunities, never knowing exactly how they would play out. While not part of my Texas legal work, they were part of my human rights journey. What could I learn? Was there some way I could help?

International human rights has been a passion of mine ever since sixth grade at Resurrection School for the same reason that civil rights in the United States has been a passion. It is about people's dignity and justice worldwide. I remember sitting by a vintage RCA floor-model radio one summer evening in my great aunt and uncle's small Pleasant Lake cottage in Michigan, listening to news reports about Salvador Allende's first run as a socialist candidate for president of Chile. I was twelve at the time.

Part of my attraction to the big idea of universal human rights is the evolving dynamism that sets measurable goals for countries. Universal health care, for example, is now widely considered a human right. The United States is still an outlier on this unfortunately. Texas won't even sign on to a federally funded Medicaid expansion program that would provide medical care to 1.4 poor families and children. Nearly 20 percent of Texas residents lack health care, three-quarters of whom are people of color.

In Europe and the Americas, international human rights courts were established by treaties to bolster the effort to enforce human rights across international borders. They have worked well, albeit slowly. It is a legal mechanism outside a country that can create change within the country. The European Court of Human Rights is particularly good in this regard. The United States Supreme Court, by contrast, will not look at or consider applying international norms.

The trips and conferences to which I dedicated some vacation time helped me understand and learn from what was happening in other countries where human rights were at risk. The trips presented a chance to show solidarity with human rights advocates abroad, to let them know they were not alone. There was nothing I could do outside the United States as a lawyer, but I could at least show up and be present as a witness to their struggle and encourage them. It surprised me how much people appreciated that gesture and were grateful. My pledge to them was that I would speak and write about their struggles when I returned home. And I did.

NICARAGUA: WHEN THE SANDINISTAS DID GOOD THINGS

The first trek—organized by a University of Texas economics professor with three Texas legislators—was in 1984 to Nicaragua and Honduras after the 1979 Sandinista revolution and during the Contra uprising to topple the new government. The Sandinistas had overthrown Anastasio Somoza Debayle, a bloody dictator and staunch US ally. His family had ruled the country since 1937.

The Ronald Reagan administration backed the Contras because of their policy that there should be no more socialist or socialist-tainted governments in the American hemispheres, something the administration feared from the new government. Cuba was enough.

Our idea was to meet with both sides, do some factfinding, and especially check out what the new government was doing in terms of human rights. We met with four Contra leaders in Tegucigalpa, Honduras, but they were all older men and seemed more intent on recovering the power and wealth they had enjoyed under Somoza. We also met with John Negroponte, US ambassador to Honduras, a country rife with human rights abuses.

Our talks with the Sandinista leaders were quite different. We met with all kinds of folks, including many from the rural community. They had hope and vision. Equitable land reform was underway, and an educational system was in the works. At the time of the revolution, 75 percent of the rural population was illiterate, which gave the country an overall 50 percent illiteracy rate. Funding was a problem because Somoza had emptied the national coffers when he fled the country.

One of the most intriguing and eloquent persons we met was Nora Astorga, an American-educated corporate lawyer who turned revolutionary and then served as Nicaraguan delegate to the United Nations. She died in 1988 at age thirty-nine.

The dreams and promise of that era are long gone, thanks to Daniel Ortega perverting the revolution and grabbing autocratic powers. He lost one election as president and wasn't going to lose again. His regime has become as much of a hell as was Somoza's, probably more so.

CHILE AND THE PINOCHET DICTATORSHIP

My second journey was to Chile in 1987 under the aegis of the National Lawyers Guild during the brutal Augusto Pinochet era after the US-supported 1973 coup that overthrew Salvador Allende, the elected president. Torture was widespread, as were political "disappearances" and killings. We know now that 35,000 Chileans were tortured and hundreds executed. Civil liberties were nonexistent, and 40,000 dissidents were held in jails throughout the 2,700-mile length of the country.

Six of us clandestinely met with courageous opposition lawyers and judges at night in upstairs windowless rooms. They were at risk just meeting with us. I admired their bravery and commitment to human rights. I did my best to lift them up with my words, but at the end of the day I could walk away—and I felt guilty about that. They did not have such freedom and were in constant danger of imprisonment, loss of livelihoods, or worse.

We observed antigovernment flash demonstrations. In one, forty people rushed up from the nearby subway, protested at a downtown army headquarters for fifteen or twenty minutes, scattered leaflets on the sidewalks and streets, and then disappeared back into the subway. They were gone by the time the police showed up.

We housed with different families in various *poblaciones* (poor, crammed residential areas of urban Santiago). The father of the small rectangular house where I stayed was at the time in prison for political reasons. They had three young kids in elementary school. His being in jail made it very tough for his wife to support the family. We accompanied her on a ten-hour overnight train ride 440 miles south to Temuco to visit him for an hour, which was the limit allowed by prison officials. She would not have been able to visit him had we not paid the train fare. That was the government's punitive intent: break up families and make it nearly impossible to stay in touch.

In the *población* where I stayed, I could see the unfinished hospital that the Allende government had been building for the people at the time of the coup. The military regime did not finish it and allowed its hulking skeleton to stand untended, deteriorating, as a symbol.

One morning while out jogging, I saw police wagons coming through the *población* and randomly grabbing young boys on the way to school. This was a common practice, I learned, to keep people on edge and in fear of the government. Parents would have to spend the day retrieving their children, which meant a loss of employment time and an expense to the family.

The regime's heavy hand was suffocating, as the government intended. The undercurrent of low-level opposition surprised me. I had never been in a country under a dictatorship like Chile's, and I could physically feel the suppression. I was so thankful when I returned to the United States that I almost wanted to kiss the ground. As difficult as it is in this country in terms of civil rights, at least we had freedom to push forward.

The people of Chile persisted and won. They eventually pushed Pinochet from power in 1990 and restored democracy. The country's judicial system finally came close to trying him for human rights abuses, but he died in 2006 before trial. The courts convicted and imprisoned sixty of the regime's notorious torturers.

PALESTINIAN TERRITORIES AND ISRAEL

The third trip was to the Palestinian territories and Israel for ten days in August 1988 during the first Intifada uprising. We were a group of seven from around the United States. We met with people in the West Bank, Gaza, and Israel. The trip was an eye-opener, in contrast to how the Israel–Palestine conflict is viewed in this country and treated by Congress.

We talked with peace advocates in Tel Aviv and with a young Israeli lawyer representing Palestinian activist leaders detained in the notorious Ansar 3 camp in the Negev Desert. She described how she would have to sneak into the camp through the tents toward the back at night to see her clients because the Israeli military had restricted attorney access. I admired her willingness to stand for justice against the odds and contrary to the political sentiment of the country at the time. We also visited with a Christian Palestinian family whom Israel had displaced from their Jerusalem home when it took over the country in 1948.

Our most captivating conversation was with the Palestinian leader Hanan Ashrawi in Ramallah. Her insight and overview of the long-simmering conflict, told from the Palestinian side, was educational and often different from the standard pro-Israel narrative heard in the United States. An academic and scholar herself, she was quite proud that the Palestinian people were so highly college-educated, with many having careers in engineering, business, and medicine.

We spent a day in Gaza and visited one of its hospitals, which was more like a clinic than a hospital. We met with a couple of families in an apartment close to Gaza's border with Egypt in the south. The grinding poverty and the dense quarters in which people had to live were shocking and awful. The same was true of the forty-year-old United Nations Palestinian "temporary" refugee camp on the West Bank that we visited. I could understand how people's antipathy toward Israel would fester.

We stayed in a small East Jerusalem hotel near the Old City walls near Herod's Gate. We explored the religious sites, of course. I expanded the tour of those sites with early jogs. One morning, out of curiosity, I jogged up an old stone stairway outside of an ancient building to a rooftop and found twenty or so Ethiopian monks saying morning prayers. It looked like they lived there. Being in jogging shorts and not modest by their standards, I quickly departed back down the centuries-worn steps.

On the last day we held a press conference, detailing our observations. The Israeli army defense radio network dutifully attended. When we departed the following morning, Israeli security sequestered us while tediously and annoyingly going through every item in our luggage until shunting us off to the plane at the very last minute as it was about to take off.

After returning to the United States, whenever we would give talks about our experiences, Israel advocates, who didn't care for our observations, would show up in the audience with adversarial comments.

IN GUATEMALA WITH JENNIFER HARBURY AND SURROUNDED BY ARMED SOLDIERS

The next mission was to Guatemala in 1992 with the human rights activist Jennifer Harbury, a friend and legal aid lawyer, to collect the remains of her husband. He had been a rebel soldier in the country's civil war, fighting on behalf of the Indigenous Maya community against the repressive government.

The army reported he had died in battle. Jennifer did not believe it and feared he was alive in captivity and undergoing torture. She wanted proof, one way or the other. Three of us, friends of hers, accompanied Jennifer, including Frances "Sissy" Farenthold.

When we arrived, we visited with the country's human rights ombudsman at night in a locked and guarded windowless room. Before daybreak, we crammed into a car and left for the five-hour drive to Retalhuleu in southwestern Guatemala, near Mexico and the Pacific, where the government claimed he was buried. A military blockade stopped us after about an hour en route; but our driver, a pathologist from the ombudsman's office, talked us through.

At Retalhuleu, which has savannah-like terrain, we met with the local magistrate, who signed off on the exhumation. Our group stood around the edge of the grave with Jennifer to witness the disinterment and see if the earth held her husband.

When the men doing the digging were just reaching a black plastic bag with a corpse, a military phalanx suddenly arrived, marching, and surrounded the cemetery. Twenty-five soldiers with rifles encircled us and the grave area. This was disconcerting, if not worrisome. The soldiers ordered that the exhumation stop, but the magistrate refused to obey.

Just then, Guatemala's attorney general, a portly man in a suit and sweating in the hot, humid midday climate, came huffing and puffing over the hillside near the grave. He had arrived by military helicopter. It was surreal. He had a heated discussion with the magistrate: a standoff between the white European power structure and the Indigenous judge. The attorney general prevailed, and we had to leave. The workers began refilling the grave.

A call from nature compelled a pit stop at the cemetery's administration building and morgue on the way out. The attorney general was there when I walked in, yucking it up with others as they stood around empty coffins. I left as quickly as possible, disgusted.

It turned out that the burial site was not the grave of Jennifer's husband, which is why the attorney general had showed up to stop us. At the very time we were in southwestern Guatemala, he was suffering torture near Guatemala City. Both the Guatemalan and American governments were complicit in the coverup. Jennifer Harbury authored an astonishing book about this titled *Searching for Everardo: A Story of Love, War, and the CIA in Guatemala*. Her activism was unrelenting. Both governments came to regret crossing her path.

Jennifer sued the country of Guatemala in the Inter-American Court of Human Rights in San José, Costa Rica, for his torture and death. The trial was in 1998. I testified about our trip and how the attorney general blocked the exhumation. The court ruled against Guatemala in 2000 and assigned damages in 2002 to her husband's children by a prior marriage, as Jennifer requested.

While waiting to testify, I was in a room with the Guatemala human rights ombudsman, whom we had met before. He talked about someone shooting at his house at nighttime and how his family had to live in the rear section of the home for safety reasons. Someone also had once shot at him while he was jogging on the beach during a family vacation. I admired his courage for living with the danger and wondered if I could show the same bravery.

TRAVELS WITH HIZMET

Then came the opportunity to travel to Türkiye in 2008 to witness the changes underway there as the new government under the Justice and Development Party seemed to offer the promise of becoming an Islamic secular democracy, solidly anchored in civil society. It was a different kind of human rights trip.

We were an interfaith group, visiting at the invitation of the Hizmet movement. Hizmet (*hizmet* means "service"), under the leadership of the Turkish scholar and preacher Fethullah Gulen, who lived in self-exile in Pennsylvania, describes itself as a faith-inspired civil society movement that seeks to create a culture of coexistence within universal, humanist values. It is committed to Türkiye having closer ties to Europe and becoming more Westernized. Hizmet functions through the work and financial underpinning of volunteers. It had become an extensive and respected movement in Türkiye, encompassing all social sectors.

It was educational and hopeful to see the democracy-related changes that the move toward accession to the European Union was helping consummate. We visited schools, hospitals, and institutions that Hizmet was creating and had dinner every night in a local home. We took breakfast at the apartment of a Kurdish family in Urfa and followed the custom of sitting on the floor around a large dining cloth. For some of us visitors, getting up was a bit tricky.

After returning from that trip, I was asked to write a book about Hizmet and Fethullah Gülen and how he had prevailed in Türkiye's courts against charges that he was undermining the secular nature of the state. I returned two times to Türkiye to do interviews. Of particular interest to me were the judicial reforms underway. The European Union invested significant resources into professionalizing the judiciary. I met with judges and prosecutors in the European Union–sponsored program, and all were proud to have been chosen as participants.

After the book's publication in early 2011, I gave speeches about the book and civil society throughout the United States, Europe, Türkiye, Canada, and Mexico. Altogether, over three years or so, using vacation

A DALLAS RESCUE IN ISTANBUL

While writing the book on Hizmet and Fethullah Gülen, I traveled to Türkiye twice to interview people. One evening before returning home the second time, I went for a stroll late one rainy evening to the nearby famous majestic Blue Mosque.

Suddenly, three police officers drove up and began questioning me. None of us spoke the other's language. I did not have my passport and began to worry about missing my flight, scheduled to leave in three hours. A supervisor arrived who knew almost a smattering of English. Communication was fraught. He kept saying. "Where from?" I kept replying, "United States"; but that did not register. I learned later the right response is "America."

Then I tried "Texas" and "Austin." No success with either; my anxiety grew.

Finally, I gambled with "Dallas." That changed everything. The *Dallas* television series was popular in Türkiye. Making that connection saved the day. After a few shared laughs and some backslapping, I was sent on my way. Whenever I tell this story to people from Türkiye, they laugh knowingly. It's always "America," of course, and "Dallas" is the key.

time, I made thirty-eight trips, traveling 140,000 miles. I met some terrific Hizmet people and visited many of their projects.

Türkiye's ten-year democracy experiment began a slow crash in 2012, as Recep Tayyip Erdoğan assumed more power and became an autocratic religious nationalist. Hizmet published *Zaman*, a respected Turkish and English daily newspaper, and operated a few media outlets, which criticized Erdoğan as he became more repressive. He then suppressed and persecuted Hizmet as he undermined civil society and weakened the newly assertive judicial system.

Erdoğan's oppression of Hizmet was, and continues to be, unrelenting. Hundreds of thousands of people in the movement lost their jobs, went to prison, or fled the country. It was the most extensive purge of public employees in world history and included judges, academics, medical staff, professionals, and labor union leaders. Erdoğan seized the *Zaman* newspaper, Hizmet schools, hospitals, and other facilities. He shut down Kimse Yok Mu ("Isn't Anybody There?"), Hizmet's renowned United Nations–certified global relief organization.

People whom I had met and interviewed in earlier years have been imprisoned. They include non-Hizmet dissidents who simply oppose Erdoğan's trajectory. I dare not reach out to them lest they suffer more repercussions. I worry about them. Many others fled the country.

Hizmet remains highly active outside Türkiye, operating schools and hosting interfaith events in multiple countries, including in the state of Texas. I am now assisting in preparing a book and legal briefing for the international human rights forum, challenging Erdoğan's persecution of Hizmet. I am not optimistic, but it is something I need to do. It's the least I can do to help.

LOS FEMINICIDAS IN CIUDAD JUÁREZ

I became involved in a different kind of international human rights endeavor at the invitation of Professor Héctor Domínguez-Ruvalcaba of the University of Texas in Austin. He was trying to do something about the brutal slayings and disappearances of thousands of young women in Ciudad Juárez, across from El Paso.

The femicide victims tended to be *maquiladora* employees abducted when leaving work late at night. A *maquiladora* (or *maquila*) is a factory in

Mexico operated by a foreign company, which, taking advantage of low-paid Mexican workers, exports its finished products to the company's home country. In the Juárez context, the companies were often American, with the owners and managers living on the El Paso side of the Rio Grande.

Between 1991 and 2023, more than 2,300 young women in Juárez were brutalized, killed, and grotesquely dismembered. Official statistics list 300 women still missing. The numbers are undoubtedly higher. Mexico did little to rein in the femicides and much to obfuscate the reality.

I authored a chapter for *Gender Violence at the U.S.-Mexico Border* titled "*¡Alto a la Impunidad!*" (End the Impunity!), published in 2010, about the prospect of petitioning the Inter-American Court of Human Rights in Costa Rica to intervene and order Mexico to solve, prosecute, and stop the femicides.

The chapter also suggested how victims' families could use Texas courts to sue *maquila* owners and operators who lived in El Paso and commuted daily to Juárez, on the ground they were doing nothing to protect their female employees despite knowing the dangers they faced.

Another professor, also involved in writing the book, and I visited the mother of a young *maquila* victim one evening. We went to explore whether the mother would consider filing a case against Mexico with the Inter-American Court about her daughter's murder and might also be willing to undertake a precedent-setting lawsuit against the *maquila* owner in Texas courts.

She lived in a small, cobbled-together ramshackle of a house, crammed against her neighbors, in a poor, ghetto-like enclave behind a Juárez factory. Such neighborhoods are where people from other parts of Mexico come to live while they work in the *maquilas*. No greenery, no yards, just desert floor. It was dark at the time and hard to find her home. There was no street lighting.

As we talked I became painfully aware that I could not shield her from retaliation if she pursued either legal action. She was already dangerously outspoken against the authorities over her daughter's slaying and the other murdered young women. She and her young son, barely a teenager, were suffering harassment and physical abuse from unknown men, even when they were walking on the dirt streets where they lived. The men would jump them, push them to the ground, and threaten the boy with death if she persisted in being vocal.

Not only could I not protect her; I would be endangering her life by enlisting her as a petitioner within either court system. I reluctantly had to ratify her suggestion that they leave Juárez and return to her hometown in southern Mexico. They had come to Juárez for employment. Leaving was the best—and likely only—protection for her and her son. Whoever was behind the slayings and atrocities had the government in tow or was in collusion with authorities. Probably both.

It was soul-crushing that I could offer no remedy for the horrific killing of her daughter. I vividly remember driving out of her wretched environs in the dark of night, turning right at the factory's red brick wall, rattled with fear that she would not survive long enough to return to her hometown. She had no phone, so we could not stay in touch. I still worry about how it all turned out for her and her son.

The professor and I also met that same night with the middle-age father of another murdered daughter (also a *maquila* worker) in a small, isolated restaurant far from his house for his protection. We reached the same heart-searing conclusion: I could do nothing other than share his pain without any consolation of justice. The evening was as depressing as it was dark.

The Inter-American Court did render judgment in 2009 against Mexico in another case, but the feminicides continued with impunity. In the end, all I could do was join others to give Mexico the bad publicity it deserved with the hope it might eventually do some good.

TAKEAWAYS: INTERNATIONAL PROBLEMS MIRROR THOSE AT HOME

My takeaway from the Türkiye and Nicaragua experiences is that, even when both countries seemed on the right track, democracy was tenuous and hard to install and maintain. Those who devised democracy had the right idea. The rule of law is what counts. We have to support it everywhere at all costs and protect civil liberties.

Even the United States, despite two and a half centuries of history, struggles with democracy to this day and will into the future. As this book goes to press, American democracy as we knew it stands on a knife's edge. A comment from Benjamin Franklin fits here. At the close of the 1787 Constitutional Convention in Philadelphia, Elizabeth Willing Powel famously asked him, "Well, Doctor, what have we got, a republic or a monarchy?" He replied: "A republic, if you can keep it."

In the international forum, the United States, even with its seriously imperfect record, must help push countries like Türkiye to where they should be and push ourselves to be true to our expressed goals.

The human rights trips were a welcome respite from the regular routine, a healthy change of pace and an opportunity to meet kindred spirits in new places. Those trips and meetings allowed for mutual self-care, which Audre Lorde tagged as self-preservation, not self-indulgence, an act of "political warfare," acquiring renewed strength against the forces of oppression.

The foreign visits gave me a profound respect for the people struggling for justice in their countries. It struck me how much gentler my life was among the global human rights community. I did not live in fear for my life or going to prison or under constant terroristic threat.

Their bravery taught me humility. They appreciated our showing up in solidarity.

One more takeaway about meeting with the mother and father of the two feminicide victims. It was miserable to witness their pain and suffering, and it was demoralizing to offer them no help or hope. I wondered as I drove back across the bridge to Texas why it had even entered my head that I could be of help under such dire circumstances, as much as I wanted to. It was a humbling lesson in raw reality.

Desmond Tutu's words from his own struggle against apartheid in South Africa bear recalling again in international human rights struggles. They offer hope and motivation: "It means a great deal to those who are oppressed to know that they are not alone. Never let anyone tell you that what you are doing is insignificant."

16

WHAT MADE TCRP UNIQUE?

Noam Chomsky, the MIT professor and public intellectual renowned for political activism and social criticism, spoke at TCRP's 2002 Bill of Rights Dinner. Afterward, he sent us a note: "I was very much impressed with what I saw and heard. I can't imagine there's another organization like the Civil Rights Project anywhere. At least, I've never come across one."

We, of course, shared his view and appreciated his affirmation. We didn't start out to be unique or try for the title. Various creative and organizing factors came into play in different ways, some of which are worth mentioning here in the hope they might inspire other civil rights and community activists.

It wasn't just that we handled more than 2,600 cases for poor and low-income Texans, some of which included comprehensive settlements and important appellate victories. It was about which cases we handled and how we handled them.

We prioritized community cases that addressed structural injustice, not Band-Aid cases that addressed the symptoms and not the causes of the structural injustice. The Band-Aid cases are very important in people's individual lives, to be sure, but we left them to other competent organizations so that we could focus our efforts.

ALL CIVIL RIGHTS IS LOCAL

Tip O'Neill, the legendary former Speaker of the US House of Representatives, was famous for pumping up the dictum "All politics is local." TCRP lived by a revised maxim: "All civil rights is local." We opted to be a statewide or local civil rights force in Texas. The national litigation stage was not for us, even though some of our cases carried national impacts. We prided ourselves on being a Texas group, protecting Texas civil rights with and for Texans. Our work was to breathe local life into the promises of human rights. In speeches over the many years, I generally built my talks around a quote from Eleanor Roosevelt, which for me epitomized our work in Texas communities. She was speaking at the United Nations in 1958 on the tenth anniversary of the adoption of the Universal Declaration of Human Rights, which she helped draft:

> Where, after all, do universal human rights begin?
>
> In small places, close to home, so close and so small that they cannot be seen on any maps of the world. Yet they are the world of the individual person; the neighborhood he lives in; the school or college he attends; the factory, farm, or office where he works, where every man, woman, and child seeks equal justice, equal opportunity, equal dignity, without discrimination.
>
> Unless these rights have meaning there, they have little meaning anywhere. Without concerted citizen action to uphold them close to home, we shall look in vain for progress in the larger world.

FOR THE COMMUNITY, ENFORCEMENT NOW AND LATER

An important aspect of TCRP's work included seeking out the community, being a part of it, and helping legally whatever organizing we could. Working at TCRP was not a nine-to-five office job. We showed up for community meetings, testified before city councils, school boards, and county commissions, and participated in demonstrations with our community partners.

We did our best to be part of whatever was of significance to a particular community organization. That lent credibility and trust. It also put us in a position where we could look at facts and measure how our legal work could help thrust progress forward. This sometimes led us to do work other than litigation but was nevertheless important and helpful to the community. Our annual human rights reports are an example.

One critical aspect of involving a community in this important work is follow-up enforcement. It is not helpful to win a case in a vacuum and then walk away with a victory only to find out a year later that the victory had not been enforced or those against whom the victory was obtained let the matter fall by the wayside.

Government is particularly adept at allowing matters to slip. A community group as the plaintiff in the lead and doing the organizing has a vested interest in the longevity of a victory. To make sure that, once victory is won, it stays won. We depended on community groups for this enforcement function, and they did it well. They could always call us back in if needed.

Our objective was to be part of the community we were working with and not see them just as a plaintiff or litigation vehicle for change but also as collaborators or, as we used to joke, "coconspirators." We were not someone those in need came to visit in an office; we were someone already out walking with the people.

Another TCRP characteristic is that we acted fast, at the speed of light sometimes, whether that meant filing litigation, holding a press event, or moving on anything else the people needed. Moving with alacrity let us try our best to fashion the narrative early on. Taking a slower path can undermine effectiveness, lose public attention, and inhibit crafting the proper narrative. Going on offense is better than being on defense or being late to the game. Not a single blade of grass grew under our feet.

A LONG, SWEET RIDE WITH THE MEDIA

TCRP embraced the media with a passion, viewing it as a vital civil rights organizing partner. Press visibility is a quintessential forum of community human rights education. It is key to raising consciousness and ginning up public support or opposition on vital issues.

We did our best to stir up public opinion and wasted no time doing so. TCRP's media job, as the justice advocate Bryan Stevenson characterized it, was to change the narrative. We did it well.

TCRP worked with both Spanish and English media when contesting an action that a local or state government agency or a private company was undertaking—or about to undertake—in the hope of preempting the issue or convincing the entity to change course. Being in Austin provided access to Spanish and English networks statewide and occasionally led to national coverage.

UNCEREMONIOUSLY SURROUNDED BY MY OWN TALKING HEADS

Despite my extensive use of the media, I did not like watching myself on television. It seemed embarrassing. There was one especially mortifying television appearance.

I was in a Montgomery Ward store one evening, taking a shortcut through the television sales section. This was back in the day when stores had various brands of floor models, all of them tuned to a single channel. I was right in the middle of the display. Local evening news was broadcasting, and suddenly an interview I had conducted with a local station appeared on the screens and a dozen or more television sets began synchronizing my image and voice. It was surprising and awkward.

I looked quickly to see if anyone noticed what was happening and might think I was showing a narcissistic streak. Fortunately, there were no other watchers; I escaped as fast as my feet could move.

Those were the days before corporate hatchet-job cutbacks on the number of reporters available to travel for newsworthy stories. It was easy enough to entice the media to a press conference with a well-timed teaser the night before. We hosted press conferences aplenty—almost weekly and sometimes twice per week.

We strove to build relationships such that, whenever the press wanted comment on a controversial civil rights matter, whether local or national, a reporter would be knocking at the door for a quick interview. We bent over backward to be accommodating, and this strategy served TCRP and our clients well.

One staffer once quipped it would be perilous to cross the path of a news camera and a TCRP representative moving toward each other. We tried to live up to that standard.

In announcing litigation or an organizing campaign, we structured the press conferences (often bilingually) around community members to amplify their voices. When appropriate, we invited local political leaders and celebrities such as Luci Baines Johnson to join in solidarity.

Reporters often tried to focus on the lawyers for comment, but we ensured that they heard the voices of the people we represented. It was as much a matter of dignity as it was empowering the community groups and individuals.

Even when fulfilling separate interview requests following a press conference, as was typical, TCRP attorneys made sure that a member or two of the community stood shoulder to shoulder with us so the message of solidarity appeared on the evening news.

For our offices along the border, the Mexican press was excellent. Their reporting was longer and deeper compared to their English peers across the Rio Grande. Spanish-language television in Texas usually presented better and more detailed coverage.

Sometimes cases came to us as a result of our media presence. The Williamson County constable religious test lawsuit, discussed in chapter 14, originated because of TCRP's intense public criticism of the county after the media had phoned for comments. The rejected applicants heard the press interview and showed up, ringing the doorbell at our offices.

Our salubrious media relationship helped us reach potential clients in rural areas and draw them to our services. This was true of expanding TCRP's VAWA outreach into East Texas. Clients came to us through our Spanish-language press work.

TCRP made it a practice to issue press releases about civil rights issues, whether local, statewide, or national. The print media would oblige us by printing op-eds that we routinely distributed, usually about six per year. Smaller newspapers were always hungry for columns to print. For twelve years I was a contributing writer for the *Texas Observer*, and for seven years with *Texas Lawyer*, which helped get the word out.

SALARIES AND TEAMWORK

Two deep philosophical issues distinguished us from other nonprofits and public interest law firms: modest salaries and team spirit. The typical capitalist view is to pay higher salaries according to skill level, the pedigree of one's education, and experience. We took the view that modest salaries attracted people committed to the cause, not to self-advancement. That was our experience, too.

There had to be some differential for lawyers because of debt incurred in law school. However, there was a loan forgiveness program for nonprofit organization attorneys that we could plug into. We also provided good staff benefits, which was helpful. I personally adhered to our modest salary philosophy. TCRP's accountant would complain that my salary was too low, which always led to an interesting discussion. My daughter, in elementary school at the time, mused one night at dinner about why we didn't have a swimming pool at the house like other attorneys. That led to another opportune discussion about values and community.

In hiring attorneys, the reputation of the law school that the applicant attended mattered less than the volunteer and community work the candidate had engaged in. An Ivy League applicant was on the same footing as anyone else. Previous volunteer and community work experience was important for other staff positions as well.

We approached all litigation as a team, both among ourselves and with community partners. We planned cases accordingly during strategy sessions. The idea was to be our own TCRP team just as much as we supported and were part of the larger community team. We did our level best to eschew attorney elitism. And we did our best to minimize internal hierarchal structures. Collegiality was our aspiration.

LAW STUDENT INTERNS ROCKED

Because they knew law student volunteers and summer interns would get on-the-ground legal experience in a just cause, TCRP had no trouble attracting fantastic young folks, sometimes as many as fifteen at a time in our offices. They all came with their own funding or simply as volunteers, at no cost to TCRP.

It was a blessing, exponentially because they increased our capacity to serve in so many respects. Sometimes, we would spend the fall months catching up with all the legal work the summer students did (and did well).

I unabashedly went a step further. Often, when one of my law school seminar students could not conjure up a topic for a paper, I would offer up whatever legal issue was broiling at TCRP. That mutually benefited us. A few seminar students joined us as interns. Over time, we employed two as staff attorneys.

During my quarter-century at TCRP, more than four hundred law students of astonishing diversity from across the country shared their time and talents, donating about 122,000 hours of legal work. The students' passion for civil rights inspired us and the clients whom they assisted. Some went on in their careers to continue the community engagement they began at TCRP. We encouraged that as much as we could. It was a pleasure to get to know them personally.

It may seem ironic, but I often discouraged idealistic young folks from going to law school. Jobs at nonprofits like TCRP are scarce. If the individual's desire was to make social change, I would suggest union or community organizing alternatives. My proffered wisdom more often than not went unheeded, which may be a good thing. I know of only two people who accepted my advice, one of whom went on to serve as a tenant organizer in New York City.

Our offices also opened their doors to interns from local colleges and universities and recruited students looking to earn college credits and do good work in the professions they were about to enter. Most of our undergraduate interns came from social work, community organizing, and paralegal programs and contributed enormously to our endeavors.

LOUDLY SINGING THE PRAISES OF VOLUNTEERS

In addition to law students and interns, hundreds of volunteers joined TCRP, and enough gratitude cannot go to them as they gifted us with their passion and talent. They increased our capacity for serving the greater good and offered us the opportunity to encourage them in future service to the community. It was an agreeable mutual relationship. Those who benefited the most were the people of Texas.

TCRP offices always found room for volunteers according to the skills and time they could devote. We did our best to tailor our tasks to them, not vice versa. We were bound together in the struggle for human rights and wanted to help expand their horizon of justice.

We also recruited volunteers from religious communities, including the Jesuit Volunteer Corps and Lutheran Border Servant Corps for our El Paso office. The Mercy Sisters (including Sister Moira Kenney, affectionately known as *La Monja*—"The Nun") provided staff for our South Texas office. Moira became quite respected within TCRP for spending six months in the federal prison camp in Bryan in 2003 for participating in the annual protest rally held at the United States Army's School of the Americas at Fort Benning, Georgia. Thousands gathered there every November to protest human rights abuses committed by its graduates who became dictators, torturers, and assassins in Central and South America. The school was closed in 2000 and reopened under a new name.

Two amazing volunteers came forward in El Paso (Gabby García) and Dallas (Cynthia Lucero) and helped get our offices off the ground there. Both were outstanding organizers.

We worked with UT Law student volunteers during spring breaks to conduct a well-attended clinic in South Texas to prepare last wills for people who could not afford an attorney. Wills are crucial estate planning tools for transferring property when the inevitable comes. If someone passes without a will, straightening out property issues later is difficult and expensive. The book's earlier VAWA and Title IX chapter also described terrific volunteer work. The list goes on.

By way of footnote, my first volunteer adventure was setting up the Monday evening pro bono East Austin Law Clinic in 1986, in cooperation with the UT Chicano Law Students Association and the Travis County Bar Association, at a neighborhood center. Eighteen lawyers signed up. After four years the local bar association took over the clinic and expanded its operation. Two volunteer attorneys became judges, and another went on to become president of the Texas State Bar.

There were so many decent people willing to help if we just asked. It was all about finding and coordinating with them. Our offices were more like organizing centers than legal silos.

COOPERATING ATTORNEYS

Likewise, TCRP extensively recruited cooperating attorneys on a pro bono basis for many of our lawsuits. They significantly augmented TCRP's litigation capacity and our impact throughout Texas. Sometimes they cocounseled with us or wrote briefs and handled appeals. At other times they took over the entire case.

This strategy had multiple benefits. One was to bring another lawyer's time, skill, and resources into the litigation. Another was to help broaden the legal experiences of attorneys in private practice so they would be more inclined to accept civil rights cases on their own. The involvement of prominent mainstream law firms likewise helped attract favorable attention from judges.

It also improved the learning curve for TCRP lawyers. We typically concentrated on crossing the murky River Styx of legal hurdles just to establish liability, which was a hard task indeed. Lawyers in private practice, however, offered great insight into how to evaluate a case monetarily for settlement or trial purposes. For our part, we showed them how to structure social change into a settlement (in addition to winning dollars if the case merited). We had a mutually helpful learning partnership.

When attorney fees resulted from a lawsuit, the cooperating attorneys usually donated their shares to TCRP's coffers as part of their pro bono work. It was a good arrangement overall.

It is heartening to note the increasing number of attorneys who handle civil rights cases these days, particularly against law enforcement abuses, many more than when TCRP got off the ground all those decades ago.

We showed our respect and honored cooperating attorneys and their law firms at our annual Texas Bill of Rights Dinners with the Kristi Couvillon Award, named after the former TCRP law clerk and Austin lawyer who met an untimely death. Law firms appreciated the TCRP imprimatur and duly noted it on their websites.

CSR QUASI-VOLUNTEERS: HELPING TCRP HUM ALONG

We sought volunteers from everywhere. One group of volunteers (perhaps "quasi-volunteers" is more accurate) came from Community Service and Restitution (CSR) programs, whereby people with low-level misdemeanor convictions, such as DWI or marijuana use, were able to pay off fines or avoid jail sentences by completing twelve to twenty hours of work with a nonprofit organization. Some chose TCRP.

Given the limited time with us, they usually performed light office duties. Some had the skills for conducting nonlegal research. Even a few lawyers who themselves were fulfilling CSR showed up, which was helpful for legal work. Our goal was to maximize whatever talent they brought to the table and to draw them, at least philosophically, into the human rights family.

My first CSR experience was with a young African American police officer, convicted of lobbing a bottle, while off duty, at a KKK march on Congress Avenue in downtown Austin. The judge thought it would be helpful for him to spend time with us, learning better respect for people's First Amendment rights, even if one had an understandably visceral reaction to unpopular advocacy. At the end of his stay, we had an interesting discussion about how much better he begrudgingly respected the First Amendment.

Some CSRs continued on with us as regular volunteers or helped with events like the annual Bill of Rights Dinner. One CSR assignee, an accomplished professional photographer, held a fundraiser for TCRP featuring his artwork.

ANNUAL HUMAN RIGHTS REPORTS

One outstanding example of volunteer assistance was TCRP's annual human rights reports. The reports addressed a variety of issues over the years, directed toward educating the larger community on what our main theme was for that year. Volunteers helped prepare and write the reports and then conducted press events surrounding each year's report. We could not have produced the reports without these volunteers.

The human rights reports were in-depth publications, typically around fifty pages, addressing issues for which litigation might not be available, either because case law was unfavorable or because a lawsuit would be prohibitively expensive or logistically impossible.

The first report zeroed in on discriminatory law enforcement practices toward the African American community in Palestine, Texas. The practices were not egregious enough to be unconstitutional, but they were bad and offensive. We introduced the report at a press conference. The *Dallas Morning News* picked up the story and ran with our report. It did not take long for the police to meet with the community and establish reforms. Shining a light on a discomforting situation can lead to positive impacts. The report accomplished what a lawsuit could not in that situation.

Other human rights reports tackled the rise in hate crimes statewide, the deficiency of disability access at Texas courthouses, and the lack of diversity in lawyers hired to assist judges on the Supreme Court of Texas and the Court of Criminal Appeals. Our report on the disparity between the funding of minority versus nonminority schools in Austin drew considerable attention and helped bring about some funding shifts—though not enough in our view.

The press was very helpful in publicizing the reports. The media gave us good mileage.

DINNER IS SERVED

A celebratory way to spread the good word, share solidarity, and raise funds was our annual Texas Bill of Rights Dinner. We held twenty-four in all. The keynote speakers were always superb, including María Hinojosa (of NPR Latino USA), Sissy Farenthold, Paul Rusesabagina (of *Hotel Rwanda* fame), Linda Brown Thompson and Cheryl Brown Henderson (*Brown v. Board of Education* students), Dolores Huerta, Senator Bernie Sanders, Reverend James Lawson, Lilly Ledbetter (namesake of the Lilly Ledbetter Fair Pay Act), Noam Chomsky, Sister Helen Prejean (*Dead Man Walking*), Senator Ted Kennedy, Sharon Robinson (Jackie Robinson's daughter), Rami Nashashibi (of Chicago's Inner-City Muslim Action Network), Jim Hightower, Michael Tigar, and Danny Glover.

TCRP honored and recognized community groups, activists, and cooperating attorneys with special awards at these dinners. As Molly Ivins grew ill and her time among us was drawing to a close, we created the Molly Ivins "Give 'Em Hell" Journalism Award and asked her to present it to Leonard Pitts, our keynote speaker, which she did in typical Mollyesque fashion.

The Bill of Rights Dinners brought media attention and enhanced TCRP's public image. Our South Texas, El Paso, and Odessa offices sponsored similar events.

LEAVE NO DOLLAR ON THE TABLE: SPECIAL PROJECTS

TCRP scouted for and grabbed every funding opportunity even remotely in sight. To that end we undertook many special matters, including projects on prisoners, veterans, police relations, economic justice, and Dreamers. We aspired to expand our reach as much as we could, particularly into rural Texas. The operative philosophy was that TCRP, if money was available for a special project that would enhance justice, would find the staff for it. And we did.

Chapter 14 describes our prisoner rights project. We also had a court program for veterans in Midland/Odessa and Central Texas, a police–community relations project in Hidalgo County, the Fuerza del Valle worker rights initiative in South Texas and El Paso, a joint consumer education effort with LUPE, and a project in Hidalgo County to help people adjust oppressive property deed contracts to avoid exorbitant interest rates and repossessions for being late on a monthly payment (they were able to convert those deed contracts into regular mortgages).

President Barack Obama created the Deferred Action for Childhood Arrivals (DACA) or Dreamers program to protect young adults whose parents brought them to the United States without legal documentation as children. In response, the Austin office organized a DACA assistance program. DACA kept them safe from deportation and provided them with work authorization for temporary, renewable periods. DACA recipients moved into a variety of occupations. Many joined the professions, especially teaching. Everyone benefited from this arrangement.

SPREADING THE GOOD WORD FAR AND WIDE

TCRP jumped at every opportunity to speak at school functions, college classes, various conferences, and continuing legal education seminars for lawyers. The idea was that getting the word out might encourage others to become involved in civil rights or at least be more supportive and change their views. This was part and parcel of our public education work, to which we were solidly committed. Sometimes these talks provided occasions to lift a powerful prophetic voice for human rights.

Thanks to an invitation from the US Department of State's diplomacy program, TCRP staff met once or twice each year with visiting judges and human rights lawyers from other countries to offer our perspectives on the state of civil rights in this country. It was fascinating to compare notes with peers. Dialogue is always good. We shared similar goals but operated under different systems with varying degrees of institutional freedom. I admired and respected the people we met. Quite often their professional challenges were more severe than ours here at home.

Not surprisingly, I spoke and wrote extensively on constitutional law for general as well as professional audiences. Besides my twenty-seven-year adjunct professor career at UT Law and nine years at St. Mary's University School of Law, for fourteen years I also taught evening undergraduate courses at UT in civil rights and famous American trials, doing my best to "corrupt young minds," as I sometimes joked when introducing students to the art of critical thinking. Teaching was a good way of staying intellectually active.

A good quantity of nighttime oil was burned authoring *The Texas Bill of Rights: A Commentary and Litigation Manual* (plus a second edition), showing how Texas courts, historically and in recent times, had favorably extended or could apply greater-than-federal constitutional protections in various circumstances.

Unfortunately, Texas courts became more conservative, rendering my treatise into a historical piece rather than a legal activist's manual (at least for the time being). Hopefully, in the future, someone else can pick up this strain of legal reasoning and run with it. I enjoyed academia and writing learned treatises, but having just one foot in the door was enough. For me personally, academia and the pragmata of life should be a bridge to each other.

For three summers (2013–2015), the University of Texas International Student & Scholar Services enlisted me as an instructor to help introduce Iraqi college students to the ideals behind democratic civil society.

As I look back over my career, one of its most unforeseen aspects was how much writing I would do. I never anticipated that. I grew into writing because of its importance. I cannot count how many times I have felt gratitude in my heart to those who patiently taught me to write. I hope I have done them honor.

The most surprising facet of my career was how many doors opened to someone with a law license. It drew respect from foes, though not their admiration. Attending law school was one of the best decisions of my life. I owe it to that "Underdog Saturday" so many years ago.

COURT-AWARDED ATTORNEY FEES

One way in which TCRP sustained itself financially was by insisting on attorney fees in successful litigation. Most laws under which we sued entitled us to claim the hourly rate that attorneys in private practice would receive calculated according to their skill and experience. We could also claim litigation expenses in most cases (paralegal time, copying costs, and experts, for example).

Court-ordered compensation for fees and costs went into our general account, which financed TCRP's overall program. The court might award $400/hour to an attorney in private practice, for example, which was certainly greater than a TCRP attorney's $30/hour salary average. The difference between what the lawyer earned from the court and received in salary would support TCRP staff and operations.

Attorney fees didn't roll in every day, of course, only when a case wrapped up. It was important to fight for every dollar to which TCRP was entitled. The balance of our income came from foundation grants and fund-raising activities, such as the annual Texas Bill of Rights Dinner.

MIDNIGHT FIRE AT TCRP'S AUSTIN OFFICE: THE COMMUNITY LIFTS US UP

Shoestring nonprofits like TCRP live with ever-present worries about break-ins and fires (whether accidental or arson). Our fear became a nightmare on October 30, 2013, when an electrical wiring glitch in a front office set fire to our Austin building at midnight and destroyed part of it. Smoke damage permeated the entire office.

No words can describe the dreaded midnight this-can't-be-true call I received from the ADT security agency and then the sinking feeling in the pit of my stomach while driving up Montopolis Drive and seeing the smoldering building and fire trucks come into view.

Fortunately, we had substantially upped our insurance a few months before—talk about serendipitous—and Texas RioGrande Legal Aid kindly offered us office space the following day. We held a teary-eyed outdoor staff meeting the morning of the fire in a drizzle next to our burned building, then were off to our temporary exile for seven months while we rebuilt. We barely missed a beat thanks to the staff, allies, our TRLA colleagues, and fortuitous insurance coverage. For a disaster, things could not have gone any better.

The fire showed the depth of community backing for TCRP. Individuals and foundations, especially the Texas Access to Justice Foundation, generously opened their hearts and pocketbooks. Community folks of all kinds showed up and gave their time on Saturdays to help refurbish as we got close to the grand reopening. It was heartwarming to see so many people pitching in.

The fire and the reconstruction offered excellent fund-raising opportunities, and people and organizations responded generously. We used the terra cotta wall tiles again in the front lobby to honor our donors—forty-six new tiles surrounding the thirty-nine originals charred by the fire. Having the office burn was not a good happenstance, but we came out of it with our feet on solid ground.

I will always remember my deeply personal conversation with the contractor overseeing the reconstruction. He made a point of commenting on our disability work when I stopped by during rebuilding. He talked about helping his paraplegic son, against the odds, compete in this country as a weightlifter and then travel to Norway to become a world-class champion. He understood our work and what the disability rights movement was about, and he helped me better understand it and be proud of what we did.

OCTOBER 30: ALWAYS AN AUSPICIOUS DAY?

The date of October 30 was never a good day for TCRP after the 2013 fire and 2015 flood. Another October 30, however, was memorable and funny. It was the birth of our second son in 1975. I was up all night when he was born, just a day or two into a criminal jury trial that I had been appointed to handle.

That morning, right in the middle of examining my own witness on the stand, I fell dead asleep with my head in my hands. I awoke when I heard the judge saying, quite loudly, "Counsel, counsel." It was unclear how long I had been asleep, so I gambled and tried to act like I was deep in thought while looking sheepishly sideways out of the corner of my left eye to see if the jurors were watching. They were.

No damage was done to my client, however. We won. I imagine the jury was sympathetic, since I managed to slip mention of my son's birth into the closing argument—always a smooth move with Rio Grande Valley juries.

So many inspiring people—and such good fortune to live on the planet with them.

Fire was not the only misfortune to beset the building. Fate struck again two years later on the exact anniversary date of the fire: a torrential storm of great magnitude hit in Austin and dumped enough water to flood our thirteen-room office. A pump extracted 350 gallons of water after we swept what we could out the back door.

THREATS, HATE MAIL, AND KIND GESTURES

Threats of violence happened, as one might expect. Following the first threat, Pharr's chief of police brought me a bulletproof vest to wear during the McAllen police litigation. He was acting on an insider tip received from a McAllen officer. That seemed a bit much. Besides, it was an old lead vest, no doubt retrieved from a storage dustbin. It was very heavy and hardly conducive attire for our hot, humid, cinder-block building bereft of air-conditioning. I stashed it under my desk.

There was no end to the hate mail that arrived for all sorts of reasons. One deeply hurtful letter blamed me for the killing of a McAllen police officer because I had sued the department. That, she said, had made the police afraid to do their jobs for fear of litigation, thereby exposing them to danger. She also published her mean diatribe as a letter to the editor in the *McAllen Monitor*. Being blamed so directly for someone's death was a piercing experience.

Then there was the older, well-dressed Anglo woman who stopped me one pleasant sunny spring afternoon as I walked down Congress Avenue, returning from the Capitol. She pointed a finger at me from about six feet away and shouted: "I know who you are, and I hate everything you do!" I kept walking and took that surprise shoutout as an unintended badass compliment and loved it.

The incident with that one angry lady paled in comparison to the generous words from many individuals, usually African Americans or Mexican Americans, in stores and other venues, often prompted by TCRP's visible media presence. We also received more than our due of cordial, heartening letters of thanks and encouragement. We made sure the staff saw these.

HELPING KEEP AUSTIN WEIRD

Every once in a while, we had a case that was just fun, such as helping the internationally famous Cathedral of Junk art installation prevail in its life-and-death struggle to keep the city of Austin from shutting it down in 2010. The owner, Vince Hannemann, began building the multistory, thirty-ton monumental sculpture in his backyard in 1988. He fashioned it from cast-offs of all sorts: bicycle parts, lawnmowers, computer components, toys, car bumpers, bottles, skis, and on and on.

The sculpture quintessentially represents the unofficial city motto "Keep Austin Weird." Cathedral of Junk has attracted more than 100,000 visitors, hosted countless weddings and parties, and has drawn worldwide media stories. TCRP board member Chuck Herring, as one might expect if you know him, was relentless in his support of the preservation effort. The city acquiesced and granted a permit.

THE SPACESHIP LANDING PAD

Like most nonprofit public service organizations, TCRP had its share of bizarre calls and letters, many of them during a full moon phase. One day, early on in my career, three rugged-looking, middle-aged guys, who could have been cast for a West Texas reality television series about oil drilling, showed up, seeking a court order against the construction of a 7-Eleven store along the expressway. Why? Because it would interfere with the spaceship that regularly landed on that stretch of land.

I gently demurred, offering unconvincing reasons (for them) why we could not take their case. They didn't take "no" kindly and two weeks later served us with an "Intergalactic Indictment." The other attorney in the office freaked out enough that he took shelter in the storage room. We did not appear for trial. Fortunately, no harm befell us. Nor were we cited for contempt of the intergalactic court.

TAKEAWAYS

More than 2,600 cases tell the tale, with the paramount message being that all civil rights is local. The key to success, of course, was the many other communities that we worked with, and those who helped lift up our mission, throughout the state of Texas.

The Spanish and English media, of course, played their role, especially when we had an important message to broadcast and print. Building relationships over many years helped us carry those messages. And the fact that we were a law firm shored up our credibility—measly salaries and all.

We couldn't have done all this without the help of our law student and undergraduate interns and cooperating attorneys. Not everyone is cut out for law school and a legal career, but many are—and we found plenty. We were blessed to receive the help of many, many amazing volunteers and our "quasi-volunteers."

Our annual human rights reports became a highlight over decades, and our Texas Bill of Rights Dinners—true celebrations of the spirit we tried to embody—did likewise. Fund-raising was a struggle, but these components of our work helped keep us on the path toward justice for everyone as well as special projects for prisoners, veterans, police relations, economic justice, and Dreamers. Regular speaking appearances at schools, conferences, and all manner of functions helped along the way, as did court-awarded attorney fees.

We had our share of lows: October 30 will always be remembered with melancholy as the date of both fire and flood. And the threats of violence and the hate mail we received were troubling to say the least. But there were also highs—kind gestures on the street, in stores, and at our offices.

There were also the funny moments, such as when we received the "Intergalactic Indictment" to save the UFO landing pad. And we will always enjoy laughing about the Cathedral of Junk campaign. Keep Austin Weird, as they say.

TCRP was indeed unique . . . and badass.

17

FINAL THOUGHTS

Keeping the Marathon Going

Robert Frost's "The Road Not Taken" sums up my personal and professional journey:

> Two roads diverged in a yellow wood,
> And sorry I could not travel both.
> . . .
> I took the one less traveled by,
> And that has made all the difference.

His poem grabbed me as a high-school senior and stuck with me. I mulled it over whenever a life-directional choice showed up. Choosing the less traveled path meant turning away from the road "with the better claim," as Frost put it, a safer and more socially accepted pathway.

Frost is spot-on. When hiking through the woods, taking the less-trekked path means a more uncertain and difficult walk. Getting lost is possible. Sometimes one must muster navigational creativity. Leaves cover hidden rocks and holes that cause a stumble. But we rely on our choice, hoping that trail may offer a brilliant sunset view or a breathtaking panorama of the canyons below.

I chose the riskier path, one I trusted would reach a more splendid sunset to share with fellow travelers. Being able to work a half-century with them for justice was an arduous but incredibly colorful journey.

The thought has crossed my mind that much of what this memoir describes happened within a unique groundswell of time from the 1960s into the early 2000s, surging with the civil rights movement. That rhythm of justice played around the world, not just in this country and Texas. The times begged for change and found it.

The groundswell has ebbed, as historically occurs. In those fifty years, society journeyed through a hopeful era of amazing human rights progress back into a repressive, divisive epoch. How long until the next groundswell or the tempo of the rhythm picks up again, and how to help it happen, are questions in front of us. Meanwhile we march on, learning how to be honed by the forces against us.

When I was teaching, I came across a quote from Eugene Debs, an indomitable leader of the labor movement in the early twentieth century, that is worthy of frequent recall: "Every struggle for justice is lost, is lost, and is lost until it is finally won." I often had to pass on that message when things got tough. It helped us keep faith and keep moving forward.

Perhaps my narrative may help point toward prospective human rights strategies when the rhythm picks up again and the cycle turns once more toward social progress. History may not repeat itself; but it can sometimes rhyme, as the saying goes.

My wish is that this memoir may encourage others to take the road less traveled. Maybe it will inspire kindred souls and young attorneys to dive into the world of grassroots organizing for justice. Above all, this memoir should offer hope. The people with whom I struggled offered hope, and I pass it on.

Civil rights work is difficult and sometimes dangerous. It demands personal sacrifice and often reordering one's life, of moving from being a do-gooder to becoming a doer of good. It is the difference between service and solidarity, working *for* or working *with*. Helping people make a difference in their lives brought me peace of mind and calmness of spirit. "Becoming proximate" to those with whom one seeks solidarity is not easy, but it is essential and rewarding in spirit.

As I reflect on my life's work, I came to see my experience as unfolding or maturing in phases, which overlapped with each other. In the beginning, what motivated me was a sense of injustice and my desire and responsibility to adjust what I could, even daring to trust that a few well-placed class action lawsuits would resolve the matter.

As I worked more closely with oppressed and marginalized communities, I began to understand better the community's own internal wisdom and culture and how to respect that. This meant sidetracking any tendency to "colonize" or prioritize what seemed the best approach to me or others as to where things should go. The job was to work with the community to discern where things should go and how to get there.

Then I began to see human rights work like the poem of Hafiz, the fourteenth-century Persian lyric poet and mystic: how to be the hole in the flute through which people can make the music of their lives, the harmony of their being.

Over the years, through dogged badassery, TCRP became a buttress against governments and individuals who would kneel on the necks of the people. We were an ally of those who bravely rose up for their rights against powerful adversaries. We did "uncomfortable things" together and made "good trouble" together, to invoke the wise counsel of Bryan Stevenson and John Lewis.

Not everyone liked everything TCRP did, which was a good sign; but everyone liked something we did, another good sign. One example was a Republican bank president who served as a TCRP board member and became a substantial donor. Who would have done this work, had not TCRP helped, especially in minority and rural communities?

Lawyers are essential and necessary in any social movement. We could offer our work to the courageous activists and people around us. Litigation is expensive. Our work came at no financial cost to those we served. It was the least we could do. We had the expertise. Not every case was monumental in the large scale of things, but it could be monumental in the context of individual lives and help them with the music of their lives, as Hafiz put it. It hurt that we could accept only a small percentage of the cases that people brought us.

Keeping TCRP's goals always in front of me and maintaining appropriate boundaries became another lesson learned from César Chávez. At the height of the Chicano movement in the late 1960s and early 1970s, a concerted effort was underway to draft him as the country's premier Chicano leader. César steadfastly resisted, insisting that his sole mission was to organize agricultural laborers. He would support all organizing efforts but dedicate himself to only one. Good boundaries.

Activists of my generation, many of whom today are leaving the playing field or will soon enough, share anxiety that the organizations that we built and nourished are changing in ways unrecognizable to us. We hope the new teams coming on board will commit themselves to painstaking grassroots organizing. It is not a nine-to-five task or a five-days-per-week effort. Human rights is a way of life, not a mere job.

It's important for us that the new team resist a certain professionalization of the nonprofit sector that appears to be underway. People these days seem to join an organization for a couple of years and then leap to another. The reasons are mixed. There are those, of course, who search for the place where they should be and that sustains them. For me, solidarity and long-term dedication were always the main goal.

Another concern that hovers over us is the strange view afoot that one need only organize through social media. Posturing on social media about justice sometimes seems out of hand and wastes precious time and energy. To be sure, social media is an excellent tool and can be a springboard into organizing. But it's just step one.

The second step of successful organizing, adjunct to social media, is putting on the shoes, hitting the pavement, talking face to face, and bringing people together. The temptation of social media organizing by itself can become a delusional dodge from the hard labors of the field. The forces arrayed on the other side have top-notch social media experts and often outperform us. But they are not experts on doing the in-person, door-to-door visiting.

Social media is one-on-one contact, often impersonal. A group meeting hears many voices and shares them in a different multipersonal dynamic, which is the first step of walking out the door together to do something. I always liked Dolores Huerta's concise maxim: "Walk the street with us into history. Get off the sidewalk."

Doing community work also means being present in the office and accessible. Working online remotely from home is convenient for staff, but not for the people. It removes staff from the community. Nor are staff available when a sudden community need arises, as often happens. It also impedes media availability. "Being proximate" means having a daily physical presence among the people. We work for the people, not for our convenience.

Another caveat, hopefully reflecting some wisdom: when we were discussing this memoir in process, Juanita Valdez-Cox, LUPE's retired executive director, commented about the new generation advocating for personnel policies to deal with burnout.

Her response, with which I agree, was: "Hell, there's no time for burnout in this work." As with any absolute statement, a qualification needs to follow. Our constant reflection should be whether we are becoming self-absorbed to the point of losing our focus on poor and minority folks. When that happens, we become co-opted and even part of the oppression that weighs heavily on their shoulders. We must not be gatekeepers for the empire of the greedy, corrupt, and powerful.

Staying connected with others who do human rights work is crucial. Mutual support should flow from us to allied spirits and back. The giving and taking, the back-and-forth, between the individual and community is a necessary cadence for human betterment. Celebrations with each other help tamp down the exhaustion that can creep up on us.

The redoubtable Molly Ivins said it perfectly: "So keep fightin' for freedom and justice, beloveds, but don't you forget to have fun doin' it." We lose only if we quit. Having fun and well-placed times to recharge are good preventative medicine.

As far as staying personally grounded in human rights work, I remember being on a speakers panel at an Austin Community College student gathering. There were four of us from different grassroots organizations.

Our presentations outlined the woes we faced, the setbacks, the baby steps forward, the surprising victories, the "blood, toil, tears, and sweat," and the daunting forces arrayed against us. During the wrap-up question-and-answer session, a young woman stood in the center of the assembly with pen and notepad in hand and asked: "How do you keep going? How did you continue doing what you're doing day after day, facing everything you face, and not burn out?"

The question was a surprise. It was the first time in all my speeches and presentations over the years that someone had stood and asked it that bluntly. I was thankful that the answers started at the other end of the table so I had time to ponder a pithy meaningful reply.

Quite surprising, each of our answers had a common thread: to have an anchor in spirituality. This reminded me again of John Lewis: "The civil rights movement was based on faith. Many of us who were participants in this movement saw our involvement as an extension of our faith."

Our group's views on spirituality were of quite different shapes and sizes but had a commonality in the fundamental grounding that kept us going and upright. I am not sure what Lewis meant by "faith" here, but we all had it in some fashion, moving forward, at times without the North Star, but always steadfast. Our focus was on others, not ourselves.

Upon retirement, my spirituality led me to serve the Proyecto Santiago immigrant congregation at St. James' Episcopal Church in Austin as an unsalaried priest. It was coming full circle in a sense, having started in the seminary as a high-schooler and returning to church ministry fifty-six years later, though not without similar structural tensions experienced the first time around. It's intriguing that a number of lawyers eventually go into ministry.

The new direction allowed me to organize a Reading Buddies program at the predominantly minority Norman-Sims Elementary School, help establish the Texas Pauli Murray Scholarship for ministry students of color, and work with the Casa Marianella refugee center to help develop an apartment housing program for asylum-seeking families.

Keeping my lawyer hat available allowed me to prepare immigrant women in the Hutto detention facility for their initial asylum hearings. Their accounts of what drove them on the perilous journey from their hometowns were often wrenching—violence from corrupt police and the cartels and often rape. The women sometimes wept as we reviewed their painful personal details as we prepared for the hearing, and sometimes I felt like crying along with them. Laying out the excruciating particulars was their only chance for asylum, and they had only thirty nervous minutes to make their preliminary case as to why they should proceed to a full hearing later. The prospect was deportation if they didn't satisfy the government's interrogator. Organizing legal workshops for immigrants is now part of my life.

The lawyer cap was also put on for preparing amicus curiae briefs in voting rights and prisoner rights cases and, for four years, assisting with KOOP 91.7 FM's Community Radio weekly Monday evening *Civil Rights and Wrongs* program. On-the-air discussions with younger human rights activists were always a pleasure. They were doing so many good things and taking their place in the community in our stead. Equally rewarding is teaching at Austin's Lifelong Learning Institute about the labor movement and civil rights in Texas. And I continue to author op-ed columns for Texas newspapers.

Physical activity outdoors was also important to grounding and self-sustenance. I took the kids camping as often as possible, including Inks Lake on weekends and New Mexico and West Texas in the summers. My daughter and I later hiked a hundred miles of Spain's Camino de Santiago in July 1989, arriving in Compostela for her birthday. The countryside solitude and open-air hiking were spirit-stimulating. There's a camaraderie among us who have walked the Camino and almost a kinship with the Spaniards who greeted us from their farms along the way, urging us on: *Buen Camino*.

Every spring for twenty-four years a group of us, family and friends, journeyed to Big Bend in West Texas and canoed the Lower Canyons. For a week, we slept under the stars on the desert floor while the Rio Grande rippled past. No tents, just the shadowy canyon walls at night and the Milky Way overhead. Full moons were particularly splendid, giving off almost enough brilliance to read a book. Cell-phone and internet service were nonexistent. Just the Big Dipper over our heads, rotating around the North Star. A few hawks glided above during the days, accompanying us down the river, with the occasional soaring eagle.

I always bunked near the river to hear the flowing water during the night. One morning, when I got up for some early coffee, I saw the telltale trail of a medium-size snake that, during the night, had slithered down the nearby sandy hill and across my sleeping bag on the way to the river. I loved it.

We built great camaraderie over the years. Two canoe buddies went on to become prominent water rights attorneys in New Mexico. We shared notes, strategies, and beer, paddling down the Rio Grande under the baking sun.

Teaching at the University of Texas gave me access to a gym, where I put in a few years on the handball courts, including once even with César

THE FLAGS ARE QUITE DIFFERENT

Occasionally while canoeing downriver we would stop to hike up a canyon wall. One time I had sprained my ankle, so I stayed behind to watch the six canoes and read. My canoe was flying a large Ireland flag, as it was St. Patrick's Day.

The Border Patrol came boating upriver, stopped, and asked if I was transporting people illegally across the river, as if that was even possible given the steep canyon walls on both sides and it being broad daylight. I replied, "No, why?" The agent pointed out how I was displaying the Mexican flag.

After I clarified that it was the Irish tricolor for St. Patrick's Day, he gave me a blank look, and the patrol moved on. Go figure.

Chávez. There was also daily jogging for thirty years until the knees demanded I switch to cycling. Runners talk about a kind of nirvana while jogging. I agree. Jogging four miles every day provided a rhythm to quietly contemplate people's cases and possible strategies and to be at peace.

For two months in 1979 we got to Spain, where Rebecca and I taught at the University of Salamanca. Living in a different country offers a perspective distinct from just visiting as a tourist. It was a pleasant time, with weekend soirées to various Spanish and Portuguese cities. Toledo, with its El Greco art, and cosmopolitan Lisbon were my favorites.

This memoir is about hope, digging down deeply into ourselves to live according to that hope, just as our courageous predecessors in justice did, often at great suffering and personal cost. That is what they expected of us. Always move forward bravely. Accompany others in their pain. Standing still in this work is moving backward.

We all should affix to our bathroom mirrors a daily reminder that, at every moment of our existence, we affect others' lives. Fred Ross, the renowned Saul Alinsky organizer, used to visit César Chávez every Saturday after César's discharge from the United States Navy. Like many others in East Los Angeles, César spent Saturdays with his pals, drinking beer and tinkering with their autos. Every Saturday Fred Ross would go by and cajole the future farmworker leader: "César, you can do better than this." One day, César finally asked, "Like what?" The rest is history. Fred Ross should be our model.

None of our heroes descended from heaven and suddenly appeared among us. Others close by helped form them into our heroes. In turn, our heroes—personal and public—help mold us, as do all those around us. They pass on to us the voices that inspired, encouraged, and grounded them, expecting us to do the same.

We all help each other build community, now and into the eras yet to come, just as those before us did. The novelist David Mitchell put it beautifully in his novel *Cloud Atlas*: "From womb to tomb, we are bound to others, past and present. And by each crime and every kindness, we birth our future."

This memoir began by honoring people from the community, our staff, and all our friends for being tenacious and hopeful partners in bending the wobbly moral arc toward justice a little more. And so it ends. It is only fitting to conclude in the same way.

A fortunate wind blew us together. Indeed! And in our bold fight together for justice, it was awesome being a badass. *¡Viva la Causa! ¡Adelante!*

Don't be satisfied with stories, how things
Have gone with others. Unfold
Your own myth, so everyone will understand
The passage, *We have opened you.*

RUMI, "UNFOLD YOUR OWN MYTH"

AFTERWORD

At the time this book is going to print, wars are escalating across the world, our democracy is shaking under the weight of oligarchy and extremism, and the climate crisis is accelerating. Many young people, who are usually the energy behind our movements, feel demoralized and demobilized. Understandably, I'm constantly asked: "What gives you hope? Why should we keep going?" The responses to these questions are different for each person, but I think many of the best answers are tucked somewhere among the pages of Jim Harrington's life story.

Here's a few of those answers for me: the world can be awful, but the fight for a better world can be joyful. Can't we, like those before us, rebuild a community of happy warriors that aren't disconnected, isolated, or burned out? And another answer: Texans before us have overcome even greater odds. How could we waste their sacrifices? The farmworkers, the litigators, the Chicanos and Chicanas—they all knew that hopelessness was not an option. They beat back abuse from sheriffs, big businesses, Supreme Court justices and senators. We could do the same, then pass along the unfinished portions of our struggle to the next generation of activists and organizers.

In Texas this not-so-distant history is all around us. If we keep this history in mind—if we measure our movements in generations and not in election cycles—I think those of us in the fight for social justice will feel less lost. I hope that some of my own story, and how it picks up from where Jim's memoir leaves off, proves useful for readers asking themselves: "What do we do now?"

I can trace a line from Jim Harrington and Chuck Herring conspiring over tacos directly to my own elections to Austin City Council and Congress. They used to meet at Las Manitas, the beloved Mexican restaurant on Congress Avenue where César Chávez once marched alongside a flood of workers from across Texas. Las Manitas helped launch my electoral career, not because I would eat there frequently (I stepped inside only once that I can recall) but because it was eventually torn down.

In 2011, the city of Austin gave millions of dollars in subsidies to White Lodging, a development corporation, to replace Las Manitas with a luxury Marriott hotel. At the time, I was an organizer with Workers Defense Project, an organization of Texas immigrant workers. Two young volunteers—Emily Timm and Cristina Tzintzun—drew heavily from the model of the United Farm Workers union to create Workers Defense Project.

One day at the Workers Defense office in East Austin, I heard from two workers that they were being paid less than the city had required on White Lodging's Marriott project. To hold the corporation accountable, I tracked down dozens more workers on their lunch breaks, and they signed a stack of sworn affidavits attesting to illegal underpayments. Of course, I got help from a bunch of people: especially an experienced organizer named Philip Lawhon from the electrical workers union and Cynthia Perez, who used to run Las Manitas with her sister. Cynthia knew the spots where everyone went for lunch now that her restaurant was gone.

Sworn testimony in hand, we took the fight to court. We didn't have much money, but we did have a great (and free) lawyer: Brian McGiverin from the Texas Civil Rights Project. Brian's director was none other than Jim Harrington. We demanded that workers be paid what they were owed and that White Lodging lose the millions of dollars in subsidies given to the Marriott hotel project.

At the time, I didn't know anything about the history of TCRP. I just wanted to beat the bullies, and I was ready to use every tool available—from the courthouse to the court of public opinion. We marched up and down Congress Avenue, in the same footsteps of the farmworkers decades before. We fought the mayor and pressed City Hall to crack down on the developer.

The big corporation hosted a counterdemonstration at City Hall. Dozens of workers marched into City Council chambers wearing "I support White Lodging" stickers. Little did White Lodging know that we had conducted Dolores Huerta–style house meetings, and we had already won some of these workers' trust and support. The sticker-wearing workers happily told the media that in fact they did not support White Lodging—they had just been required by their employer to come to City Hall. When elected officials found out that these workers supported our cause, and not the developer's agenda, the shady tactic backfired and momentum shifted to our side. Nothing was more fun than winning at the game that the bullies thought they'd rigged.

Finally, in 2013, our coalition of trade unionists, civil rights organizers, and our poor and working-class members were victorious. White Lodging had to pay back millions of dollars for their indiscretions. The same progressive coalition that had been built a generation before us was finding its power once again.

Our David-versus-Goliath victory inspired my 24-year-old self to run for City Council in 2014. We spoke to thousands of voters at their doors and in the streets, and I won by a 30-point margin. But within moments of this big win, Texas's right-wing election deniers sued me. Their conspiracy theories about election fraud and unreliable voting machines were unprecedented in our city. I didn't know where to turn for help when a couple of lawyers told me they wanted to lead my volunteer legal team: Chuck Herring and his spouse, Ginny Agnew, with Jim Harrington quietly chipping in $200 to the legal defense fund.

After forty years in the struggle, Jim and company simply had not quit. They were supporting the next generation to pick up where they left off. Whether we fully knew it or not, our movement of young organizers in Texas had picked up the torch. We felt the momentum. With their help, the lawsuit was thrown out, and we felt unstoppable.

We continued Jim's efforts to support workers in Austin and beyond: we raised the minimum wage for city workers, built new unions, and passed paid sick day policies. We promoted police reform ordinances that were overwhelmingly approved at the ballot box. With help from lawyers at TCRP, we united cities to sue the state to block Texas's anti-immigrant laws.

But despite years of successful work after the White Lodging fight, our communities were still sliding backward. In many ways, everyday Texans had fewer rights and less power in 2024 than we had in 2014, from the rollback of worker protections to the gutting of the Voting Rights Act.

Eugene Debs long ago said: "Every struggle for justice is lost, is lost, and is lost until it is won." What Debs failed to say is that after the victories come even more painful losses. Our true test is not whether we reach victory but whether we concede to the defeats that come after the win. That's why I think that Debs's quote is not as good as this Jim Harrington maxim: "We lose only if we quit."

Staring at a mirror in my congressional office, I considered quitting. My first-ever local law—guaranteeing rest and water breaks for workers in the sun—had been nullified by the Texas state legislature and Governor Greg Abbott. What was the point of being the first person from the movement, and the first person of color, to be sent to represent my city in Congress if we were going backward instead of forward?

I was angry and discouraged. But instead of turning inward I put that energy toward what our mothers and fathers in the movement did—in the tradition that has been passed down to us.

We called for a thirst strike on the steps of the US Capitol. Dozens of organizations and unions, and a hundred fellow Texans, came to the nation's capital to protest. Dolores Huerta herself kicked off the strike. We stood in the sun without water, and we heard testimony from those who had lost loved ones to heat stroke while on the job. The best speech all day was delivered by a young farmworker with the UFW.

Two days later, then-President Joseph Biden went on television to announce the White House's efforts to protect workers from the heat, and one year later the president released his administrative heat-and-rest rule to protect not only Texas workers but also millions more across the country. Our defeat in Texas, at the time of this writing, will transform into powerful labor law for the whole nation. However, I also know there is a good chance that such rules could be reversed by a future antiworker president. This no longer brings me despair. Instead, I know that this is how civil rights movements work. With every short-term win comes another backlash. That backlash must then be defeated for longer-term transformation. My hope comes not from knowing that we will see victory in our lifetime but from the faith that we are a small part of keeping the struggle for justice alive across generations.

The regressive actions of Governor Abbott—just like Captain A. Y. Allee and Judge O. P. Carrillo—will wind up being historical footnotes. They'll be remembered as minor villains at best. The real Texas history will be about another group of workers waving red flags emblazoned with black eagles, again standing behind a president watching equality and fairness signed into law. We should all be proud—as Jim is—whenever we help them get there. That's my hope.

GREG CASAR

United States Representative, 35th Congressional District of Texas

ACKNOWLEDGMENTS

I acknowledge and profoundly thank all those with whom I had the privilege to associate—brave clients, stalwart staff, devoted grassroots activists, pro bono attorneys and law clerks, volunteers, and family—without whom nothing described in these pages could have happened.

Thanks to those who helped with this memoir: Sarah E. McGavick, Mia Uribe Kozlovsky, the University of Texas Press staff, freelance copy editor Jon Howard, S. Kirk Walsh, Niki Garcia-Holmes, Mary Keenan, Isabel Castro, Margot Marshall, Amelia Headley Lamont, and Tim "Carlos" Anderson for editing suggestions; to Rebecca Flores, Wayne Krause Yang, Jaime Ortiz, Juanita Valdez-Cox, Peter Hofer, Joe Richard Flores, Paulina Baca, Alex Moreno, Deborah Hiser, and former TCRP staff for jogging my memory and providing details; and to Rolando Pérez for editing ideas and patio brainstorming. And thanks also to everyone who offered encouragement when they found out this project was underway. Special gratitude to everyone who made this badass journey possible—and fun.

The list of people and groups with which I worked is long and itself would fill a volume. Some groups were ad hoc and small; others were more established. Some appear by name, but scores of others are not individually identified. Omission of anyone by name is sometimes due to aging memory, but more often for privacy or brevity. I thank you all.

RESOURCES

This is not a bibliography. Books, videos, websites, and so on abound about the farmworker movement and civil rights struggles in Texas. The few entries below contain detailed information particularly pertinent to this memoir that might not readily appear in web searches. They provide helpful summaries or backstories.

Life with the Texas Civil Rights Project, and the South Texas Project before that, has been public enough that media accounts abound reporting on legal cases, controversies, writings, press conferences, and the like. To the extent that any cases or events laid out here pique further interest or research, a Google search will work well enough.

The labor archives at Wayne State University house many files from the South Texas Project years (1973–1983) under the United Farm Workers (Texas) file; and the University of Texas at Arlington archives papers from TCRP during the author's tenure there (1990–2016).

Arionus, Steve. "Interview with Jim Harrington." https://crbb.tcu.edu/interviews/299/interview-with-jim-harrington (June 13, 2016); https://texashistory.unt.edu/ark:/67531/metapth987624 (excerpts).

Balladares, Victor Ruben, and Katherine Kuehler Walters. "Casso, Ramiro Raúl (1922–2011)." Texas State Historical Association, April 28, 2021. www.tshaonline.org/handbook/entries/casso-ramiro-raul.

Bluejack, Barbara. "Keeping the Tradition Alive: The Texas Civil Rights Project Turns 15. An Interview with TCRP Director James Harrington." *Texas Observer*, October 7, 2005. www.texasobserver.org/2052-keeping-the-tradition-alive-the-texas-civil-rights-project-turns-15-an-interview-with-tcrp-director-james-harrington [https://perma.cc/Y7M2-FNYC].

Campney, Brent M. S. "'A Bunch of Tough Hombres': Police Brutality, Municipal Politics, and Racism in South Texas." *Journal of the South-*

west 60, no. 4 (Winter 2018): 787–825. Project MUSE. doi:10.1353/jsw.2018.0016. https://scholarworks.utrgv.edu/cgi/viewcontent.cgi?article=1054&context=hist_fac.

Denison, Dave. "A Victory for Farmworkers." *Texas Observer*, May 17, 1985, 6.

Flores, Rebecca, and Alfredo Santos, eds. "Farm Worker Comme196 moration: Starr County Melon Strike and March." *Farm Workers 2016* (50th anniversary commemorative issue). *La Vos*, 2016. www.lavoznewspapers.com/UFW_Program_2016_inter__.pdf.

Flores, Rebecca, with Juanita Valdez-Cox and James C. Harrington. "The Farmworkers of Texas." In *Mexican American Civil Rights in Texas*, ed. Robert Bruschetta and J. Richard Avena. Chapter F. East Lansing: Michigan State University Press, 2021.

García, Thomas Ray. "Remembering the Pharr Riot, February 1971." January 31, 2021. https://iberoaztlan.com/articles/remembering-the-pharr-riot-february-1971.

García, Thomas Ray. Edited by Abigail Vela. "Op-Ed: The Pharr Riot and the Need for Mexican-American Studies." February 7, 2023. https://truchargv.com/pharr-riots.

Guajardo, Miguel A., and Francisco J. Guajardo. "The Impact of *Brown* on the Brown of South Texas: A Micropolitical Perspective on the Education of Mexican Americans in a South Texas Community." *American Educational Research Journal* 41, no. 3 (Fall 2004): 501–526.

Harrington, James C. "From La Casita to LUPE." *Texas Observer*, December 3, 2004.

Harrington, James C. "From the Protest Line: Why Are You There?" Excerpted from *Preaching Black Lives (Matter)*, ed. Gayle Fisher-Stewart, 133–149. New York: Church Publishing, 2020.

Harrington, James C. "Reflections of a Human Rights Advocate." *The Fountain*, March 1, 2014. https://fountainmagazine.com/2014/issue-98-march-april-2014/reflections-of-a-human-march-2014.

Jiménez, Francisco E. "LUPE's Legendary Executive Director, Juanita Valdez-Cox, Retires." January 14, 2023. https://myrgv.com/local-news/2023/01/14/long-legacy-lupes-executive-legendary-director-retires.

King, Michael. "Point Austin: Introducing the Constitution. Texas Civil Rights Project Remains a 20-Year Work Still in Progress." *Austin Chronicle*, October 1, 2010. www.austinchronicle.com/news/2010-10-01/point-austin-introducing-the-constitution.

La Unión del Pueblo Entero. "About La Unión del Pueblo Entero." https://lupenet.org/about.

Oliver, John. "Farmworkers: Last Week Tonight with John Oliver (HBO)." YouTube. www.youtube.com/watch?v=41vETgarh_8.

Pardo, Guadalupe. "The 'Animals' of McAllen PD—A History of RGV Policing," ed. Josué Ramírez and Abigail Vela. July 29, 2022. https://truchargv.com/mcallen-pd.

Ripps, Geoffrey. "The Battle for Farmworker Compensation." *Texas Observer*, January 13, 1984, 7.

Sims, Dave, dir. *Voices of the UFW in Texas*. 2016. https://utsa.hosted.panopto.com/Panopto/Pages/Viewer.aspx?id=e6b254e2-f3f8-4b4e-b626-ad7f01076bce.

United Farm Workers Texas Photograph Collection. UTSA Libraries Special Collections. University of Texas at San Antonio. https://digital.utsa.edu/digital/custom/ufw.

Zazueta-Castro, Lorenzo. "Pharr Riots' Anniversary Marks Watershed Moment in Valley History." *McAllen Monitor*, February 6, 2016. www.youtube.com/watch?v=jAG7Qr157zA.

INDEX